THE ORIGINS OF
SOUTHERN COLLEGE FOOTBALL

THE ORIGINS OF
SOUTHERN COLLEGE
FOOTBALL

HOW AN IVY LEAGUE GAME BECAME A
DIXIE TRADITION

ANDREW McILWAINE BELL

LOUISIANA STATE UNIVERSITY PRESS

BATON ROUGE

Published by Louisiana State University Press
www.lsupress.org

Designer: *Mandy McDonald Scallan*
Typeface: *Sentinel*

Cover image: The 1888 Wake Forest football team. Courtesy Special Collections and University Archives, Wake Forest University, Winston-Salem, North Carolina.

Library of Congress Cataloging-in-Publication Data
Names: Bell, Andrew McIlwaine, 1970– author.
Title: The origins of Southern college football : how an Ivy League game
  became a Dixie tradition / Andrew McIlwaine Bell.
Description: Baton Rouge : Louisiana State University Press, 2020. |
  Includes index.
Identifiers: LCCN 2019055112 (print) | LCCN 2019055113 (ebook) | ISBN
  978-0-8071-7120-2 (cloth) | ISBN 978-0-8071-7411-1 (pdf) | ISBN 978-0-8071-7410-4
  (epub)
Subjects: LCSH: Football—Southern States—History.
Classification: LCC GV938 .B39 2020 (print) | LCC GV938 (ebook) | DDC
  796.3320975—dc23
LC record available at https://lccn.loc.gov/2019055112
LC ebook record available at https://lccn.loc.gov/2019055113

In memory of

Alfred Kelley "Dickie" Dudley,

a Hampden-Sydney Tiger

for all eternity

Southern football players play with a reckless abandon, a wild fanaticism that's rarely found in players from other parts of the nation.

—WILLIAM "PUDGE" HEFFELFINGER,
Yale guard, three-time All-American, and the nation's
first paid professional player

CONTENTS

Illustrations follow page 72

THE ORIGINS OF
SOUTHERN COLLEGE FOOTBALL

INTRODUCTION

Southern college football today is a multibillion-dollar enterprise. Colossal stadiums that can hold more than one hundred thousand ticket holders tower over the South's landscapes like modern-day Roman amphitheaters. On game day, most are filled to capacity with rabid fans who spend their hard-earned money on everything from concessions and club seating to VIP parking and souvenirs. One of the highest-paid coaches in history is the University of Alabama's Nick Saban, who earned an eye-popping $8.3 million during the 2018–2019 season. (Dabo Swinney surpassed Saban in 2019 by signing a ten-year deal with Clemson worth $93 million.) Saban is worth his weight in gold to his employer, since his success on the gridiron has produced higher enrollment numbers for Alabama and a substantial increase in the school's endowment.

The conference Saban represents, the Southeastern Conference (SEC), collects more than $450 million annually from bowl games and TV deals, which is then divvied up between its fourteen member schools. Sales of officially licensed merchandise generate additional revenue. Five of the ten best-selling college brands at Walmart, the nation's largest retailer, are SEC schools. The introduction of the College Football Playoff, in 2014, has added another cash cow to the South's already sizeable herd. ESPN is shelling out $7.2 billion over twelve years for broadcast rights to the playoff, which so far has been dominated by southern teams.[1]

With so much money at stake, it is easy to see why college football is often derided as a shady business operation run by greedy university and National Collegiate Athletic Association (NCAA) officials. Civil rights historian Taylor Branch likes to remind people that college athletes do not get paid for putting their bodies at risk, despite generating huge sums for private companies and public institutions. "Slavery analogies should be used carefully," Branch writes. "Yet to survey the scene—corporations and universities enriching themselves on the backs of uncompensated young men, whose status as 'student-athletes' deprives them of the right to due process guaranteed by the Constitution—is to catch an unmistakable whiff of the plantation."[2]

Perhaps Branch is right. Maybe it is time to start paying college athletes a fair wage for taking risks that make others rich. I do not address that question in this book. Instead, I have attempted to provide a partial explanation of why college football is popular in the South by examining the game's early development in the region. Money, after all, is only a symptom of the South's football madness, not an explanation of its cause. Southern college football would not be a multibillion-dollar enterprise without the support of countless fans who buy tickets and merchandise and stay glued to their TVs whenever their favorite team is playing. But what motivates these fans to spend so much of their precious time and money on something that, in the grand scheme of things, has no bearing on whether they succeed or fail in life? The book of Matthew (6:21) teaches, "For where your treasure is, there will your heart be also." If this is true, then we must first tackle the question of why college football arouses such heartfelt passion among southerners before we can understand why the game is lucrative below the Mason–Dixon Line.

One reason is the region's unique history. Violence was part of the southern experience from the very beginning, largely (but not exclusively) due to a dependence on unfree labor—first in the form of indentured servitude and then of chattel slavery. Keeping these laborers in line required a tolerance for violence that gradually wormed its way into the South's cultural fabric. There also was the disastrous defeat during the American Civil War, which left southerners with a massive inferiority complex. With their way of life in shambles, they looked to northern institutions for guidance on how to rebuild their society. Northern universities, in particular, were seen as bastions of enlightenment, with curricula and methods that could be reproduced at southern schools. When organized or "scientific" football became popular at places like Yale and Harvard, southern educators—many of whom were either Yankee transplants or locals trained at northern schools—insisted that the game be played on their campuses too. A minority of southerners, concerned with the dangers of football, pressed for its abolition. Others believed it could be made safer through bureaucratization and rule changes. Young southerners considered football a modern and exciting sport that heralded the dawn of a new golden age for Dixie.

There was also what I call the "Sir Walter Scott effect." For centuries, southerners imagined their region as the last remaining stronghold of aristocratic privilege in America, an enchanted land inhabited by fair damsels and men of chivalry championing virtues from a bygone era. As football's popularity grew in the late in the late 1800s and early 1900s, southern journalists routinely employed Arthurian metaphors when writing about the new sport. Players were "padded knights" or "long-haired knights of the football arena" performing in front of "lovely young women, escorted by gallant young cavaliers." These descriptions reinforced the myth of the swashbuckling southern aristocrat, which in turn expedited the South's acceptance of a game that previously had been identified with northern colleges.[3]

Scientific football was introduced on southern campuses during a period of rapid industrialization and urbanization in the northern states. In the South, despite the efforts of visionaries such as Henry Grady who were pushing for the creation of a "New South," most people continued tilling the soil just as their fathers and grandfathers had done. They were cognizant of the fact that northerners were, by and large, wealthier and better educated than most southerners, a painful truth that lowered their self-esteem. The success of football teams at local colleges and universities not only provided relief from the boredom of agrarian life but also gave southerners something to be proud of in a region that was often ridiculed as dull-witted and underdeveloped.

In addition, football helped southerners find common ground with their fellow Americans, in the same way that baseball would for many immigrants in the first half of the twentieth century. And it helped southerners resolve a conundrum that stemmed from the unique experience of losing a war: how to embrace the future without letting go of the past. College traditions that paid homage to the Old South were invented out of whole cloth, even as they captured the energy and spirit of the New South.

Of course, the game, in one form or another, had been part of the southern experience for as long as anyone could remember. When the English settled Jamestown in the seventeenth century, they were amazed to discover Powhatan Indians playing football, though the Powhatan version of the game was less violent than the various types of mob football games that had been played in English towns and villages for centuries. "They make their Goals as ours only they never fight nor pull one another down," noted Henry Spelman, an English teenager who was sent to live with the Powhatan. The chaos and violence of mob football in England horrified elites, who had failed in their repeated attempts to have the activity banned. Aspiring English gentlemen in the American colonies were equally repulsed by football. "Games played with the ball, and others of that nature, are too violent for the body, and stamp no character on the mind," Thomas Jefferson advised his nephew.[4]

Young Englishmen and Americans continued playing football anyway. The game was too much fun and gave them a much-needed opportunity to blow off steam. Soldiers in both the American Revolution and the Civil War played football when they were not fighting battles. Winslow Homer, who worked as an illustrator for *Harper's Weekly* before he became a world-famous painter, drew a sketch of Union soldiers engaged in a mob football match, which he captioned *Holiday in Camp* (figure 1).

Football became more organized when it moved into secondary and postsecondary schools in both England and the United States. Students attending Westminster, Harrow, Eton, Rugby, and other English preparatory schools created their own versions of football, which they subsequently took with them to university. But since multiple sets of rules made it difficult for students from different schools to compete against one another, in 1848 an attempt was made at Cambridge to establish a uniform football code. Unfortunately, squabbling continued even after the Cambridge rules were approved.

In October 1863, representatives from several schools and football clubs gathered at the Freemason's Tavern in London to take another stab at coming up with a standardized version of the game. They drafted a list of thirteen rules and established a governing body called the Football Association (FA) (*soccer* is a derivation of the word *association*). Not everyone was happy with the new rules, however, and a splinter group, keen on preserving what it viewed as a "manlier" style of play, distanced itself from the FA and founded the Rugby Football Union.[5]

In the United States, football followed a less refined route. By 1827, first- and second-year students at Harvard were battling one another in a violent annual contest known as "Bloody Monday," which gave the sophomores an opportunity to haze the incoming class of freshmen. It occurred each year on the first Monday of the fall term, when faculty were normally preoccupied with meetings. Yale's version was called the "annual rush." Princeton students played "balldown," a game with two teams of twenty-five players, who were allowed to catch kicked balls but not to run with them. Northeastern prep schools produced their own versions of football. Gerrit Smith Miller, a student at Epes Sargent Dixwell's Private Latin School in Boston, organized the Oneida Football Club during the Civil War. Miller's club played on Boston Common against makeshift teams from other local schools and never lost a game. These contests produced the famous "Boston Game," which would have a profound impact on the development of American football. A marker honoring the Oneida Club was erected on Boston Common in 1925. The inscription reads, "On this field the Oneida Football Club of Boston, the first organized football club in the United States, played against all comers from 1862 to 1865. The Oneida goal was never crossed."[6]

Like their cousins across the Atlantic, northeastern college students eventually grew tired of the endless varieties of football and adopted a uniform set of rules in the 1870s and 1880s. No single person contributed more to this effort than Walter Camp, the "father of American football." Camp had discovered the game while attending Yale and dedicated his life to refining and promoting it, even after he became a family man and a busy executive at the New Haven Clock Company. He wanted football teams to function like well-engineered timepieces, with each individual component working in tandem with the others in a precision display of order and efficiency. Camp's influence on the development of southern football cannot be overstated. It is no coincidence that a number of prominent southern universities—including Alabama, Georgia, and South Carolina—founded football programs in 1892, one year after Camp published his magnum opus, *American Football.*

But the story of southern college football, like the story of the South itself, begins in Virginia. The state's proximity to the Northeast and its unique role in the founding of the United States has traditionally made it a catch basin for ideas and people moving from north to south. Virginia college students caught wind of the sport that was taking over northern campuses before their peers further south did.

My narrative begins at Washington and Lee University in Lexington, Virginia, which is where I found some of the earliest documented evidence of southern college students playing football. Melvin Smith, a retired meteorologist who has painstakingly compiled data on games played from the mid-nineteenth century through the 1890–1891 season, has unearthed a reference to a soccer-like contest, scheduled for October 1869 between W&L and the Virginia Military Institute, that was canceled due to bad weather. Had the match occurred, it would have been recorded as America's first intercollegiate football game. Instead, that distinction that belongs to students from Rutgers University and Princeton University, who played each other a month later. Jerry Ratcliffe, a sports journalist for the *Charlottesville Daily Progress,* found a passing reference to an 1871 game between the University of Virginia and Washington and Lee while researching a book on Cavalier football; unfortunately, he was unable to track down any details. "I had hoped that perhaps someone who read my book might have had some kind of information passed along through family history or something of that nature that would enhance our knowledge of that early game, but to no avail," Ratcliffe told me.[7] At any rate, we can say with confidence that Virginia is not only the birthplace of presidents but also the birthplace of southern college football.

At this point, I think it would be useful to disclose my biases and some of the methods I used to produce this study. First, I am a graduate of the University of Alabama and thus a loyal Crimson Tide fan. And that is why I did not spend a lot of time writing about the history of Alabama football. To the extent that they can, historians should present the past as it was, without letting their personal predilections skew the narrative. Also, I am continually reminded by friends and family that there are other teams out there besides Alabama. I did my best to include brief histories of as many southern Division 1 Football Bowl Subdivision programs as possible, but if I overlooked your alma mater or a game you feel was crucial to the development of football in the eleven former Confederate states, I humbly beg your pardon. I will try to do better in the next edition of this book . . . assuming there is one.

Second, I use the term "Ivy League" in certain places to describe the northeastern schools that invented American football, even though that league did not officially exist until the 1950s. I did so for the sake of convenience and under the assumption that most readers would understand my meaning. I also alternate between the ancient and modern names of certain schools. Auburn, for example, was founded as the Agricultural and Mechanical College of Alabama. But I found the task of typing out this antiquated name every time I wanted to discuss Tiger football to be both arduous and unnecessary. Auburn is a household name; A&M College of Alabama is not.

Finally, this book is as much a story of America in the Gilded Age and the Progressive Era as it is a history of southern college football. I realize that by embedding a pigskin history inside of a general history of the United States I risk alienating some hardcore football fans and professional historians, who will be disappointed that I did not spend more time discussing their favorite topics or make more explicit the connection between certain historical events and the game of football. But that is a risk I am willing to take in order to begin the process of patching a hole in the historiography. Most of the football books I read while researching this one provide a microscopic view of the sport's origins without discussing the larger social and political trends of the period, an approach that, in my view, shortchanges readers.

Southern college football did not germinate in a historical vacuum, any more than jousting did in medieval Europe or cricket did on the Indian subcontinent during the nineteenth century. Sport is a useful cultural text that can help us better understand a society's customs, aspirations, and shortcomings, when presented in a far-reaching, macrohistorical context. Consider this: If, one hundred years from now, a football historian writing about a game from our own time failed to mention Donald Trump's presidency, mass shootings, climate change, immigration, or any number of other contemporary political issues, his or her readers would still be able to tell what happened on the playing field—which team won, who gained the most rushing yards, and so forth. But they would have little understanding of what else besides football might have been on the minds of the players and fans. If all history is the history of thought, as R. G. Collingwood argued, football history requires its practitioners to get inside the heads of the people who played and supported the game, an exercise that perforce includes trying to understand the times in which they lived.[8]

I chose football as a prism through which to examine the transformation of the United States from a laissez-faire society to a bureaucratized one, because football underwent a similar metamorphosis during the same period. Gilded Age football was a brutish, amateurish pastime played by young men who were eager to test their mettle in a world they believed owed them nothing. Progressives fashioned it into a sport governed by committees and rules, which made it safer and more acceptable to middle-class Americans. Football as we know it today is a reflection of the values and assumptions of people who were alive during these two momentous periods of change. If there is any lesson for the current generation to be gleaned from this study, it is that football is part of our national heritage that many of our forebears—whether rightly or wrongly—thought worth preserving.

This is not to suggest that football as we know it should be bequeathed to the next generation. In fact, the discovery of neurodegenerative diseases caused by head injuries, such as chronic traumatic encephalopathy, makes it hard to imagine that football in its current form will survive. What seems likelier is that future generations will play a less risky version of the sport, using improved technology and new rules that place a greater emphasis on safety. And that is how it should be. Football, after all, has never been a static, motionless game but one that is constantly moving and adapting to changing circumstances, both on and off the field. In other words, it has continually been reshaped by the broader cultural and political currents of American life.

An increasing number of journalists and historians are writing books that explore the intersection of history, politics, and college football. Sally Jenkins's *The Real All Americans* (2007) is a fascinating account of how football restored the pride and dignity of Native Americans attending the Carlisle Indian School in Pennsylvania at the turn of the century. (I present a similar argument in this book, only with southerners rather than Indians as the focus of attention.) Warren St. John's runaway best seller *Rammer Jammer Yellow Hammer* (2004) shines a spotlight on the Alabama Crimson Tide's colorful fan base even as it probes the deeper mystery of why southerners are obsessed with college football. Ray Glier's *How the SEC Became Goliath* (2012) has been endorsed by sports journalists across the South for its warts-and-all look at how better recruiting, better coaches, and bigger bank accounts have transformed the SEC into the nation's most powerful college football conference. Tony Barnhart's *Southern Fried Football* (originally published in 2000) is a lighthearted compendium of notable games and players, mostly from the twentieth century. John Sayle Watterson's *College Football: History, Spectacle, Controversy* (2000) is a much more serious scholarly effort that traces the evolution of college football from an Ivy League extracurricular activity to a multibillion-dollar industry that has become virtually indistinguishable from the professional version of the game.

Leo Andrew Doyle's 1998 doctoral dissertation, *Causes Won, Not Lost: Football and Southern Culture, 1892–1983*, is essential reading for anyone interested in understanding the history of southern football. Many of the arguments contained in Doyle's work are reprinted in this study, a demonstration of my respect for his pioneering research. For example, Doyle ingeniously draws parallels between nineteenth-century southerners and twentieth-century Cubans and Japanese. All three groups were subjugated by the United States military and all three "embraced a symbolically important cultural pastime of an economically and technologically superior rival."[9] (As it turned out, postwar Japanese and Cubans were more interested in baseball than in football.) It is easy to miss the postwar South's susceptibility to northern influences when one focuses exclusively on the region's well-documented history of resistance to racial integration and the expansion of democracy. Doyle's work demonstrates that there is more to the story.

Two books by Ronald A. Smith—*Sports and Freedom* (1988) and *Pay for Play* (2011)—share a common theme: amateur athletics have never existed at the collegiate level. Once presidents and other university stakeholders figured out that successful sports teams made higher education palatable to the general public and brought in piles of cash, says Smith, any serious efforts aimed at reforming college athletics were doomed to failure. Wealthy alumni, university trustees, bloated athletic department bureaucracies, and quiescent faculty perpetuate a system that is only occasionally sidetracked by token attempts at reform.

Brian M. Ingrassia presents an equally gloomy thesis in *The Rise of Gridiron University* (2012). He argues that progressive educators immediately saw the potential of football as a bridge between the knotty intellectual pursuits of university life and the comparatively glib interests of the hoi polloi. By providing regular folk with a connection to the local college, football ensured the survival of institutions that might otherwise have collapsed. Unfortunately, these educators failed to realize they were creating a monster that would come to dominate campus life and leave them feeling more estranged from the public than ever.

Michael Oriard's *Reading Football* (1993) focuses on print journalism's role in shaping public perceptions of football. The heavy press coverage and heterogeneous accounts of early games, says Oriard, allowed diverse groups of readers to see themselves and their concerns reflected in the action on the field. Falling mostly within the realm of cultural studies, *Reading Football* nevertheless provides important information on the media-generated myths surrounding football that will pique the interest of historians.

In 2013, Susan Reyburn and the Library of Congress released *Football Nation: Four Hundred Years of America's Game.* Reyburn's subtitle says it all—football has replaced baseball as the nation's favorite pastime, a cultural change not lost on *Washington Post* reporter Mary McGrory, who in the mid-1970s wryly observed, "Baseball is what we were. Football is what we have become."[10] How much longer football will remain America's game has yet to be seen, but Reyburn's book is a must-have for sports fans. Her research is impeccable and her writing sublime.

Two southern classics deserve special mention: Zipp Newman's *The Impact of Southern Football* (1969) and Fuzzy Woodruff's three-volume *A History of Southern Football, 1890–1928* (1928). Woodruff was there when wobbly-boned collegians with scruffy hair and handlebar mustaches put on uniforms resembling long underwear and trampled each other with vicious plays like the flying wedge and the turtleback. Newman was a sportswriter for the *Birmingham News* who dutifully recorded games and events he thought would interest his readers. Regrettably, neither man ever received training as a scholar, which shows in their work. Both Woodruff and Newman fumbled a number of important facts and, worse yet, failed to cite their sources, an unforgiveable transgression among professional historians.

Of course, it is easy to criticize authors who lived in the pre-internet era for not always getting their facts straight. The only group easier to bash is those of us who can Google the answer to any question under the sun at any time of day or night. For the mistakes contained in the chapters that follow, I take the customary responsibility. I am keeping my fingers crossed that they are few and far between.

Using a patchwork of sources that often contradicted one another or were maddeningly short on details (such as the Woodruff and Newman books), I have done my best to piece together an accurate history of southern football's formative years. In doing so, I consulted published collections of primary sources, student yearbooks, old newspapers and magazines, athletic department records, church records, university trustee records and meeting minutes, personal papers and letters, manuscript collections, speeches, and a bevy of secondary material, including peer-reviewed books and articles as well as team media guides, which helped me fill in the missing details of key games. I also consulted a series of books called *Football Vault(s)*, commissioned by Whitman Publishing in Atlanta, that are the product of a joint effort between sports journalists, athletic department personnel, and librarians at a number of Division 1 schools. Although geared toward sports fans, these books contain invaluable information for football historians, including facsimiles of primary sources—game day programs, ticket stubs, team photographs, student newspaper articles, and more. I used them judiciously, and I carefully cross-referenced the stories they contain, knowing that my use of nontraditional source materials would likely raise a few eyebrows in academic circles.

The Origins of Southern College Football is a book I have been thinking about and researching for the better part of a decade. Along the way, certain people have helped me get it off the ground, and I wish to acknowledge their efforts here. Librarians, the unsung and underpaid heroes of the scholastic world, deserve first mention. Julia Bradford and Rebecca May helped me locate sources and images housed in the Z. Smith Reynolds Library at Wake Forest University. Lisa McCown, C. Vaughan Stanley, and Seth McCormick-Goodhart uncovered materials kept in the Leyburn Library at Washington and Lee University. Anne Causey, Margaret Hrabe, Irvin Jordan, Heather Riser, and the UVA Digital Production Group helped me navigate the university's special collections. Matthew Turi at the University of North Carolina at Chapel Hill; Judee Showalter at Randolph-Macon College; Rusty Tryon at Louisiana College; Brandon Lunsford at Johnson C. Smith University; Tim Pyatt at Duke University; Shannon Steffey at UVA-Wise; Margaret Vaverek at Texas State; Will Ritter at Greensboro College; Shanee Murrain at the University of West Georgia; Kelly Spring and James Stimpert at Johns Hopkins; Marina Klarić, Kevin Ray, and Terry Brown at the University of Alabama; Carl Van Ness at the University of Florida; Teresa Gray at Vanderbilt University; and Kirk Henderson at Georgia Tech also contributed time and materials. Kyle Kondik, director of communications for the UVA Center for Politics (and a fan of the Ohio University

Bobcats), read an early draft of the manuscript and offered invaluable suggestions and edits. So did Tyler Anbinder, professor of history at the George Washington University and Raymond "Skip" Hyser, a Gilded Age/Progressive Era specialist who teaches at James Madison University in Harrisonburg, Virginia. A Georgia undergraduate student named Wells Armes was kind enough to send me pictures of a plaque honoring a Georgia player named Von Gammon that hangs in UGA's Butts-Mehre Heritage Hall, a gift to the Bulldogs from the Virginia Cavaliers. Thank you, Wells. My editor, Rand Dotson of Louisiana State University Press, is a true southern gentleman. He took a chance on me many years ago when I was shopping my first manuscript, *Mosquito Soldiers,* and has remained a caring and enthusiastic cheerleader ever since. The LSU Press team is unmatched, and I thank Neal Novak, senior editor; Laura Gleason, production manager; sales and marketing manager James Wilson; and freelance copy editor Todd Manza.

And finally, I tip my hat to the young men who suit up in plastic armor and chase after a striped leather ball every autumn, out of love for the game, their fellow students, and the colleges they attend. Gentlemen, the story of your country and the players and coaches who came before you is on the pages that follow. I hope you enjoy reading it as much as I enjoyed putting it together.

CHAPTER ONE

RUDE BEGINNINGS IN THE OLD DOMINION

O n October 26, 1872, the editors of the *Southern Collegian* commented on a new pastime gaining ground among their fellow students at the Washington and Lee University in Lexington, Virginia: "Foot-ball is now all the rage. The game as played on the campus, with about a hundred on each side, is very exciting sport, and doubtless fine exercise," they opined. "Among the possibilities of the game, however, broken noses and shins must be reckoned prominent." Although unsure of the new sport's rules, the *Southern Collegian's* editors were confident they knew genuine athletic talent when they saw it: "We do not see among all of the kickers, if that be the correct term, anyone who equals Tom Hanna in lifting the ball into the air, or one who could, in the charge, keep by the side of 'Goob' Swanson . . . in our estimation, the successful rival of the mythical 'Old Brook,' who is so famous in the foot-ball annals of Eton."[1]

In reality, Tom Hanna and Goob Swanson were playing a game that was crude by Eton standards. Etonians had codified their famous "Field Game" (roughly speaking, a cross between soccer and rugby) in 1815, the same year the Duke of Wellington defeated Napoleon on the plains of Waterloo. By 1872, they were familiar also with English Football Association rules and the more recently drafted Rugby Football Union rules. Even the rough-and-tumble "Wall Game" at Eton was more organized than any of the early football games at Washington and Lee, which were little more than chaotic clashes between mobs of rowdy male undergraduates. Everyone on campus was welcome to join in the fun. Victory belonged to the player who could kick, slap, punch, or headbutt the ball, as well as the opposing team, the hardest. Might made right. Rules and team sizes were largely irrelevant.[2]

Washington and Lee's version of football, like others found in English-speaking countries around the world, was an offshoot of England's ancient mob games. One such game, Royal Shrovetide Football, has been an annual event in the town of Ashbourne, Derbyshire, for the past eight hundred years. There are few rules for Shrovetide football other than the scoring method, which requires players to tap the ball three times against one of two millstones positioned on opposite ends of town. Players can advance the ball in any manner they see fit and there is no limit to the number of people who can participate (figure 2).[3]

Old Brook[e] was a fictional character from *Tom Brown's School Days,* a nineteenth-century best seller written by the Englishman Thomas Hughes that was the *Harry Potter* of its day. Instead of quidditch, though, readers were spellbound by Hughes's account of a real-life game played at the eponymous Rugby School in Warwickshire, England, the author's alma mater. *Tom Brown's School Days* describes Old Brooke as the "Cock of the school," who happens to be "the best kick and charger in Rugby." In addition to misspelling his name, the *Southern Collegian*'s editors had goofed by placing Old Brooke at Eton rather than at Rugby, but the character was as familiar to their generation as Ron Weasley is to modern-day *Harry Potter* fans.[4]

During a visit to the United States in 1871, Hughes was invited by Cornell students to participate in one of their football games. Although he was accustomed to a certain degree of confusion on the playing fields of Rugby, the author was caught off guard by the sheer chaos he encountered at Cornell. "All who cared to play collected into two irregular crowds, unorganized and leaderless, and stood facing one another," Hughes noted. "Then a big, oddly-shaped ball arrived, somebody started it with a kick-off, and away went both sides in chase, wildly jostling one another, kicking, catching, throwing, or hitting the ball, according to fancy, all thoughts more bent, seemingly, upon the pure delight of the struggle than upon any particular goal."[5]

Football looked equally primitive on other college campuses. A few years before the *Southern Collegian* commented on the sport's growing popularity at Washington and Lee, Rutgers University defeated Princeton University 6–4 in what is generally considered the nation's first intercollegiate game. Before the contest began, the teams had agreed to abide by a set of modified FA rules, which were honored more in the breach than in the observance. Fifty players smashed into one another (as well as through a fence upon which fans were seated) in a seesaw contest stemming in part from an argument over a stolen Revolutionary War cannon. The game also featured an early version of the bone-crunching flying wedge play—a subject we shall return to in a later chapter.[6]

One year later, in November 1870, a group of students at the University of Virginia gathered on a grassy area in the center of campus known as "the Lawn" to play football after their math class was canceled. One eyewitness described the event as "a crowd of coatless youth engaged in what seemed . . . the insane sport of rushing together, and trying to kick each others' hats off." He joined the game out of curiosity and was promptly kicked "on the shins and on the knees."[7]

The legendary coach John Heisman recalled playing a similar version of football as a boy growing up in the oil fields of Western Pennsylvania: "The game we played in Titusville was only a species of Association football. Of rules we observed few, having few. Signals we had none—needed none, wanted none. We butted the ball, punched it, elbowed it and kicked it. Incidentally, many were the butts, punches, kicks and assorted socks that fell short of the ball and found lodging on us."[8]

American football, like the nation itself, was slowly emerging from a primordial ooze of provincialism and violence. The United States was still a backwoods, balkanized country in the nineteenth century, which contributed to the development of different versions of football across regions. Each locale played by its own set of rules. The historian Robert Wiebe famously described the United States during this period as "a nation of loosely connected islands" inhabited by people who rarely left their own island.[9] This was especially true for southerners living in communities that were poor, rural, and—after 1865—struggling to recover from the effects of a disastrous war.

The shadow of the Civil War loomed large in Lexington during the 1870s. Robert E. Lee, the Confederacy's greatest general, had served as president of what was then known as Washington College from the end of the war until his death in 1870. When Lee passed away, the board of trustees voted to change the name of the school from Washington College to Washington and Lee University and to appoint Lee's son George Washington Custis—also a Confederate general—as his successor. The Virginia Military Institute, home of Thomas "Stonewall" Jackson, the Confederacy's second-greatest commander, was less than a mile away. VMI cadets' hearts and thoughts were never far from Jackson or from the ten cadets who had died at the

Battle of New Market, trying to stop a federal invasion of Virginia's Shenandoah Valley.[10]

In the autumn of 1873, fifty VMI cadets took on an equal number of Washington and Lee students in a football "series" that lasted six "innings" (students from both schools better understood the rules of baseball, which had been introduced in Lexington in the 1860s). W&L won the series 4–2. The contest took place on VMI's parade grounds, directly across the street from the W&L campus. The editors of the *Southern Collegian* complimented the cadets' performance but also complained that the large number of players on each side made it difficult to identify the truly talented athletes. "Another objection is that the ball was not on the ground enough, thus making the game fist-ball, instead of foot-ball," they griped. "We hope the players will remedy these two objections, and have many more games before the cold weather comes."[11]

Football was a welcome diversion from the grim news of the day. The residents of Memphis, Tennessee, were struggling with a deadly yellow fever epidemic that would ultimately claim two thousand lives. A railroad construction company called the Crédit Mobilier had recently been found guilty of defrauding the federal government and paying hush money to crooked congressmen in their quest to build part of the first transcontinental railroad. Jay Cooke's banking house—a major financial firm with close ties to the Grant administration—had collapsed that same autumn, triggering a nationwide financial panic that sent businesses and agricultural prices into a tailspin. Millions of people lost their jobs as companies across the land went bankrupt. The Panic of 1873, as it would later be called, was largely the consequence of a post–Civil War railroad bubble, and it ushered in an economic depression that would last until nearly the end of the decade.[12]

The downturn lasted even longer in the South and devastated the region's agricultural economy. Tenant farmers and sharecroppers found it increasingly difficult to repay debts they owed to landowners as crop prices plummeted. State tax revenues evaporated. Railroad companies laying much-needed track through isolated rural areas failed. And Republican politicians who had promised southern voters a new age of prosperity based on the expansion of railroads were left with egg on their faces.[13]

Not that white ex-Confederates had ever trusted Republican promises. Most viewed the party's southern office holders as unwelcome interlopers acting on behalf of a tyrannical Congress. They were still in shock over the fact that their former slaves and northern enemies were now their political lords and masters. And blame for this turn of events rested squarely with Congress, which in their eyes was an American version of England's infamous Rump Parliament, the legislative body responsible for the trial and execution of King Charles I.

By the time Washington and Lee students began playing football, the South was in the third and final stage of a federal reconstruction program that had kicked off during the Civil War (figure 3). Reconstruction had initially been controlled from the White House. Abraham Lincoln issued a Proclamation of Amnesty and Reconstruction in December 1863, allowing 10 percent of the registered voters in each southern state to form new governments, provided they abolished slavery and took an oath to uphold the Constitution. The president's 10 percent plan was considered too lenient by some members of his own party, however, and a tougher reconstruction plan was subsequently passed by both houses of Congress. Lincoln deftly avoided a protracted political struggle by exercising a pocket veto. He explained to the public (somewhat disingenuously) that he did not wish to get tied down to a single plan of reconstruction.

After the Civil War ended and Lincoln was assassinated, Republicans on Capitol Hill ran out of patience with presidential reconstruction. They were particularly upset by what they saw as neo-Confederate nose thumbing at federal authority and wrested control of reconstruction from Andrew Johnson, Lincoln's presidential successor.[14] Johnson, like Lincoln, supported policies that he supposed would bring a quick rapprochement between the North and the South. Former Confederates were granted generous pardons, land confiscated during the war was returned to rebel owners, and Congress was pressured to readmit the southern states to the Union with virtually no preconditions. Southerners began to believe that they might escape punishment for waging a war that had resulted in 620,000 deaths and left many thousands more injured and traumatized. Joseph Addison Waddell, a Virginia resident and historian with close ties to Washington and Lee, summed up how many of his fellow southerners felt during this period: "At the close of 1865, our people flattered themselves that they would be left to attend to their own affairs, under the Constitution of the United States, without further molestation."[15]

"Radical" Republican congressmen like Thaddeus Stevens of Pennsylvania and George Boutwell of Massachusetts had other ideas. They wanted the federal government to dismantle the southern political dynasties they blamed for the war and to provide greater protection to black voters who were being attacked by white vigilante groups. President Johnson himself eventually became a target of radical wrath and was impeached by the House of Representatives during the last full year of his presidency. The final straw for Congress came when ten former Confederate states, taking their cue from the Johnson White House, stubbornly refused to ratify the Fourteenth Amendment, which granted citizenship to native-born black people. The amendment also stripped rights from some native-born whites who had supported the Confederacy, and it repudiated Confederate debts and claims for compensation stemming from the loss of slaves.

Over Johnson's objections, Congress placed the ten recalcitrant states under military occupation and ordered them to draft new constitutions, with input from black men twenty-one and older but without the participation of white ex-Confederates who were disenfranchised by the Fourteenth Amendment. This action signaled the end of presidential reconstruction and the beginning of a new phase known as Congressional or "Radical" reconstruction. Compared to what had come before, it was the best of times for many southern blacks and the worst of times for many southern whites.

A total of 265 African American men were chosen to serve as delegates to the various constitutional conventions mandated by Congress. African Americans held a majority of the seats in the Louisiana and South Carolina conventions and close to 40 percent of the seats in Florida. Elsewhere their numbers were lower but still significant—20 percent in Alabama, Georgia, Mississippi, and Virginia and half that number in Arkansas, North Carolina, and Texas. Southern white Republicans ("scalawags") and their northern Republican allies ("carpetbaggers") held an overall majority of seats.[16]

These election results sparked a backlash from southern bigots, who wanted a return to the antebellum status quo. When twenty-four African Americans were elected to the Virginia constitutional convention (out of a total of 105 delegates), the conservative *Richmond Enquirer* lamented "the elevation of the illiterate Negro over the head of the educated and intelligent white man, a form of despotism so horrible and loathsome, that by comparison with it, the domination of the soldier may be regarded as a blessing." The *Mobile Advertiser and Register* dismissed Alabama's convention as a collection of "wooly heads, empty heads, stolid ignorance and base venality." Other conservative newspapers derisively described the assemblies in their states as "black and tan," "bones and banjo," or simply "mongrelized" conventions.[17]

In reality, the black and white Republican conventions produced state constitutions that were in many ways remarkably enlightened documents. All of them guaranteed political and civil rights for every citizen, regardless of skin color. Whipping was banned as a punishment for crime. Voters were permitted to cast secret ballots instead of having to voice their picks in front of potentially hostile registrars. Other clauses were drafted on behalf of orphans, the poor, the mentally ill, and married women with property.

One issue in particular proved to be a political football: the racial integration of schools. Republicans in most states were divided over the matter, while Democrats stood united against it. Even some African American delegates, who personally opposed segregation, were forced to admit that most white *and* black southerners preferred to have their kids taught in separate schools. The Republican Party did not press the issue, in no small measure due to the ambivalence of its black members, who were more concerned with getting their children enrolled in school than with holding out for integrated classrooms. Black reticence and white hostility worked in tandem to keep southern schools segregated—a bitter legacy of Reconstruction that would remain unchallenged until the second half of the twentieth century.[18]

Washington and Lee University at the time, like a majority of U.S. colleges, did not admit African Americans—or most other Americans, either. In fact, fewer than 1 percent of the population attended college in the 1870s as most people could not afford to quit working for four years in order to study Euclidean geometry, Sappho's poetry, and other intellectual esoterica. Consequently, the all-white, all-male, elitist student body at W&L felt comfortable making racist and sexist remarks that would never be tolerated on a modern college campus. For example, the same issue of the *Southern Collegian* that covered Goob Swanson's football heroics included a racist joke about the supposedly low academic standards of historically black Lincoln University in Oxford, Pennsylvania. (In reality, Lincoln would produce many gifted academicians, including Supreme Court Justice Thurgood Marshall and the poet Langston Hughes.) Women were also the butt of crude jokes. A subsequent issue of the *Collegian* noted that Washington and Lee suffered from a "scarcity of beavers on the Campus" during football games.

Southern colleges in the nineteenth century were bastions of cultural and ethnic homogeneity, and the students who attended them were overwhelmingly male, white, and Protestant. "White" however was a more complicated racial descriptor than it is today. Between the mid-1800s and the 1920s, "white people" were divided into additional subcategories, such as "Slav" (Eastern European), "Celt" (Irish), or "Anglo-Saxon" (primarily British).[19] Because most nineteenth-century college students self-identified as "Anglo-Saxon," they were keen on copying the customs of Anglo-Saxons living in Britain, which included kicking a leather ball across a grassy field.

Southern Anglo-Saxons, however, were a unique subspecies with their own peculiar customs and cultural hang-ups. Between 1619 and 1865, they had become dependent upon a race-based system of slavery that spawned a culture of violence and contempt for people of African descent. Ironically, this same system contributed to their disdain for one another, a fact noted by Professor John Hope Franklin in an influential article published at the height of the civil rights struggle: "The rule of tyranny by which [southerners] lived naturally fostered an independence and self-sufficiency—one is tempted to call it an individual sovereignty—that would, on occasion, burst out in all its fury in their quarrels with each other."[20]

Contemporary historical scholarship supports Franklin's thesis. Slavery was indeed buttressed by a culture of violence that bled into many other facets of southern life, including the southern collegiate experience. Rex Bowman and Carlos Santos, for example, have shown how dangerous the University of Virginia was in the years leading up to the Civil War. As the authors discovered, the spoiled sons of rich merchants and plantation owners who attended UVA beat their slaves, their professors, and one another with such frequency and ferocity that the school nearly closed on more than one occasion.

On a more positive note, UVA deserves credit as one of the first southern universities to adopt football. Apart from the pickup game played on the Lawn in November 1870 (which was dutifully recorded by the editors of Virginia's college magazine), sportswriter Jerry Ratcliffe has uncovered a tantalizing reference to an 1871 game between UVA and Washington and Lee that could very well have been the South's first intercollegiate contest. Unfortunately, the details of this early game have been lost to history.[21]

Although compelling, Franklin's thesis misses some other key causes of southern violence. Honor—a concept that has largely disappeared from the modern American zeitgeist—played an equally important role in normalizing bloodshed. Honor meant more than simply gaining the respect of friends and family; it was the glue that held southern society together. Men without honor were not admitted to the ranks of the elite, had a harder time obtaining credit, were not elected to office or given leadership positions in the military, and, worst of all, were considered lesser men, lacking in courage and integrity. With so much at stake, a southern man could be expected to fight—and even kill if necessary—to preserve his honor.[22]

Violence was also part of a complicated cultural legacy bequeathed by Scots-Irish immigrants. Between the late 1690s and the American Revolution, hundreds of thousands of Scots had left northern Ireland and settled on hardscrabble plots of land in and around the Allegheny and Appalachian Mountains. Persecuted in the Old World for their national origins and religious beliefs, the Scots-Irish brought to the new one a reflexive hostility toward outsiders that frequently led to violent encounters. Their enemies were as much English elites living along the eastern seaboard as they were Indians on the frontier or slaves toiling on plantations. Over time, as Scots-Irish immigrants were fully absorbed into the American mainstream, these attitudes and values became associated with southern culture.[23]

Of course, not every southern affair of honor ended in bloodshed. Disagreements were often settled on football fields rather than on dueling plains. In the spring of 1874, "without any warning," members of the Virginia Military Institute Cadet Football Club stormed the gates of Washington and Lee and challenged the students to a game on VMI's home turf. The men of W&L "were not to be backed out" and immediately dispatched thirty-five players to VMI's parade grounds, where, "much to the surprise and disgust of the cadets," they managed a 4–3 upset. The *Southern Collegian*'s editors gleefully taunted their neighbors with sarcastic quips: "We propose to have a championship game of marbles with [VMI] soon. May be, the cadets play that game better. However, it doesn't matter; we will play you at anything, gentlemen, that you can play. How would mumble-peg do?"[24]

Such prideful boasts were common in the nineteenth-century South (as they are in many areas of the South today). They also were at odds with the religious principles endorsed by a majority of southerners. Visitors to the region were often surprised to discover an intense religious sentiment that ran as deep as the Mississippi River. One English tourist described the South as "by a long way the most simply and sincerely religious country that I was ever in." A majority of southerners self-identified as Baptist (whether Two-Seed-in-the-Spirit, Regular, Southern, Primitive, Free Will, or something else), but Lutheran, Episcopal, Methodist, Presbyterian, Orthodox Jewish, Catholic, and other Protestant services were also popular, as were nondenominational revival meetings. Interestingly, church membership varied by locale. In some rural areas, only one in ten inhabitants belonged to a church, while in other locations the number was closer to 60 percent. City dwellers tended to join churches at a higher rate than country folk. But church membership was not always an accurate indicator of a community's religiosity. Plenty of southerners who prayed and attended services on a regular basis never bothered to join a church.[25]

Nevertheless, most colleges in the nineteenth century were affiliated with one Protestant denomination or another, whose members shared a common desire to keep the King James Bible as part of the curriculum. At Washington and Lee, a school established by Scots-Irish Presbyterians, local ministers took turns leading "daily religious exercises" on campus, and students were encouraged to attend a church of their choice on Sundays. Robert E. Lee, whom many southerners regarded as a model of manly Christian virtue, requested construction of a new chapel at Washington College during his presidency. The board of trustees responded by building a brick and limestone Victorian structure that was finished in time for the commencement exercises of 1868. Lee regularly attended services there with students and used the lower level of the chapel as office space.[26]

Church on Sunday and classes during the week left students with limited time for leisure activities. Saturday was different. It was the one day of the week when they could play games without fear of being reprimanded for neglecting their studies or breaking the Sabbath. As a result, college football games were frequently played on Saturday. Federal rules governing television broadcasting rights cemented this tradition in the twentieth century, but it was born in the nineteenth, out of practical necessity.[27]

On Saturday, October 10, 1874, football players from Washington and Lee once again locked horns with VMI cadets for town bragging rights. The series ended in a 1–1 tie, but W&L's players were convinced that they had been hornswoggled—the Institute had supposedly fielded eight extra men during the first game. "We were rather surprised at our friends' attempting to cheat us," griped the editors of the *Southern Collegian*.[28]

The editors might have been less surprised if they had been paying closer attention to current events. Cheating and corruption were pervasive in the years following the Civil War, a period historian Mark Summers has aptly described as "the era of good stealings." Men like William "Boss" Tweed in New York City and Michael "King Mike" McDonald in Chicago controlled powerful political machines that circumvented the democratic process through graft, bribery, and backdoor shenanigans. Tweed, in particular, took dirty politics to a new low, stealing a princely sum from the Big Apple that, in today's dollars, would amount to somewhere between $1 billion and $4 billion.[29]

The nation's capital was equally corrupt, especially during Ulysses Grant's presidency (1869–1877). Although Grant himself was honest, he surrounded himself with morally bankrupt men who were eager to profit from their high-ranking positions. Grant's secretary of war, for example, was forced to tender his resignation after he was caught taking bribes from a defense contractor. The president's private secretary, a man named Orville Babcock, was accused of abetting the so-called Whiskey Ring, a group of federal agents and grain distillers who conspired to steal whiskey tax revenues from the government. Grant's attorney general and his secretary of the interior would also eventually resign under a cloud of suspicion. Additional scandals further eroded the public's trust in both the Grant administration and the Republican Party.[30]

Corruption was also a major problem in the South. Black and white officials who had ridden to power on a wave of Republican reform were eager to take advantage of their positions while they still could. Like unscrupulous politicians elsewhere, they shamelessly fleeced taxpayers through crooked financial schemes and shady backroom deals with corporate executives. They also raised taxes on the wealthy in order to pay for new government programs, thus further antagonizing southern elites, who had been opposed to congressional reconstruction from the very beginning.[31]

By the time football began gaining traction on southern campuses, reconstruction was in retreat. Although Republicans managed to score big victories in the early 1870s with passage of the Fifteenth Amendment and the Enforcement Acts (designed to protect African American voters), their white constituents were tired of trying to fix the mess down South. They wanted Washington to focus on other issues, such as the economy, which had grown steadily worse following the Panic of 1873. Political scandals turned voters away from the Republican Party and fueled the creation of third parties. Democrats smelled blood and pounced, picking up legislative seats and governorships in several key northern states during the 1873 elections. The following November, they gained control over the House of Representatives for the first time since before the Civil War and won nineteen of twenty-five gubernatorial races.[32]

In the South, an assembly of Democrats, former Whigs, and opportunistic scalawags banded together to "redeem" their states from Republican rule. By 1875, they had succeeded in gaining control over all but three—Florida, South Carolina, and Louisiana. Violence was employed to intimidate political opponents. In Mississippi, for example, "Redeemers" threatened and murdered black Republicans while federal officials remained on the sidelines. On Election Day 1875, most African American voters in Mississippi stayed away from polling places out of fear for their safety. As a result, Democrats were able to seize both houses of the state legislature and pressure Republican governor Adelbert Ames, a former Union general, into resigning.[33]

Northern apathy and racism aided the efforts of the Redeemers. Even the president of the United States confessed to being weary of trying to change southern hearts and minds. "Let Louisiana take care of herself, as Texas will have to do," Grant told a reporter. "I don't want any quarrels about Mississippi State matters referred to me. This nursing of monstrosities has nearly exhausted the life of the [Republican] party. I am done with them, and they will have to take care of themselves."[34]

Many northerners agreed. The Thirteenth, Fourteenth, and Fifteenth Amendments seemed sufficient recompense for the crime of slavery. The freedpeople would have to work out the rest for themselves. Northern Anglo-Saxons were keen on reconciling with their southern racial kinsmen and moving the country forward. They also were opposed to prolonging reconstruction on cultural grounds as much as on racial ones. Black Republican rule had become synonymous with corruption, cronyism, and—worst of all from the standpoint of many northern conservatives—*socialism*.[35]

James Pike, a reporter for the *New-York Tribune* who had been a vocal opponent of slavery prior to the war, published a book on South Carolina politics, in 1874, entitled *The Prostrate State*. Unsurprisingly, Pike's book includes racist language and ideas that were common in many nineteenth-century publications. But it also questions the wisdom of giving political power to *any* race of men who do not own property, arguing that such persons inevitably try to topple the existing social and economic order while feathering their own nests with taxpayer dollars. "[South Carolina's legislators] pick your pockets by law," the journalist railed. "They rob the poor and the rich alike, by law. They confiscate your estate by law . . . They do all simply to enrich themselves personally. The sole, base object is, to gorge the individual with public plunder. Having done it, they turn around and buy immunity from their acts by sharing their gains with the ignorant, pauperized, besotted crowds who have chosen them to the stations they fill, and which enable them thus to rob and plunder."[36]

Similar views could be found on the pages of the *Nation*, an influential northern periodical that had at one time endorsed congressional reconstruction. In 1874, the *Nation*'s editors warned that the reconstruction acts had emboldened "a few designing men, with the aid of the Negro vote, to plunder the property holders." Unless South Carolina reversed course, the "dangerous, deadly poison" of socialism would transform the Palmetto State into an "African San Domingo."[37]

Socialism, which for many people had become synonymous with black Republican power, posed a threat to America's burgeoning industrial order. The United States could only become an economic powerhouse if every state committed itself to capitalism and kept the laboring classes under control. Southern Redeemers were willing to play ball. They wanted African Americans (a majority of whom were agricultural workers living in southern states) and poor whites to return to the fields and leave governing to those who had traditionally held power.

In the meantime, the Redeemers' privileged sons were away at college, learning how to play football. During one intramural game played at Washington and Lee in the 1870s, nineteen students from Kentucky took on a team comprised of twenty-four Texans and Tennesseans. (Most W&L students at the time were from former Confederate states.) According to the editors of the *Southern Collegian*, "The box-toed sons of the blue grass region outkicked the combined forces of Tenn. and the Lone Star to the tune of six to two." The Tennessee-Texas team blamed its poor performance on the absence of several star players and poked fun at the Kentuckians, joking that "men who came from a great mule country ought to kick well."[38]

Of course, football was just one of many athletic diversions on campus, and it would be wrong to suggest that the game was as popular in the nineteenth century as it would become later, in the twentieth. The early kicking version was primarily a distraction, a way for students to blow off steam between classes. Rules were lax, and the large number of participants made the game feel more like a boys' summer camp activity than a formal sport. Boating and baseball were also popular at Washington and Lee, and both these pastimes were better organized than football. Students worked hard at honing their skills between matches by swinging bats and rowing boats. Baseball, in particular, was a crowd pleaser that had first been introduced by Union soldiers during the Civil War. There also was a general interest in English university athletics. The *Southern Collegian* wanted its readers to be aware of the "outdoor sports" favored by students at Oxford: "throwing the cricket-ball, Yards Flat race, throwing the hammer, broad jump, hurdle race, one mile to quarter mile flat races, stranger's race, half-mile handicap, sack race, consolation race, handicap, putting the stone, ratting, foot-ball, cricket, &c."[39]

In 1876, three events occurred that would help ensure the long-term success of southern college football. The first was a presidential election. With Grant's time in office winding down, Republicans nominated an Ohio attorney and former Union general named Rutherford B. Hayes to be their party's standard bearer. Democrats chose New York Governor Samuel J. Tilden, an honest reformer who was best known for tackling political corruption in the Empire State. On Election Day, Tilden won the popular vote and came within one electoral vote of winning the White House by capturing 184 electoral votes versus Hayes's 165. Twenty electoral votes remained in dispute, however, nineteen of which were in southern states still occupied by federal troops—Louisiana, South Carolina, and Florida. The twentieth was in Oregon. Both sides refused to surrender, and the country was thrown into a constitutional crisis. There was serious talk of a second civil war.

Congress appointed a special commission to break the impasse. It consisted of eight Republicans and seven Democrats. Unsurprisingly, the commission voted 8–7 in favor of Hayes and awarded him all twenty of the disputed votes, and with them the presidency. Democrats were furious. In order to keep the peace and to hold on to power, Hayes promised to shower the South with post office jobs and public money for infrastructure improvements. More importantly, the president-elect pledged to withdraw the last federal troops from the South, effectively ceding control of the region to Redeemer-Democrats.[40]

Most white southerners were satisfied with what would later become known as the Compromise of 1877. With the long nightmare of reconstruction behind them, they could go back to managing their own affairs and refashioning the social and political order that had existed before the war. They also were delighted to be on friendly terms with their northern countrymen again and became more tolerant of Yankee ideas and immigrants. Young southerners, especially, were eager to embrace northern customs, causing angst among their elders, who were still haunted by memories of the Civil War. Southern college students soon would be exposed to a bureaucratic version of football, then developing in northern schools, that symbolized the scientific and organizational spirit of the age.[41]

The second major football-related event of 1876 occurred when a Connecticut teenager named Walter Camp set foot on the campus of Yale. Camp was strong and smart and took an immediate shine to the manly game that had become popular at Ivy League schools. It seems fitting that the "father of American football" began his playing career the same year the nation celebrated its centennial. During the first one hundred years of its existence, the United States resembled a bush league operation to many observers in other Western nations. Camp and his generation would move the United States from last place to first, thus setting the stage for the advent of what Henry Luce would later refer to as the "American century."[42]

Finally, 1876 was also the year that America's first research university, Johns Hopkins, in Baltimore, opened its doors to students. No one at the time could have guessed how important the school would be to the development of southern college football. "The question has frequently been asked . . . whether America is ready for a university such as the Johns Hopkins claims to be, or expects to be in a few years," noted the editors of the *Southern Collegian*. "We are not only ready for a National University, but we are really in need of one."[43]

CHAPTER TWO

YANKEE INGENUITY

During Walter Camp's freshman year, representatives from Yale, Harvard, Princeton, and Columbia gathered at the Massasoit House in Springfield, Massachusetts, to create a standardized version of American football based on the Rugby Football Union code. The group was able to ratify sixty-one rules (most of which were borrowed directly from the RFU's rule book) and establish the Intercollegiate Football Association (IFA), a primitive ancestor of the National Collegiate Athletic Association. It also agreed that games should henceforth be played with watermelon-shaped rugby balls rather than the round Association footballs that were harder to clutch while running.[1]

The results of this historic meeting represented a coup for Harvard, which had successfully blocked a previous attempt to turn American football into a soccer knockoff. The nation's oldest college had remained on the sidelines in October 1873, when representatives from several other schools huddled at the Fifth Avenue Hotel in New York City to codify the kicking game. Harvard men preferred tackling and ball carrying, both of which were allowed under the "Boston Game," a rough-and-tumble pastime invented by New England prep school boys that had been popular in Cambridge ever since a ten-year-old ban on football there had been rescinded. But the Boston Game was considered child's play next to rugby. Crimson players had gone gaga over the sport when they were first introduced to it, in 1874, by men from McGill University, an English-speaking college located in French-speaking Canada. With Harvard leading the charge, rugby's popularity had spread like wildfire across northeastern campuses in the months leading up to the Massasoit House meeting.[2]

A year after the rugby game was codified, a massive labor strike plunged the nation into chaos. It began in Martinsburg, West Virginia, in July 1877, when employees of the Baltimore & Ohio railroad responded to a series of wage cuts by refusing to move B&O trains. The governor of West Virginia—a former Confederate officer named Henry Mathews—initially believed that his state militiamen could handle the protest. But when they expressed sympathy for the strikers instead of cracking skulls, Mathews requested reinforcements from Washington.

News of the strike quickly spread to other cities, triggering an orgy of violence and destruction. In Baltimore, an enraged mob threw bricks and paving stones at Maryland troops, who panicked and opened fire, killing ten and wounding twenty-three. In Pittsburgh, rioters ducked bullets, looted stores, and torched railroad property—twenty-five people died. In Chicago, dozens more were killed in street battles between police and protesters. Railroad traffic across the country ground to a halt. Employee anger boiled over in other towns and cities along major rail lines, including Albany, Buffalo, Cincinnati, Kansas City, St. Louis, and San Francisco.

The country appeared to be going off the rails. The protests lost steam once federal troops intervened, but by then at least one hundred people were dead and millions of dollars' worth of property had been destroyed. Many Americans attributed the unrest to the spread of radical foreign ideas, particularly those espoused by the Paris Commune, a left-wing group that had seized control of the French capital at the end of the Franco–Prussian War.[3]

Thus, few raised any objections when the last federal troops were withdrawn from the South in 1877 and Redeemer governments replaced Republican ones that were widely seen as corrupt and socialist. Washington's retreat signaled the end of Reconstruction and, with it, the end of a southern black renaissance that had begun fourteen years earlier with the Emancipation Proclamation. Some African Americans could see the writing on the wall and responded to the Redeemers' counterrevolution by voting with their feet. In the late 1870s, tens of thousands of them living in the Mississippi Delta migrated to Kansas. It was the beginning of a massive exodus that would change the character and culture of areas outside the South in the years that followed.[4]

In 1878, Walter Camp attended the second meeting of the Intercollegiate Football Association and suggested that team sizes be reduced from fifteen players to eleven. Camp's support for eleven-man teams likely came from his knowledge of a game played in December 1873 between Yale and a group of Eton alumni, during which both sides, at the British players' behest, fielded eleven players. Yale men found that they preferred the more open style of play, while Camp believed a smaller team might also make it easier for players to obtain faculty permission to travel. The IFA stiff-armed his proposal.[5]

That same year, yellow fever—a virus transmitted by *Aedes aegypti* mosquitoes—swept through the Mississippi River valley like a scythe, harvesting between sixteen thousand and twenty thousand souls. Victims in the advanced stage of a yellow fever infection bleed from the nose and mouth; suffer excruciating headaches, fever, and jaundice (hence the name yellow fever); and, worst of all, vomit half-digested blood resembling coffee grounds, a consequence of internal hemorrhaging. The pandemic had started in New Orleans and traveled along the South's waterways and rail lines, spreading as far north as Indiana, Illinois, and Ohio.

The Deep South, however, bore the brunt of the suffering. Thousands of people in Louisiana, Mississippi, and Tennessee were infected with the virus and died in agony. In the city of Memphis alone there were five thousand confirmed yellow fever fatalities. Urban residents fled in terror but were shocked to find that in some places their rural neighbors had turned against them. Bands of vigilantes in sparsely populated communities turned away refugees at gunpoint in order to check the spread of the plague. The pandemic illustrated the need for a more rigorous southern public health system, which would gradually take shape in the coming years. Southerners understood that their region would never prosper until it modernized.[6]

The South's yellow fever nightmare seemed a world away to Walter Camp and other northeastern university students, who were doing their best to learn the finer points of rugby football. "Being bound by no traditions, and having seen no play," Camp recalled in later years, "the American took the English rules for a starting-point, and almost immediately proceeded to add and subtract, according to what seemed his pressing needs." Harvard's match with McGill allowed its students "to explain the knotty points [of rugby] to a small degree, but not enough to really assist the mass of uninitiated players to an understanding." With only a rudimentary grasp of English rugby, American players improvised.[7]

During an 1879 game against Harvard, Princeton assigned two men to protect the ballcarrier and thus stumbled into the concept of offensive blocking. Camp, who happened to be officiating the contest, rebuked Princeton's captain for employing an illegal move. Princeton players continued blocking anyway. The technique proved so successful that Camp's own Yale adopted it later in the season. In May, the University of Michigan inaugurated Midwestern college football by playing Racine College at the White Stockings' baseball park in Chicago. Michigan won the game by a score of 1–0. News of college football was beginning to travel out of the northeast along the telegraph lines and railroads that were driving America's industrial revolution.[8]

Football made a giant leap forward in 1880, when Camp convinced the IFA committee to replace the rugby scrum with a line of scrimmage. Instead of starting each play by having teams crowd the ball in a tangled mass of flesh, Camp's scheme involved a single player kicking or "heeling" the ball backwards into the arms of a quarterback. The committee also changed its mind about Camp's earlier proposal for eleven-man teams and reduced the size of the playing field from 140 yards to 110.

Camp's scrimmage idea initially looked like a stroke of stupidity. Teams quickly figured out that it allowed them to hold on to the ball indefinitely, thus robbing their opponents of any chance at scoring. During the 1880 and 1881 seasons, Princeton and Yale bored their fans to death by playing "block games" in which the offenses for both teams were able to force ties by refusing to kick, score, or turn over the ball. Something had to be done.

Camp's ingenious solution was a system of downs that gave the offense three chances to move the ball five yards. If the effort was successful, the cycle started over again; if unsuccessful, the offense had to turn the ball over to the other team. Not long afterward, lines were painted on football fields in five-yard increments as a way of measuring progress. In combination with separate vertical lines, a distinctive grid pattern began to take shape, resembling an ancient cooking device known as a gridiron. American football became known as "gridiron football" for this reason.[9]

While Camp was busy hammering out the rules for gridiron football, Kentuckians were discovering the joys of the old rugby game. In what some say was the first college football game in the South—a dubious claim, at best—Centre College took on Kentucky University (now Transylvania) in April 1880 at City Park in Lexington, Kentucky. Kentucky U. crushed Centre 13 3/4–0. (The following year, the team lost to a rookie squad from what would become the University of Kentucky.) Charles Thurgood, a divinity student from Melbourne, Australia, had introduced Kentuckians to the basics of rugby and had added his own novel way of keeping score: a point system that counted each touchdown as a quarter point. In contrast, the attendees of the 1876 Massasoit House meeting had determined that each football "goal" would count as four touchdowns, a far more confusing scoring method that would later be replaced with one similar to Thurgood's. Thus, the Bluegrass State—by way of Australia—can justly be described as the birthplace of football's points-based scoring system.[10]

Ten days prior to the Centre College–Kentucky University game, Wabash, Indiana, became the first city in North America to be illuminated by electricity. When the Brush Electric Light Company threw the switch on four large arc lamps it had installed on the Wabash County courthouse, sparks flew and brilliant columns of light penetrated the Midwestern night sky, astonishing a crowd of ten thousand that had turned out to witness the historic event.

It was an age of scientific wonders. Thomas Edison put his incandescent bulb into mass production the same year that Wabash switched on the lights. Alexander Graham Bell had only recently invented the telephone. Professor Thaddeus Lowe, already famous for his balloon experiments during the Civil War, took out a patent on an ice machine that would ultimately make industrialized food production possible. There were oil pipelines running through Pennsylvania, a transatlantic telegraph cable connecting Europe and America, a transcontinental railroad linking the eastern and western portions of the United States, and enormous factories that were gobbling up natural resources and generating obscene wealth for a handful of investors. Nearly all of these advances were the result of Yankee ingenuity, a point not lost on southerners, who desperately wanted their region to achieve a similar level of prosperity.[11]

But it was hard to get rich farming, especially under the South's oppressive crop lien system. Under the lien system, the average southern farmer, short on cash, had to borrow the supplies he needed from a local merchant, who agreed to wait until harvest for repayment of the principle, plus interest. If the farmer did not make enough money from the sale of his crops to cover his debts (a common occurrence), the merchant would force him to take out a new lien against the following year's harvest. The farmer would then have to borrow additional supplies from the merchant in order to make it through another season. And so it went, year in and year out, until the farmer found himself drowning in a sea of red ink. Lawrence Goodwyn describes the South's crop lien system as a "debasing method of economic organization" that evolved out of the devastation of the Civil War.[12] By the time Lee surrendered at Appomattox, Confederate currency had become worthless, emancipation had nullified the South's huge investment in slaves, southern banks were failing, and Union armies had wrecked the region's infrastructure and left tens of thousands of families without a primary breadwinner. In the absence of sufficient capital, southern agriculturalists had no choice but to go along with an economic system that made them slaves to their creditors.

In response to this situation, farmers in Lampasas County, Texas, had founded a grassroots organization, in 1877, that would eventually become known as the Southern Farmers' Alliance. By the middle of the 1880s, there were more than three hundred suballiances in Texas alone and a burgeoning Midwestern movement that referred to itself simply as the Farmers' Alliance. A separate Colored Farmers' Alliance sprouted up alongside the other two organizations. All three supported initiatives that were designed to lift farmers out of poverty, such as marketing cooperatives and a "subtreasury" plan—essentially, a proposal for a new government program that would allow farmers to store their crops in federal warehouses and borrow money at low interest rates until agricultural prices peaked. Alliance members also demanded higher taxes on the rich; a liberal monetary policy in the form of "free silver" (putting more money into circulation causes inflation, which in turn makes it easier for borrowers to pay off pre-inflationary debts); government control over railroad, telephone, and telegraph companies; and the direct election of U.S. senators by their constituents rather than by state legislatures.[13]

Even so, plenty of southerners were prepared to abandon farming altogether in favor of more lucrative professions. College offered them a way out. In the new industrial economy, men with university degrees were needed to manage factories, work in chemistry labs, design new machines, and teach college-level courses. And no institution of higher learning had greater appeal to southerners in the last quarter of the nineteenth century than Johns Hopkins University. Part of the reason was geography. Johns Hopkins is located in Baltimore, a city close to the Mason–Dixon Line, which has traditionally served as a cultural bridge between North and South.

The school also appealed to southerners because of its high percentage of southern faculty and the fact that its founder had set aside scholarship money to educate men from Maryland, Virginia, and North Carolina. In the late nineteenth century, southern alumni returning to their home states to fill academic posts "founded Hopkins 'colonies' from Virginia to Texas."[14] By 1896, no fewer than sixteen southern colleges employed three or more Hopkins graduates as faculty members. Roughly twice that number had at least one Hopkins-trained professor on the payroll.

Southerners crammed into classrooms to hear lectures delivered by brilliant teachers like Edward Renouf and Ira Remsen, two chemistry professors from New York, who, like many American faculty at the time, had earned their doctorates in Germany. German universities were well respected in the United States because of their affordable tuition, well-stocked libraries and laboratories, and rigorous curricula. Historians estimate that between nine thousand and ten thousand American scholars studied in Germany from 1815 to 1914. Johns Hopkins had been planned as America's answer to the German research university.[15]

Remsen had been poached from Williams College in Massachusetts for the purpose of building a chemistry department at Hopkins. Southerners flocked to his lectures because of his friendly teaching style and mastery of a subject they considered "a means of upward social mobility." At a time when medicine was still struggling to emerge from the scientific dark ages, chemistry offered its practitioners sound science as well as promising employment prospects. Ninety-five of the 202 chemistry PhDs produced during the Remsen era (1879–1913) came from southern states. Remsen's colleague, Edward Renouf, was another popular chemistry professor at Hopkins. When not teaching, performing lab experiments, or rolling cigarettes with one hand, Renouf was handling matters related to his role as president of the athletic association and acting director of the university gymnasium.[16]

Johns Hopkins students began playing football in the autumn of 1881. Walter Canfield and John Glenn formed a football club that practiced at Druid Hill Park in Baltimore. No meaningful games were scheduled during the inaugural season, due to the team's inexperience and rudimentary knowledge of the rules. That same semester, Richmond College (University of Richmond) played its first series of intercollegiate games against

Randolph-Macon College in Ashland, Virginia. Because it allowed twenty players on each side, Richmond's version of the sport was dubbed "twenties football." Richmond won the series 3–0.[17]

In September, President James A. Garfield died from wounds he had received two months earlier at the hands of a paranoid schizophrenic named Charles Guiteau. Guiteau had supported Garfield during the 1880 presidential campaign and expected a cushy government job in return. When the president instead called for an end to the spoils system, an enraged Guiteau purchased a handgun and shot Garfield as he stood waiting for a train in Washington, DC. The assassin had hoped that Garfield's running mate, Chester A. Arthur, would put the brakes on reform and continue doling out party patronage once he became president. Ironically, it was Guiteau's heinous act that convinced Arthur, once a "Stalwart," or opponent of civil service reform, to change his mind. Before his presidential term ended, Arthur signed the Pendleton Act into law, establishing the nation's first competitive civil servant exams.

Civil service reform was just one of many changes sweeping the nation in the 1880s. Immigrants were flooding into the United States in search of economic opportunity and religious and political freedom. Italians, Eastern Europeans, Greeks, Hungarians, Chinese, Russians, Jews, and other newcomers were culturally and ethnically dissimilar from the Northern and Western Europeans who had originally settled the United States. A nativist backlash led to the passage of the Chinese Exclusion Act (1882) and, later, the National Origins Act (1924), which would restrict immigration from areas outside of Northern and Western Europe, until the act was abolished in 1965.

The new immigrants provided the sweat equity for American industrialization, which was creating a prosperous middle class even as it undermined traditional gender roles. As farms gave way to factories, male workers were required to spend more and more time away from their families, under the watchful gaze of supervisors. Consequently, home and work became separate spheres, with the former managed almost exclusively by women. The segregation of bourgeois women proved to be a double-edged sword—they were denied the social and economic opportunities afforded to men but also gained a group cohesion and self-awareness that would gradually lead to their emancipation.[18]

Conservatives worried that the economic prosperity of the Gilded Age—Mark Twain's tongue-in-cheek name for America's industrial era—was creating a generation of namby-pamby men who were incapable of preserving the republican liberties they had inherited from their forebears. European philosophers had long warned about the dangers posed to free societies by commercial luxuries. Once men became addicted to the good life, so the thinking went, they gradually lost the self-restraint and manly virtue that were necessary for responsible citizenship. Commercial luxuries, as well as "bicycle-riding, bloomer-wearing, college-educated, job-holding New Women," threatened American masculinity and thus the future and stability of the American republic.[19]

College life was thought to be particularly emasculating. Young men who spent the bulk of their time with their noses in books were at risk of becoming "over-civilized, effete, and lazy." Both faculty and parents believed that students needed to engage in vigorous athletic activities in order to stay out of trouble and strengthen their bodies. At Johns Hopkins University, students wrestled, participated in gymnastic events, and played baseball, football, lacrosse, tennis, and tug-of-war. They also briefly flirted with cricket, until it was decided that "this branch of out-door sport was not suited to the stalwart Hopkinsians."[20]

In the autumn of 1882, Hopkins's football team played its first real game against the Baltimore Athletic Club. BAC players like Tunstall Smith and "Dr. Iglehart" turned the game into a "bloody contest," punishing Hopkins 4–0. The next game was a snowy Thanksgiving Day showdown with the U.S. Naval Academy. It was the beginning of an annual Hopkins–Navy Turkey Day tradition that would last for nearly a decade. Because the players were unaware of Camp's recently introduced system of downs, the game quickly became gridlocked. Hopkins managed to hold Navy to a 0–0 tie during the first half, but the cadets broke it open in the second, scoring two touchdowns. They returned to Annapolis bragging about their shutout victory over Hopkins's hapless eleven.[21]

Further north, Walter Camp and the IFA were still fine-tuning the rules of football. In December 1883, the committee adopted a new points-based scoring system. Under the new rules, a touchdown would count as four points, the goal afterwards as two, safeties also as two, and a field goal as five.[22]

The United States was divided into four time zones that same year.

Traditionally, each community had established its own local time based on the rhythms of life and the movement of the sun, but railroad companies insisted on a uniform timekeeping system that would allow them to move people and freight more efficiently. Clocks across the country were adjusted to accommodate rail schedules. A few years later, the IFA standardized the length of a football game to one hour and forty-five minutes—two forty-five-minute halves, with a fifteen-minute break in between.[23]

Both football and the American way of life were being transformed by a rush toward standardization, specialization, and uniform timekeeping. Socializing, in the agrarian past, had frequently been connected to work-related activities such as barn raisings and quilting bees, but in the modern industrial era, leisure and work were strictly segregated. The concept of the "weekend" emerged. Employees with discretionary income sought amusing diversions when they were not at their jobs. Men like Phineas T. Barnum, co-owner of the Barnum & Bailey Circus, and Captain Paul Boyton, proprietor of the first amusement park on Coney Island, cashed in on the growing demand for popular entertainment. Sports, too, were considered part of the entertainment world. Baseball games, boxing matches, and horse races attracted large crowds and generated healthy box office receipts. Newspapers began including details of these events in special sports sections, which further stimulated public interest.

Walter Camp was determined to keep his favorite sport from getting left behind. He advised football team managers to rent out large venues like the Polo Grounds in New York in order to make games feel like larger-than-life spectacles. In 1889, Camp teamed up with a journalist named Caspar Whitney to select the first "All-America" football team. It was a brilliant publicity move. By shining a spotlight on individual players, Camp and Whitney gave football fans a stronger emotional connection to the game. Their idea was so successful that it was soon adopted by every other college sport. As men of character, strength, and intelligence, All-American football players embodied the nation's highest ideals.[24]

They were also men who could survive in an era of "social Darwinism," a nineteenth-century philosophy based on the teachings of Herbert Spencer, an English academician responsible for the phrase "survival of the fittest." Inspired by Charles Darwin's theories on natural selection, Spencer reasoned that human beings, like every other living thing on the planet, benefitted from cutthroat competition. Competition weeded out weaklings and gave the strongest and smartest individuals a chance to thrive, thus improving the health and vitality of the community as a whole.

Spencer's most enthusiastic American disciple (besides the steel magnate Andrew Carnegie) was a political/social scientist at Yale named William Graham Sumner. Sumner enjoyed "a wider following than any other teacher in Yale's history" and was at the height of his academic career when Camp and others were inventing the rules of football. (Camp married Sumner's sister, Alice, in 1888.) During one of his more pungent lectures, Sumner blasted progressive economists for being "frightened at liberty, especially under the form of competition, which they elevate into a bugbear. They think it bears harshly on the weak. They do not perceive that here 'the strong' and 'the weak' are terms which admit of no definition unless they are made equivalent to the industrious and the idle, the frugal and the extravagant."[25]

Sumner's ideas complemented those associated with "muscular Christianity." Two British authors, Charles Kingsley and Thomas Hughes (the same Hughes who played football at Cornell in 1871), were the leading proponents of this idiosyncratic spiritual movement, which had originated in England. Muscular Christians believed the church needed a strong dose of rugged "masculinity" to offset the "emotional, feminine" worship style that had become common at too many parishes. For them, Jesus was as much raging bull as sacrificial lamb. Hughes's book *Tom Brown's Schooldays,* which was set at Rugby School and included a detailed description of the unique game played there, was suffused with muscular Christian themes. The author told a Harvard audience, in 1870, that his popular fictional characters belonged to "the brotherhood of muscular Christians" and that after "considering the persons up and down her Majesty's dominions to whom the new nickname has been applied, the principles which they are supposed to hold, and the sort of lives they are supposed to lead, I cannot see where [Tom Brown] could in these times have fallen into a nobler brotherhood." Muscular Christians in America worried that the new wave of non-Protestant immigrants, the growth of U.S. cities, and the proliferation of cushy desk jobs were turning good Christian men into Caspar Milquetoasts. Anglo-Saxons, in particular, needed to reinvigorate themselves through strenuous exercise and manly exhibitions. The Young Men's Christian Association (YMCA), the birthplace of basketball and volleyball, is the muscular Christian movement's most memorable achievement.[26]

Few southerners had time to entertain highfalutin ideas like the decline of Christian masculinity. Most were fixated on feeding their families and saving their farms from foreclosure. They watched in awe as Yankee capitalists like John D. Rockefeller, J. P. Morgan, and Cornelius Vanderbilt amassed huge fortunes and built opulent estates that made the South's antebellum plantation houses look like corrugated tin shacks. At the beginning of the Civil War, U.S. industrial output had lagged behind much of Western Europe's. By the end of the century, American corporations—most of which were located north of the Mason–Dixon Line—were producing more goods than Great Britain, France, and Germany combined.

Southerners also took note of the problems that accompanied such growth, including labor demonstrations that occasionally turned violent. One such episode occurred in Chicago's Haymarket Square, on May 4, 1886, when police tried to disperse a crowd of activists that had gathered to protest the killing of two McCormick Reaper plant workers the previous day. Toward the end of the protest, an unidentified person in the crowd threw a bomb at police, who responded by firing their weapons. By the time the smoke cleared, fifty people were wounded and ten lay dead, including six police officers.

Although the Haymarket protest had been planned by a relatively small number of radicals, the American public blamed organized labor as a whole for the fiasco. Membership in the Knights of Labor—a group that traditionally had opposed anarchism while countenancing some radical ideas, such as abolishing the wage system—plummeted from seven hundred thousand to one hundred thousand in only four years' time. The more conservative American Federation of Labor arose from the ashes to take its place. The AFL was willing to work within the capitalist system to secure basic worker rights, such as higher wages, safer working conditions, and shorter hours for its members.[27]

The same year that the Haymarket incident occurred, Harvard rejoined the IFA after a twelve-month hiatus. Harvard's faculty had banned football in 1885 over concerns the sport was getting out of hand. Players were constantly fighting and flouting rules without penalty. There were also the health risks associated with new power plays like Princeton's "V trick," a forerunner to the infamous flying wedge play later developed by Harvard. As the name suggests, players lined up behind the ball in a goose-like V formation, with the center at the V's apex. Once the ball was snapped, the quarterback tossed it to the fullback, who rushed downfield surrounded by a protective triangle. (A similar scheme was employed during kickoffs, with the quarterback carrying the ball instead of the fullback.) Legend has it that William "Pudge" Heffelfinger, the Yale All-American who would go on to become the nation's first professional player, devised a brutal but effective method of stopping the V trick play. Once the V was on the move, Heffelfinger would charge toward it at full speed, vault over its lead blockers, and land "his two-hundred pounds knees-first on the astounded ballcarrier."[28]

While northern footballers were busy bashing in each other's brains, a young Georgia newspaper editor named Henry Grady, who had made a name for himself as a pundit and national correspondent, accepted an invitation to address the prestigious New England Society of New York. It was the first time such an honor had been bestowed upon a southerner. Anxious to attract Yankee investment and heal the sectional wounds caused by the Civil War, Grady heralded the arrival of a "New South" that combined a solemn reverence for the past with an optimistic view of the future. "We have sown towns and cities in the place of theories, and put business above politics," the journalist intoned. "We have learned that one Northern immigrant is worth fifty foreigners and have smoothed the path to Southward, wiped out the place where Mason and Dixon's line used to be, and hung out the latchstring to you and yours." By the end of the speech, Grady had his audience in tears with a quote from Daniel Webster, who had addressed the very same club forty years earlier: "Standing hand to hand and clasping hands, we should remain united as we have been for sixty years, citizens of the same country, members of the same government, united, all united now and united forever."[29]

Grady's speech exaggerated the South's virtues and glossed over its many problems, including the all-too-obvious racial one. The Georgia journalist told the New England Society that African Americans in southern states received a fair share of public school funds and enjoyed "the fullest protection of our laws, and the close friendship of our people." Grady was not entirely off base, for it was true that most southern blacks *were* treated reasonably well by whites . . . as long as they "knew their place" and did not attempt to improve their station in life. Or, as Frederick Douglass put it in a speech he delivered at around the same time as Grady, the black man's "course upward is resented and resisted at every step of his progress." African Americans were stuck in a Catch-22: if they remained poor and ignorant, they reinforced racial stereotypes; if they became educated and affluent, they were despised for their impudence.[30]

Black stereotypes were a source of entertainment for students at Johns Hopkins University. When the school's athletic association ran low on funds, the Alpha Sigma Alpha Fraternity organized a minstrel show that raised two hundred dollars. "The performance was a 'howling' success," beamed the authors of the *Hopkins Medley.* "Wasn't 'Cotton,' with his chicken-pie and his Kangaroo Dance, the star of the Troupe?" added the *Hopkinsian.* Minstrel shows, which featured white performers in blackface mimicking the dialect, gestures, and songs of African Americans, had been part of the nation's cultural fabric since at least the 1830s. They reinforced damaging stereotypes and provided white audiences with a smug sense of their own supposed racial and cultural superiority.[31]

Professor Edward Renouf was president of the athletic association at the time of the Alpha Sigma Alpha minstrel show. His vice president was a young chemistry graduate student from Milledgeville, Georgia, named Charles Holmes Herty. After graduating from the University of Georgia (UGA) in 1886, Herty had enrolled in Johns Hopkins to study chemistry. Under Ira Remsen's tutelage, Herty spent four years learning inorganic chemistry, the history of chemistry, "theoretical" chemistry, and "chemistry of the compounds of carbon." His dissertation was entitled "The Double Halides of Lead and the Alkali Metals," the results of which were published in the prestigious *American Chemical Journal,* a periodical founded by his advisor. Herty stayed active during his time at Hopkins by singing in the glee club, running track, and participating in gymnastics. He also played baseball, but he showed a decisive lack of talent in this area, finishing dead last during the 1888 season with a batting average of .151 and a fielding average of .455.[32]

One of Herty's pals at Hopkins was a history doctoral student from Alabama named George Petrie. Petrie had originally enrolled at Hopkins to study languages but changed his major after taking a class taught by

Herbert Baxter Adams, another product of the German university system. Petrie also fell under the spell of a visiting professor from Wesleyan (and later Princeton) named Woodrow Wilson, who taught government at Hopkins during the summer months. As an undergraduate at Princeton, Wilson had coached the first Tiger football team organized under Massasoit rugby rules. As a professor at Wesleyan, he arranged coaching sessions for Wesleyan players, attended practices, and occasionally traveled with the team when it went on the road. Wilson's enthusiastic support for Wesleyan football helped revive the school's 1889 season, which began with "a disastrous series of defeats" but ended on a high note with a number of "widely hailed victories."[33]

Petrie and Wilson shared similar backgrounds. Both men were southerners and both were the sons of Presbyterian preachers (Wilson knew Petrie's father). In addition, Wilson's brother-in-law, Isaac Axson, and Petrie rented rooms in the same Baltimore boarding house. The future president would occasionally stop by their house when he was in town. During one such visit, Wilson was amused when Petrie showed off a ludicrously oversize coat he had bought on sale and had refitted by removing the buttons from the chest and sewing them under the right sleeve. Petrie was starstruck by Wilson, who was ten years his senior, and in later life remembered him as a "dynamic teacher" who had a habit of stressing important ideas by pointing with "his right fore-finger . . . and by twitching the end of his nose, with an up and down movement."[34]

Another Hopkins history major taken with Wilson was Frederick Jackson Turner. "Dr. Wilson is here. Homely, solemn, young, glum, but with that fire in his face and eye that means that its possessor is not of the common crowd," Turner wrote to his fiancée in the winter of 1890.[35] That same year, the U.S. Census Bureau announced the disappearance of the American frontier, prompting Turner to pen what is arguably the most influential historical essay ever written, "The Significance of the Frontier in American History." For Turner, American freedom and prosperity had traditionally depended on the westward movement of the nation's citizens. On the frontier, they encountered new economic opportunities and developed a self-reliance and restless energy that made democratic government possible. For more than three hundred years, people in the East who were trapped in lousy jobs and denied access to the levers of power had been able to make a fresh start by moving west. The implication was that the closure of this historical safety valve had left the nation circling the drain.

Turner's frontier thesis is no longer fashionable in academic circles, but for decades it shaped Americans' view of themselves and their past. It also provided a convincing—if overly simplistic—explanation for the many problems associated with the Gilded Age. Northern Anglo-Saxons, in particular, were worried about the labor strikes, demographic changes, and wild economic swings of the period. The society they had managed for centuries appeared to be slipping out of their control. They also were unhappy with the regimentation and dreariness of life in the new industrial era. Open-air exertion was gradually disappearing from people's daily lives as a consequence of urbanization and rapid advances in transportation and communications.

They turned to athletic competition and outdoor recreation for relief. As the 1890s unfolded, Americans became obsessed with physical activities—walking, cycling, rowing, riding, fishing, fencing, swimming, and more. These activities provided a way for white citizens, in particular, to demonstrate their "racial fitness." Teddy Roosevelt challenged American men to live the "strenuous life" (the title of one of his speeches) and American women to bear at least four children in order to avoid committing "race suicide." German immigrants had helped lay the groundwork for the fitness craze, years earlier, by introducing Americans to gymnastics. The modern version of the sport had been developed by Friedrich Ludwig Jahn as a way of promoting German unity and patriotism. By the late nineteenth century, gymnasiums, or "gyms," had become a common sight in cities and small towns across the United States.[36]

Colleges and universities contributed to the fitness fad by building gyms and adding physical education courses to their curricula. Campus sports soon became so popular that a "combative team spirit became virtually synonymous with college spirit" and "athletic prowess became a major determinant of institutional status." In 1861, Amherst College in Massachusetts became the first school to hire a full-time professor of hygiene and physical education. Harvard followed suit eighteen years later by appointing Dudley Allen Sargent, a one-time circus acrobat and Yale Medical School student, to a similar position.[37]

Sargent's tenure at Harvard represented a "turning point for physical education as a profession." He developed a fitness system based on pulley-weight machines (some of which Sargent himself designed) that could be adjusted for each individual's skill level. He also created a series of "mimetic exercises" that copied the movements of athletes and manual laborers. Sargent's ideas were so popular that he founded a teacher-training program at Harvard in 1884. By the beginning of the twentieth century, no fewer than 270 colleges were offering P.E. courses to students, thanks to the efforts of Sargent and other like-minded fitness enthusiasts.[38]

Southerners wanted their schools to be every bit as modern and sophisticated as northern ones. If Yankee educators considered physical education important, then it would have to be part of the curricula at southern colleges, too. In the 1880s and early 1890s, departments of physical culture spread like kudzu across the region. Many of the colleges they were attached to had themselves been established just a few years earlier by the Morrill Land-Grant Acts. Justin Morrill, a Republican congressman from Vermont, had introduced the original bill in 1862, granting federal land to states for the purpose of founding universities dedicated to agriculture and the mechanical arts (engineering). Schools such as Mississippi State, Texas A&M (Agricultural and Mechanical), the University of Arkansas, and Virginia Tech owe their existence to the Morrill Acts.

The land-grant universities were launched at a time of crisis. Industrialization had improved Americans' lives in many respects, but it had also left them anxious about the nation's future. The explosive growth of cities and factories had transformed formerly virile Anglo-Saxon men into pasty-faced dandies. The immigrants arriving from Eastern and Southern Europe in record numbers seemed far more energetic and self-assured. Some of them were also spreading radical European ideas that posed a threat to capitalism and social stability. Abysmal working conditions were fueling sympathy for these ideas—as well as strikes that periodically turned violent. The closing of the frontier heralded the end of westward territorial expansion and American democracy. And, as a result of new scientific management techniques and economies of scale, U.S. corporations were producing more than the domestic market could absorb. There was talk of a new, more aggressive foreign policy as a solution to the nation's woes. An American empire not only would open up new markets for corporations but also might deliver fresh souls to Protestant churches and give American masculinity a much-needed kick in the pants. Moreover, in a world governed by social Darwinism, the United States needed to seize its fair share of overseas territory before Europe claimed it all.

The South had its own unique set of challenges. The Confederacy's defeat during the Civil War had left the region with a massive inferiority complex. It was obvious that northerners were, by and large, better educated, wealthier, and more successful than southerners. Future southern prosperity would depend upon emulating northern methods and embracing northern ideas. From an educational standpoint, that meant transforming the region's colleges and universities into schools that could rival the great institutions of the North, such as Harvard and Princeton, where a new, scientific version of football was being developed.

CHAPTER THREE

DIXIE'S FOOTBALL PRIDE

On October 18, 1888, a crowd of between ten and fifteen thousand people descended on Raleigh for the next-to-last day of the North Carolina State Fair. The turnout shattered all of the fair's previous attendance records. Special trains were bringing in tourists from across the state. Most were heading straight from the train depot to the fairgrounds to gawk at wondrous exhibits like Professor Nowitzky's Indian medicine and phrenology show and the Hume, Minor, & Company multipiano display. W. T. Blackwell & Company's exhibit featured a wall built entirely from packages of its world-famous Bull Durham Smoking Tobacco, along with two pyramids constructed from hunks of long-cut and plug-cut tobacco. Passersby lingered at Mr. Harris's poultry pen to inspect his huge forty-four-pound turkey, which was rumored to be the state's biggest. They also eyeballed Major Tucker's Jersey cattle herd, with its magnificent prize bull.

At midday, Senator Zebulon Vance addressed a crowd that had gathered at the fair's grandstand. Vance, a former Confederate governor of North Carolina, knew that most of the voters in his audience were farmers, and he tailored his speech accordingly. *How could American cotton growers compete with Egyptian ones who were willing to work for as little as eight cents a day?* he thundered. *Farmers were the victims of corporate trusts, monopolies, and bad government policy. Yankee robber barons were getting rich off the backs of North Carolina farmers . . .* and so on. "The Senator's speech struck the popular chord," reported the *Raleigh News and Observer.* "It was like 'Our Zeb'—honest, noble, sincere, outspoken, fearless and manly."[1] At the conclusion of Vance's speech, the crowd settled in to watch the afternoon horse races. The third race turned out to be the most exciting, with Honeysuckle and Bequest running neck and neck down the stretch until Bequest edged ahead, crossing the finish line first by two lengths.

Later that same day, a group of students from the University of North Carolina at Chapel Hill and Wake Forest assembled on the racetrack infield to participate in what would be the first intercollegiate football game in North Carolina history. As a result of a misunderstanding, Wake Forest brought along a team of students from various classes to play against a UNC team made up entirely of sophomores. No one fully understood the rules of the game. Each team fielded fifteen players even though IFA regulations stipulated eleven. The result was an ugly, ad hoc contest resembling a cross between rugby and soccer. The spectators and media loved it anyway. The *Raleigh News and Observer* described the game as "one of the most interesting features of the whole fair." Wake Forest triumphed by a score of 6–4. Over the next few weeks, football mania tore through the Old North State like a tornado. "North Carolina is thoroughly alive with interest on the question of football," beamed the *News and Observer*. "It is having a rage, and is springing into popularity everywhere. Raleigh . . . is already wild on the subject, and crying for more."[2]

The enthusiasm for college football in North Carolina was part of a growing national interest in popular entertainments. Industrialization had created a burgeoning middle class with discretionary income and an appetite for stimulating diversions. Nineteenth-century Americans were seeking exciting spectacles that would break up the monotony of daily life. They flocked to Buffalo Bill's Wild West show to witness shooting and roping demonstrations by frontier legends such as Annie Oakley and the great Sioux chief Sitting Bull. Traveling circuses were bringing clowns, acrobats, and exotic animals to communities large and small. The Great Coney Island Water Carnival featured high divers, log rollers, championship swimmers, and other aquatic athletes, including a team of "water football" players. Land-based athletic contests were also popular, especially baseball, boxing, and football.[3]

Organized baseball had officially launched in 1846, in Hoboken, New Jersey, with the triumph of the New York Nine over the Knickerbocker Base Ball Club. The sport's popularity had steadily climbed in the North before soaring on both sides of the Mason–Dixon Line at the end of the Civil War. Northern migrants traveling through the rubble of southern communities encouraged local ballplayers to keep swinging for the fences.

As part of his master plan to revitalize Dixie, Henry Grady, in 1885, helped to establish a professional southern league. The Georgia journalist was savvy enough to know that cities with big league baseball teams attracted media attention and were considered important commercial hubs.

Before long, small towns across the South were fielding teams of their own, staffed by brash young upstarts and older players past their prime.

Baseball was also a hit on southern college campuses. The University of North Carolina baseball team scored its first win against an all-star club from Raleigh, two years after the Civil War ended. Students at Randolph-Macon College in Ashland, Virginia, were pleased as punch when one prominent periodical included baseball in its list of sports "shown to have rooted out many of the vices common in college life." Further north, students at Washington and Lee University were thrilled when their "college nine" scheduled a game against the Monticello B. B. Club from the University of Virginia. Although they were worried by rumors that the UVA club had been "practicing every day for the last month," W&L students remained cautiously optimistic that their team would shine on game day.[4]

Boxing was less popular on college campuses, perhaps because of its reputation for savagery (even by nineteenth-century standards) and its close association with Irish Catholic immigrants. Although bare-knuckle prizefighting had been banned in most states, the practice continued in the shadows of saloons, gyms, and backcountry arenas. The most famous prizefighter of the era was the Irish American champion John L. Sullivan. Sullivan had started his career by crisscrossing the country and offering money to anyone who could stay in the ring with him for four rounds. Between 1882 and 1892, the Boston pugilist with the handlebar mustache pummeled anyone who was brave enough to accept his challenge. Rank-and-file southerners admired Sullivan and turned out in force when he fought Jake Kilrain in Mississippi, in one-hundred-degree heat, for a mind-boggling seventy-five rounds. The bare-knuckle bloodbath received heavy press coverage.[5]

In the fall of 1888, however, North Carolinians were more interested in football than in prizefighting. After the matchup at the state fair, students from Wake Forest and Chapel Hill decided that future games should be played under IFA rules. This decision sat well with Trinity College (Duke), which challenged UNC to a game on Thanksgiving Day. Football had been brought to Duke by its thirty-year-old president, John Franklin Crowell. As a student at Yale, Crowell had taken a part-time job as a reporter covering Yale's athletic events for both the student newspaper and the *New Haven Morning News*. His passion for college sports (football especially) stemmed in part from his conviction that athletics served as an "effective bulwark against the social and individual vices incident to collegiate life," which he listed as "sensual indulgence, mollycoddling . . . gambling . . . drinking and carousing." Crowell had kept up with the career of his fellow Yalie Walter Camp and possessed an expert knowledge of IFA rules. In the weeks leading up to the Thanksgiving Day contest, he relentlessly drilled the Duke team in the fundamentals of football and even found time to write an article for the *Raleigh News and Observer* explaining the rules and history of the game.[6]

At two p.m. on Thursday, November 29, fans began filing into the baseball park at Raleigh's athletic field to witness North Carolina's first "scientific" game of football. The price of admission was twenty-five cents for men and fifteen cents for women and children. Fans were impressed with the bright new uniforms worn by players on both sides (Duke was rumored to have spent more than one hundred dollars on their team's duds). The Tar Heels won the coin toss and elected to receive. Not much else went their way the rest of the day. Stonewall Jackson Durham and Tom Daniels each scored touchdowns for Duke, putting their team on top 12–0 by halftime. Tempers flared. Two players got into a spat, which, according to Crowell, nearly ended in "an old-fashioned duel." UNC hung tough in the second half but could not find a way to score. Duke punched in another touchdown shortly before the game ended, making the final score 16–0.[7]

Later that day, members of both teams joined a delegation of students from Wake Forest for a conference at the Yarborough House Hotel in Raleigh. The purpose of the meeting was to establish a North Carolina intercollegiate football association modeled on the one created at the Massasoit House in Massachusetts. Davidson College also had been invited to send delegates, but Davidson's fuddy-duddy faculty refused to allow its students to participate.

Jealously between the schools in attendance resulted in gridlock. When the group failed to elect a single officer after casting eighteen ballots, a decision was made to draw lots. The presidency of the association fell to Duke, a Wake Forest student was chosen secretary, and a UNC man became treasurer. That night, North Carolina hosted a victory party for Duke that was attended by an influential state newspaper editor and UNC law school graduate named Josephus Daniels. Daniels shook hands with Crowell and congratulated him on Duke's big win. "I responded that apparently the mantle of Yale had fallen on [Duke]," Crowell recalled in later years. "That victory had a moral effect far beyond the importance of the score: it gave notice that the little college up in Randolph [County] had come out from under."[8] In other words, football had put Duke on the map, just as Crowell hoped it would.

Further north, the University of Virginia football program was also gaining steam. A former Princeton player named H. Reid Rogers had been elected president of Virginia's Football Association in 1887 and was teaching UVA students the finer points of the game. His efforts paid off on November 20, 1888, when Virginia trounced Pantops Academy, a local boys' school, by a score of 20–0 in UVA's first "official" game. A few days later, the university eleven traveled to Alexandria and defeated a joint team made up of students from Episcopal High School and the Virginia Theological Seminary. Virginia was humiliated on December 8, however, when Johns Hopkins came to town and delivered a 26–0 knockout blow.

That same season, UVA decided to change its school colors. Players had been wearing gray and red uniforms that symbolized the bloodstained uniforms worn by Confederate troops during the Civil War, but these were hard to see when football fields turned muddy. When the question of team colors was raised during a student meeting, someone in the crowd snatched an orange and blue scarf off the shoulders of a football player named Allen Potts and shouted, "How will this do?" Cavalier colors have been blue and orange ever since. Potts had evidently acquired the scarf the previous summer while participating in a crew race in England, where tradition held that rowing clubs swap scarves at the end of their regattas. Researchers believe Potts's scarf came from the Grosvenor Rowing Club, which supposedly used orange paint on its boats as a cheap substitute for gold paint (the club's official colors are gold and blue).[9]

During the early years of southern football, UVA and other colleges were not picky about whom they played against. High school teams, independent football clubs, and other amateur groups were routinely added to season schedules. As noted earlier, Johns Hopkins's first real game was against the Baltimore Athletic Club. In the years that followed, Hopkins took on the Druid Athletic Club, Gallaudet (a college for the hearing-impaired, located in Washington, DC), and a team from the Baltimore Medical College. After beating UNC–Chapel Hill at the North Carolina State Fair, Wake Forest played the Raleigh Football Association, another independent club without a college affiliation. Teams nowadays recruit star athletes and carefully plan their season schedules in order to maximize their chances of winning. But in the nineteenth century, football was a slapdash, amateurish sport that attracted men of all shapes and sizes with varying degrees of athletic talent.[10]

In December 1889, Furman University made history by playing Wofford College in South Carolina's first intercollegiate football game. Wofford was coached by a Yale graduate named Edwin Kerrison, who led his team to a 5–1 victory on Spartanburg's Encampment Grounds. Despite his Yale pedigree, it is unclear how much Kerrison actually knew about scientific football, since the final score was a numeric impossibility under IFA rules. It could be that Kerrison was fully aware of IFA regulations but chose to play by a different set of rules, based on a request from Furman. According to a report published in the January 1890 edition of the *Wofford College Journal*, "The Wofford team wished Association rules to govern the game, but Furman protesting, after some discussion, it was decided to play the old rough-and-tumble game." What exactly was "the old rough-and-tumble game"—one played by some variation of IFA rules or English Football Association rules, or something else entirely? Unfortunately, the answer to this question appears to have been lost in the fog of history.[11]

In the autumn of 1890, Charles Herty arrived in Athens, Georgia, to begin working as a chemist for the Georgia Agricultural Experiment Station. It was not the same sleepy southern hamlet Herty remembered from his undergraduate days at Georgia. There were new buildings under construction, freshly paved sidewalks, and state-of-the-art electric streetlights. Local factories and businesses were humming. Henry Grady was optimistic that Athens would become the next major American manufacturing center, the "Lowell of the South," as he liked to call it, a reference to the booming textile mills that had put Lowell, Massachusetts, on the map earlier in the century. Herty quickly mastered the duties of his new position, having performed similar work in graduate school. He also befriended a number of UGA students and faculty.[12]

As Herty was getting settled in Athens, the Virginia Cavaliers were making history as the first southern team to play—and to be massacred by—the Princeton Tigers. The final score of the exhibition game played in Baltimore was 115–0.[13] UVA fans breathed a sigh of relief a few weeks later, when their team shredded Randolph-Macon 136–0 at home in Charlottesville, but the lesson from their loss to Princeton would echo across the South for two decades: southern teams, no matter how talented, were no match for north-eastern powerhouse programs.[14]

In October, President Benjamin Harrison signed the McKinley Tariff into law. Like most Republicans, Harrison and the bill's chief sponsor, Congressman William McKinley of Ohio, believed that high tariffs (or taxes on imports) boosted the U.S. economy by making American goods less expensive than foreign ones. Consumers would naturally choose the cheaper option, so the thinking went, thus stimulating the growth of domestic manufacturing.

High tariffs had never been popular in the South, however. A majority of southerners believed that tariffs gave northern manufacturers an unfair advantage (what we might call "corporate welfare" today). Southerners also were opposed to the idea of taxing one area of the country for the exclusive benefit of another, especially one that already possessed a disproportionate share of the nation's wealth. Furthermore, they knew that high tariffs nearly always led to retaliatory tariffs from foreign countries that purchased southern agricultural products such as cotton and tobacco, thus harming their sales.[15]

Both of these crops played a critical role in Tennessee's economy. But bragging rights, not tariffs, were on the minds of those who attended the 1890 Thanksgiving Day game between Vanderbilt and the University of Nashville. It was the Volunteer State's first intercollegiate football contest. The game had stemmed from a challenge issued by Nashville students, who wanted to put their intramural football skills to the test by playing students from another school. The president of Vanderbilt's athletic association, a chemistry professor named William Dudley, took Nashville's challenge seriously and scheduled a meeting in the school gymnasium that was attended by 150 students.

For Dudley, nothing less than the pride of the university was at stake. The students dithered at first. Was there enough time to prepare for the game? Didn't Nashville's considerable experience give it an unfair advantage? In the end, it was decided that Vanderbilt men did not take guff from Nashville braggarts. The challenge would be accepted.

Elliott Jones, a student who had seen "organized" football played at a prep school in Massachusetts (and also owned a book on football) was elected captain of the team. Jones readied his men for battle, and on Thanksgiving

Day they crushed Nashville 40–0. R. H. Mitchell, who "had a way of squirming and twisting his way through opposing tackles," wore down the Nashville defensive line. Horace Bemis stiff-armed his opponents and gained the most yards for Vanderbilt, primarily by running outside. That evening, the two schools' debate teams went head to head in the Vanderbilt chapel. When the judges briefly left the room to decide a winner, a few cheeky Vandy students placed the game ball—which had been painted with a large "40 to 0"—in the church pulpit, causing a joyful noise to erupt from the pews.[16]

Football quickly replaced baseball as Vanderbilt's most popular sport. Large crowds began turning out for games. Money from ticket sales filled the athletic association's coffers. And winning became the most important thing—even more important than good sportsmanship.

Teams discovered that one way of stacking the odds in their favor was to recruit paid professionals, or ringers, to help them win. Ringers were usually enrolled in classes to avoid raising suspicions, though few bothered to show up for class. Vanderbilt's early teams, for example, included a suspicious number of older dental and medical school students. Plenty of other colleges employed the same trick. A University of Nashville team dominated by "medical students" ended up in a brawl with players and fans from an opposing team. Although canes, knives, and pistols were drawn, no one was seriously injured during the ruckus. Duke students were reprimanded for recruiting a 220-pound townie they found working in a Durham train yard. When the story broke, Wake Forest students made fun of their unscrupulous in-state rivals: "[Duke's] center rush is like President Crowell's interest in foot-ball—abnormally developed."[17]

Corruption was also a problem at many northern universities. Walter Camp at one point controlled a slush fund worth $100,000 that was purportedly being used to "tutor" Yale athletes. Camp turned a blind eye when a twenty-five-year-old "freshman" who became team captain received free tuition, a luxury dorm suite, and permission to run campus cigarette and baseball scorecard businesses on the side. A separate class of ringers known as "tramp athletes" were brought in for big games and sometimes "found themselves matriculated at different universities weeks or months later."[18]

At the root of this chicanery was a love of money. Ticket sales were generating big bucks, and so were side bets. A reporter covering a matchup between Yale and Princeton in 1880 observed a group of students on the sidelines conspicuously waving handfuls "of greenbacks in the air, loudly calling for bets." Alumni from Harvard and Princeton were doing the same thing on the floor of the New York Stock Exchange a week before their two schools went head to head during the 1893 season. Dudley Sargent, a zealous supporter of college sports, predicted that gambling would be "the bane of competitive contests." Even Walter Camp, no stranger to financial misdeeds, worried that the availability of so much easy money might cause players to start fixing games.[19]

But there was little Camp could do to stop it. College football was operating in a largely unregulated business environment and growing by leaps and bounds every year. By 1890, the annual Harvard–Yale game was attracting twenty thousand spectators, a huge number by the standards of the era. The annual Thanksgiving Day matchup between the two best teams in the East, a tradition begun in 1876 by the IFA, was also pulling in record crowds. Camp's colorful accounts of these games were reprinted in newspapers across the country, further arousing public interest in football and earning the author a princely sum for his efforts.[20]

A month after Tennessee's first intercollegiate game, Sitting Bull was killed during a botched arrest attempt at his home in South Dakota. The U.S. government wanted him brought in over his refusal to denounce the Ghost Dance movement, a political/spiritual awakening among western Indians who were pushing for a revival of ancient native customs. When federal agents came to arrest the former Wild West performer, a band of his followers launched a defensive counterattack that ended with the deaths of twelve people, including Sitting Bull himself.

Two weeks later, soldiers from the U.S. Seventh Cavalry—the same unit that had been decimated by Sitting Bull's army at Little Big Horn—tried to disarm a group of Lakota Sioux who were making their way to the Pine Ridge Reservation. As the troops closed in, a nervous Indian discharged his weapon, either by design or by accident, triggering an instant barrage of return fire. By the time the shooting stopped, at least 150 Indians—including women and children—lay dead on the ground, alongside twenty-five soldiers. The Wounded Knee Massacre sounded the death knell for Indian resistance to U.S. encroachment. By 1890, "disease, military defeat, and dislocation" had reduced a once proud people to a pitiable husk of humanity. Some would later find success playing football for the Carlisle Indian

School in Pennsylvania, under the tutelage of Coach Glenn Scobey "Pop" Warner.[21]

The following year, Harper & Brothers (today's HarperCollins) published Camp's *American Football*. The first edition of the book featured an attractive cover embossed with an American flag and two gold eagles clutching footballs. It was an instant best seller. "The progress of the sport of football in this country, and a corresponding growth of inquiry as to the methods adopted by experienced teams, have prompted the publication of this book," Camp explained in his preface. Most of the chapters in *American Football* contain dry details on playing positions, but two of them are somewhat livelier—one on training methods and another, entitled "A Chapter for Spectators," that explains the game's jargon. Photographs of star players from Yale, Princeton, and Harvard further enhanced the book's appeal.[22]

American Football was an immediate hit on southern campuses. In the summer of 1891, the University of Georgia hired Charles Herty to teach chemistry, at a salary of $1,200 per annum. George Shackelford was a Georgia student at the time and never forgot the day that Professor Herty walked out onto the school's military drill field—which also doubled as an athletic field—carrying a copy of Camp's book. Shackelford and a group of his fellow students gathered around Herty to hear him explain how scientific football was played up North. They decided to form a team of their own and to transform the drill field into a proper gridiron. In later years, Shackelford recalled the team's first practice: "Dr. Herty simply tossed the football in the air and watched us scramble for it. He selected the strongest looking specimens for the first team. Luckily I was the one who recovered the ball and thus I was assigned a position." Herty's Darwinian coaching style included forcing his players to take cold showers and to go on three-mile runs before breakfast. No games were scheduled for 1891, due to a lack of suitable opponents.[23]

Football fans in Tennessee, meanwhile, were finding greener pastures that season. On November 21, a team from the University of Tennessee traveled to Chattanooga to take on a scrappy squad from the University of the South (Sewanee) in what was UT's intercollegiate debut. Tennessee's captain and starting halfback was a former Princeton player named Henry Denlinger, who had originally been hired by the university to teach gym. The Sewanee team was captained by Alex Shepherd, a seasoned lineman who had at one time played football for the Lawrenceville School in New

Jersey, a private high school located a few miles from Princeton. Roughly one hundred people braved a rainstorm to watch Sewanee thump UT 26–0. No one knew it at the time, but Tennessee had been beaten by an emerging powerhouse. Before the decade ended, Sewanee would establish itself as one of the greatest southern football programs of all time.[24]

On January 30, 1892, the University of Georgia played intercollegiate football for the first time. A train carrying a team from Mercer College, along with two carloads of rowdy Mercer students and fans who had hopped aboard at various stops along the Macon and Northern Rail Line, arrived in Athens at lunchtime. Georgia's campus was decked out in red and black. Students from both schools hooted and hollered as a crowd of curious spectators perambulated across the grounds. Laughter erupted when "Sir William," an ornery goat that had been selected as UGA's mascot, was led across the gridiron. (Following Yale's lead, Georgia would eventually replace Sir William with a bulldog.) By three p.m., more than a thousand people were eagerly awaiting kickoff.

The Georgia defense came out swinging and hit Mercer for a three-yard loss on its opening play. On second down, Mercer again failed to gain any yardage. On third down, the school turned the ball over to Georgia and sent in a defensive unit that played as poorly as its offense. UGA halfback Frank "Si" Herty—Charles's cousin—broke through the anemic Mercer line for a touchdown on Georgia's very first offensive play. Herty scored again a few minutes later. The most exciting defensive play of the day occurred when George Shackleford lifted a Mercer ballcarrier into the air and carried him over the goal line for a Georgia safety. Although the final score was recorded as a 50–0 Georgia win, UGA's right tackle, A. O. Halsey, thought that the victory would have been even more lopsided if the official scorekeeper had not run down to the liquor store twice during the game and "missed out on ten [additional Georgia] points."[25]

Georgia's next game was against a tenderfoot squad from Auburn (then known as the Agricultural and Mechanical College of Alabama), coached by Charles Herty's graduate school chum, George Petrie. When Petrie arrived on campus in 1891, Auburn students were playing a version of mob football similar to the one that had been popular at Washington and Lee twenty years earlier. Petrie was unimpressed. He detested the chaos of mob football and immediately set out to teach students the basics of the scientific game, while also passing along a few tips he had learned from the Virginia Cavaliers during a recent trip to Charlottesville. In addition, the proud Virginia alumnus selected UVA blue and orange as Auburn's team colors. Petrie had been invited by Herty to referee the Georgia–Mercer game but declined the offer, sending one of his team captains to do the job instead. He was not shy about challenging UGA to a game, however. The primary motivation was his friendship with Herty, but Petrie was shrewd enough to know that Auburn would benefit from the publicity surrounding a big game between two neighboring state universities.[26]

The contest was scheduled for February 20, 1892, in Atlanta's Piedmont Park. Petrie and UGA's team manager cut a deal with the *Atlanta Constitution* beforehand: in return for covering most of the teams' expenses and providing free publicity, the newspaper would be allowed to keep half of the money from ticket sales. Prices were set at fifty cents for adults and twenty-five cents for children. On game day, crowds gathered at Union Station to greet the special team trains arriving from Athens and Auburn. The UGA train got there first. It was filled with nearly three hundred rambunctious passengers sporting red and black outfits. They were welcomed by a large group of local Georgia fans, who accompanied them to the nearby Kimball House hotel. The Auburn team showed up next, dressed in gray cadet uniforms, and marched to the Kimball House like a company of battle-hardened Confederates. Both teams and their fans raised such a hullabaloo in the hotel lobby that other guests rushed from their rooms to see what all the fuss was about.[27]

Atlanta was delirious with football fever. Collegiate colors adorned the city's downtown buildings. Shopkeepers peddled team merchandise. Brass bands paraded through the streets. At 3:27 p.m., Sir William appeared on the playing field in a hat with black and red ribbons and a UGA blanket thrown over his back. Although popular, Sir William had not been everyone's first choice as mascot. Some Georgia students had voted for "Old Tub," a blind former slave who made a living selling apples and peanuts on UGA's campus.

Auburn's "mascot" turned out to be an African American janitor named Bob Frazier, who paraded up and down the sidelines dressed in a cream-colored suit, an ascot, and derby hat. Treating black southerners in such a degrading fashion reinforced the myth of the "happy darky," a cringe-inducing stereotype that had carried down from the antebellum era. How Frazier may have felt about his position is unclear, although the fact that he was often drunk while performing suggests that he was far from happy. Still, as strange as it may seem to the enlightened modern reader, the notion that he may have derived a modicum of satisfaction from being the center of attention (in the same way that "Blind Jim" Ivy did for many years, as a de facto cheerleader for Ole Miss) cannot be dismissed out of hand. Over the course of many generations, black and white southerners developed complex relationships that did not always conform to black and white stereotypes. They occasionally developed a genuine affection for one another that transcended the cultural expectations of their time, and ours.[28]

The Auburn–Georgia game kicked off at 3:30 p.m. Auburn's opening play was a V trick that resulted in a five-yard gain for the Tigers, but they were unable to score on the drive. The Georgia offense ran sweeps in response, which also proved pointless. At halftime, the score was 0–0. Early in the second half, Auburn recovered a Georgia fumble, which the Tigers were able to parlay into a touchdown and a two-point conversion. Auburn's secret weapon was a 210-pound engineering professor named Floyd Mc-Kissick, who, when faced with a fourth and goal situation, grabbed Auburn halfback Richard "Dutch" Dorsey and rammed him through a wall of Georgia defenders and into the end zone (the Tigers' "push play"). A short time later, a defensive tackle for Auburn scooped up another UGA fumble and ran fifty-five yards for a touchdown. The final score was Auburn 10, Georgia 0. Thus ended the first intercollegiate game in Alabama history and the opening match of the "Deep South's oldest rivalry."[29]

Legend has it that a popular Auburn cheer originated during this game, when a Civil War veteran in the stands lost control of his pet eagle. The bird, which had supposedly been retrieved from a battlefield in Virginia, was said to have soared majestically over the playing field during an Auburn drive, prompting fans to shout "War Eagle!" in support of their team. In a strange twist, the eagle fell out of the sky and died immediately after the game ended, but not before a college football tradition was born. This story is almost certainly apocryphal, but that has not stopped legions of Auburn fans from retelling it (and several other tall tales) when asked to explain the origins of the "War Eagle" battle cry. Currently, a trained golden eagle or bald eagle flies over Jordan–Hare Stadium before each home game to rally the Auburn faithful.[30]

CHAPTER FOUR

"FOOT BALL IS BRUTAL
AND DANGEROUS"

n March 1892, football debuted at the North Carolina College of Agriculture and Mechanic Arts (NC State), when eleven players wearing pink and blue uniforms defeated a team of local high school students from Raleigh Academy by a score of 12–6. Nearly two hundred people attended the game, "including an unusual number of ladies." An NC State professor served as umpire, along with a "Mr. Prince, of Wake Forest," who had to leave at halftime to catch a train. According to the *Raleigh News and Observer,* the "school boys averaged 125 pounds and the college men about 160." The NC State students used their superior mass to grind down the Raleigh Academy's defensive line.[1]

In July, violence at Andrew Carnegie's steel mill in Homestead, Pennsylvania, alarmed the nation. The trouble had begun when Carnegie and his plant manager, Henry Clay Frick, attempted to settle a labor dispute by replacing union workers with scabs. A gun battle ensued between the sacked employees and a contingent of Pinkerton guards who had been hired by Frick to provide security. Sixteen people were killed before the governor of Pennsylvania crushed the revolt by sending in a force of eight thousand state militiamen. Public sympathy lay with the workers until a deranged anarchist named Alexander Berkman tried to assassinate Frick at his offices in downtown Pittsburgh. Berkman's assassination attempt made it seem as if the Homestead Strike had been part of some larger left-wing conspiracy.

During the same month, the Populist Party nominated for president a former Union general named James Weaver. Leonidas L. Polk, a North Carolinian and former Confederate officer, had been a leading contender for the party's nomination, until he died suddenly in June 1892.[2] Most of the party's supporters were Farmers' Alliance members who felt they were being left behind in the new industrial economy. The party was also backed by union workers who shared the farmers' loathing for corporations and their political allies. "The fruits of the toil of millions are boldly stolen to build up colossal fortunes for a few, unprecedented in the history of mankind," read the party platform. "And the possessors of those, in turn, despise the republic and endanger liberty. From the same prolific womb of governmental injustice we breed the two great classes—tramps and millionaires." The Populists favored an end to public subsidies for private companies, "fair and liberal" pensions for U.S. veterans, immigration restrictions, government ownership of railroads, higher taxes on the rich, and other proposals designed to narrow the gap between rich and poor.[3]

These ideas made sense to many southerners who lived in rural areas and resented the growth of "an impersonal, amoral, urban-centered, non-southern, industrial society." In their eyes, the simple agrarian republic they had inherited from their ancestors had been hijacked by a handful of silk-hatted money-grubbers. Talented stump speakers like Georgia's Tom Watson appealed to black and white southerners alike who were fed up with getting left behind in the "heartless, tireless, pitiless race for wealth."[4]

But great speeches were not enough to convince most people to vote for a third-party candidate, and on November 8, 1892, Grover Cleveland was elected to a second, nonconsecutive term as president. Cleveland's victory was partially attributable to the "solid South's" overwhelming support for Democrats during every election cycle. The eleven former Confederate states contributed 112 of the 277 electoral votes that gave Cleveland his second term. Cleveland's Republican rival, Benjamin Harrison, finished in second place with 145 electoral votes. James Weaver came in a distant third with only 22 electoral votes and 8.5 percent of the popular vote. Neither Harrison nor Weaver carried a single southern state.[5]

Football debuted that autumn at the Virginia Agricultural and Mechanical College (Virginia Tech), when a team from the St. Albans boys' school in Radford took a ferry across the New River and made the quick trip up to Blacksburg in a caravan of horse-drawn surreys. On October 21, W. E. Anderson scored the first touchdown in Virginia Tech history while leading his team to a 14–10 victory over St. Albans. The lads from Radford exacted revenge eight days later by winning 10–0 in a game that had to be cut short due to a squabble over the rules. Virginia Tech students at the time were required to join the Corps of Cadets, an obligation stemming from language in the Morrill Land-Grant Acts, which stipulated the teaching of military science at land-grant schools. Tech cadets had spent the year leading up to their matchup with St. Albans, playing rugby in a field behind Barracks No. 1, the site of today's Lane Hall.[6]

In November, students at the Georgia School of Technology (Georgia Tech) played in their first game, against Mercer College, and lost 12-6. Tech students had become interested in football after seeing archrival Georgia lose to Auburn in Piedmont Park. They asked Earnest West, an adjunct physics professor, to serve as their coach and to play halfback. Unfortunately for West, Tech finished the 1892 season 0-3 after losing to Mercer, Vanderbilt, and Auburn. He was replaced the following season by Leonard Wood, an army surgeon who had assisted in the capture of the Indian chief Geronimo and would later command the First U.S. Volunteer Cavalry regiment (the "Rough Riders") during the Spanish–American War. The thirty-two-year-old Wood not only coached Tech but also played fullback for the team. In addition, he refereed games between other schools and kept his friend Walter Camp informed about the sport's growing popularity below the Mason–Dixon Line: "Foot ball is all the rage down here."

Wood led Georgia Tech to a 2-1-1 record during his first season as the team's coach/fullback, which included a 28-6 paddling of the Georgia Bulldogs in Athens. According to at least one source, an overzealous UGA fan who had grown tired of watching his team get steamrolled by a middle-age ringer threw a rock at Wood and hit him in the head, creating a three-inch laceration, which Wood himself stitched up when he returned to his hotel room. Wood's teammates also were supposedly targeted by angry Georgia fans, who hurled bricks and stones at the end of the game.[7]

At three p.m. on November 11, 1892, eleven men from Tuscaloosa gathered on a Birmingham, Alabama, baseball field for the University of Alabama's inaugural football game. They were coached by Eugene Beaumont, a native Texan, who had discovered football while attending the University of Pennsylvania. Their opponents were pimple-faced high school kids coached by a Professor Taylor, who also played center for his team. Alabama snuffed Taylor's teenagers 56-0. The next day, the university went head to head with the Birmingham Athletic Club, another one of Taylor's teams. Although Bama scored the only touchdown of the afternoon, the BAC ended up winning on an incredible sixty-three-yard field goal kicked by J. P. Ross, an Irish rugby player, in the closing minutes of the game. Under IFA rules, field goals counted as five points while touchdowns were worth only four. BAC fans celebrated the victory by carrying Ross off the field on their shoulders.[8]

Football had been introduced to the University of Alabama ("the Capstone") by W. G. Little, a Sumter County, Alabama, native who learned the basics of the game while attending Phillips Academy in Andover, Massachusetts (figure 4).[9] Little had planned on attending Yale after finishing high school, but a death in the family forced him to return home and enroll at Alabama instead. Little's fellow Bama students were impressed with his cleats, canvas suit, and suggestion that they form a genuine Yankee-style football team of their own.[10]

During the same semester, Harvard stunned the college football world by introducing a dangerous new play called the flying wedge. At the beginning of the second half of the 1892 Harvard–Yale game, a Crimson player named Bernard Trafford lined up on the forty-five-yard line for the kickoff. Trafford's teammates stood twenty yards behind him, split into two groups of five and positioned on opposite sides of the field. They were in motion before Trafford kicked the ball, charging downfield like a herd of buffalo and moving toward the center of the field in the shape of a V. By the time they reached the forty-five-yard line, Trafford had performed what amounted to an onside kick and tossed the ball to his halfback. Harvard's flying wedge then continued downfield, providing protection for the halfback and trampling Yale's stunned defense.[11]

Watching from the sidelines that day was a twenty-seven-year-old classics professor named Alexander Bondurant, who had recently taken a sabbatical from his teaching job at Ole Miss in order to study at Harvard. Bondurant was instantly smitten by the sport he considered a "union of letters and athletics."[12] For his generation, college football players were what American men were supposed to be: tough as nails and sharp as tacks.

But even the smartest and toughest players had a hard time stopping the flying wedge play. The *New York Times* described it as "half a ton of bone and muscle coming into collision with a man weighing 160 or 170 pounds. What is the result? The victim is generally sent sprawling with his nose broken or his chest crushed."[13]

Credit for the flying wedge play belongs to Lorin Deland, a Boston businessman, who dreamed it up one day while sitting in a library reading books on Napoleonic battlefield tactics. Before long, southern teams were employing the flying wedge and other "mass-momentum" plays, such as the turtleback, which, as the name suggests, grouped offenses into a fast-moving oval shape.[14]

The rookie team from South Carolina College (the University of South Carolina) was too green to employ mass-momentum plays during its first game. On Christmas Eve 1892, a hastily assembled squad of South Carolina students (plus two nonstudents) traveled from Columbia to Charleston to play Furman. Football had been on the minds of South Carolina students for three years, following Wofford's victory over Furman in Spartanburg. They became even more interested in the sport after learning that Duke had demolished Furman 96–0 in a game played under IFA rules. They were a ragtag band of rebels with a will to fight and little besides—football had not been approved by South Carolina's faculty, there was no coach, no money for train tickets, and no uniforms. The team did not even have a mascot. Worst of all, the players had no experience, a fact that became painfully obvious to all when they were thrashed by Furman 44–0 at the Charleston baseball park.[15]

On December 28, delegates from eight schools—Alabama, Virginia, Wake Forest, North Carolina, Tennessee, Sewanee, St. John's College in Maryland, and Johns Hopkins—gathered at the Exchange Hotel in Richmond, Virginia, to decide the future of southern college football. From this meeting came the original Southern Intercollegiate Athletic Association (SIAA). The association elected officers and drafted an eight-page constitution.[16] As part of its plan for tackling corruption, "very rigid rules were adopted against professionalism." From now on, only legitimate college students would be allowed to play baseball and football. The SIAA was split into two divisions, Northern and Southern, with UVA, Wake, UNC, St. John's, and Johns Hopkins in the Northern Division and Alabama, Tennessee, and Sewanee in the Southern. The SIAA baseball and football championships were to be played annually in Richmond, with a seventy-five-dollar trophy going to the winner of each sport.[17]

The dominance of Upper South schools like UVA and Johns Hopkins may help explain why this early version of the SIAA failed to take root. Dr. William Dudley, a professor of chemistry at Vanderbilt, enjoyed greater success two years later, when he revived the idea for a southern conference, during a meeting at the Kimball House hotel in Atlanta. Dudley's SIAA included Deep South programs like Alabama, Auburn, Georgia, Georgia Tech, and Vanderbilt. It would go on to grandfather two of today's most dominant football conferences, the Atlantic Coast Conference (ACC) and the Southeastern Conference.[18]

While delegates from white schools were meeting in Richmond, students from Biddle University (today's Johnson C. Smith University) and Livingstone College, both in North Carolina, were participating in the very first game between two historically black colleges (figure 5). In December 1892, Smith players crowded into a "colored" train car for the forty-five-mile ride from Charlotte to Salisbury, North Carolina. The game was played in a cow pasture that had been converted into a makeshift playing field; a thin layer of snow made it difficult to see the gridiron marker lines. Unlike their opponents, who were new to the game, Smith students had been playing intramural football for two years and were confident in their abilities as a team. At halftime, they were ahead by a score of 5–0. W. J. Trent recovered a fumble and scored a touchdown for Livingstone in the second half, but the play was overturned by a student referee from UNC–Chapel Hill, who also happened to be Livingstone's head coach. Smith was able to run out the clock and escape with a 5–0 win.[19]

In the 1890s, a growing number of black southerners were attending college and studying subjects—including football—that previously had been off-limits to them. Within two years of the Smith–Livingstone matchup, students at Howard University and Lincoln University were battling each other on the gridiron for institutional bragging rights, as were their peers at Atlanta University and Tuskegee. Atlanta Baptist, Morgan College, Virginia Union, and other schools quickly followed suit and formed teams. Black educators were mostly supportive of athletics on campus, which they believed built character and would eventually open the door for greater acceptance of African Americans in all facets of public life (a strategy known as "muscular assimilation"). Only a handful of skeptics, such as Professor William Pickens at Talladega College in Alabama, worried that black success on athletic fields would create a stereotype of African Americans as physically gifted but incapable of intellectual or moral superiority over whites (a prophecy that was fulfilled several decades later, with the assistance of a national media fixated on race).

Black collegians, on the other hand, were proud of their football teams and worked hard to keep them afloat. Livingstone players pooled their money and purchased a single regulation uniform from Spalding, which women from the Livingstone Sewing Department reverse engineered and mass produced. Players at the Oklahoma Colored Agricultural and Normal University (today's Langston University) had to pay for their own uniforms, which they ordered out of a Sears, Roebuck catalog.[20]

Many of these students' friends and relatives back home, meanwhile, were doing their best to avoid being killed. Between 1882 and 1899, more than 2,500 African Americans were executed by white lynch mobs, frequently for exaggerated or imaginary transgressions. The historian Edward Ayers found lynching to be most common in areas along the Gulf Coastal Plain, between Florida and Texas, and in the cotton-rich counties of Arkansas, Mississippi, Louisiana, and Texas. These regions were sparsely populated, and all of them experienced rapid increases in the number of African American residents at the end of the Civil War. Weak law enforcement and poor communication with the outside world made whites who lived in these areas fearful of black strangers. Local African Americans, undoubtedly looking out for their own safety, often would refuse to vouch for the newcomers, especially if a crime had been committed. Vigilante justice served as a crude substitute for proper law enforcement and simultaneously strengthened the racial pecking order. Black southerners lived in dread of saying or doing anything that might provoke the wrath of a white mob.[21]

They had good reason to be concerned. When a black journalist named Ida B. Wells condemned the practice of lynching on the pages of her independent newspaper, the *Memphis Free Speech and Headlight,* she was forced to flee north for her safety. Wells's office was ransacked by an angry mob during her absence.[22]

Besieged by prejudice and the constant threat of violence, black southerners carried on the best they could with the business of rearing their families and building institutions that served the needs of their communities. Both objectives took a hit in 1893, however, when a major economic crisis engulfed the nation.

A host of factors caused the panic, including economic weakness abroad, a domestic railroad bubble, and a steep drop in agricultural prices. In May 1893, the National Cordage Company went into receivership, triggering a collapse of the stock market. Banks began calling in loans. Railroad companies went bankrupt. Companies cut wages and laid off workers. By winter, the unemployment rate had risen to 18 percent. Hundreds of banks failed, including thirty-eight southern ones and 115 in western states. Agricultural prices, which had already been struggling, dropped through the floor. Armies of unemployed men, unable to support their families, began riding the rails in search of work. It was the worst economic depression anyone could remember, leading many to question whether American democracy could survive.[23]

And yet there were signs of life among the wreckage. In Illinois, the World's Columbian Exposition (also known as the Chicago World's Fair) opened to popular acclaim, after three years of planning and construction. A magnificent White City had been erected to showcase the technological marvels of the era. Visitors were astonished to hear the sound of an orchestra in New York playing through a telephone receiver. They were equally impressed with Thomas Edison's kinetoscope, an ingenious device that showed moving pictures (or "movies"), as well as the world's first all-electric kitchen. New brands and products were on display everywhere, including Juicy Fruit gum, Cracker Jack, and Shredded Wheat cereal. There seemed to be no limit to what mankind could accomplish through the power of science and industry.[24]

Scientific football, meanwhile, was continuing its triumphant march across Dixie. In the autumn of 1893, Dr. Charles E. Coates—another chemistry professor educated at Johns Hopkins—invited Louisiana State University students to form a team. Coates was new to Baton Rouge and was surprised to learn that LSU students were ignorant of scientific football. He remembered the game from his days at Hopkins and thought it might help boost school spirit. His knowledge of the rules, however, was limited. Coates and an entomology professor named Harcourt Morgan (who would later become president of the University of Tennessee and then chairman of the Tennessee Valley Authority) did their best to instruct LSU students in the basics of the game. "Morgan and I did the coaching quite poorly," Coates recalled in later years. "I taught the boys the [Deland] flying wedge and the turtle back."[25]

In New Orleans, meanwhile, a former Yale quarterback named Thomas Bayne and his brother, Hugh, were doing all they could to get football off the ground at Tulane University. After convincing Tulane students to support a team, Thomas took on any task that needed doing. He scrounged up a football (not an easy feat in nineteenth-century Louisiana), erected goalposts, painted lines, sold tickets, coached, refereed, and even chose Tulane's green and blue color scheme. The school's first varsity game was played against Bayne's own Southern Athletic Club on November 18, 1893. It was a sad and rainy affair for Tulane, which lost 12–0 to a team captained by their own coach.[26]

Tulane and LSU played in Louisiana's first intercollegiate game the following week, on a cold, overcast day in New Orleans. Eager to ensure a competitive contest, Bayne had traveled to Baton Rouge ahead of time to help his friend Coates whip his team into shape. LSU's quarterback and team captain was a Union Parish, Louisiana, native named Ruffin Pleasant, who would later serve as governor of the Bayou State. Aware that LSU needed some sort of color scheme, Coates went with Pleasant and a handful of other players to a local shop that had stocked up on purple and gold ribbons for Mardi Gras. "So we adopted the purple and old gold, bought out the stock, and made it into rosettes and badges," Coates recalled. "Purple and old gold made a good combination and we have stuck to it ever since." The team decided to call themselves the "Louisiana Tigers" as a tribute to the New Orleans Zouaves and the Donaldsonville Cannoneers, who had fought like tigers during the Civil War.[27]

On game day, fans cheered, whistled, and blew tin horns, creating a cacophony of noise on the sidelines. Each team was given the opportunity to pick its own referee. Tulane selected Coates and LSU returned the favor by choosing Bayne. Tulane opened the game with a flying wedge play, which the *Daily Picayune* described as "very prettily done." Two minutes into the game, Hugh Bayne breached the Tigers defensive line and bolted into the end zone for a touchdown. Tulane kept LSU pinned to the mat for the rest of the day, scoring seven additional touchdowns and three two-point conversion kicks, for a 38–0 win. Despite their humiliating loss, Tiger players comported themselves as gentlemen and congratulated the victors before quietly boarding a train for the return trip to Baton Rouge.[28]

Football was also off to a slow start at Ole Miss that fall, in part because the team was in such poor physical shape. None of the thirty students who turned out for the first practice was able to finish a four-mile run. There was also a strong antifootball sentiment among some faculty and students, who considered the game a dangerous frivolity. The team plowed ahead anyway under the leadership of Professor Bondurant, who ran two practices a day—one before classes started and another after they ended. Bondurant was assisted by J. W. S. Rhea, a fellow graduate of Hampden-Sydney College in Virginia, who, unlike Bondurant, had actually played football as a student. They both made sure Ole Miss players were well fed and well rested. A ten p.m. curfew was strictly enforced, and the team was asked to abstain from tobacco, coffee, tea, and alcohol. Bondurant also encouraged his men to grow out their hair as a way of protecting their noggins. And he chose Mississippi's color scheme, a combination of Harvard red (Harvard students had selected crimson for their team in 1875) and Yale blue, based on Bondurant's belief that "it was well to have the spirit of both these good colleges."[29]

Mississippi's first game was played at home, on November 11, against a team from Southwestern Baptist University (now Union University). The atmosphere was relaxed. Ole Miss students met their rivals at the Oxford train station and gave them a tour of the city in a horse-drawn carriage. Fans applauded both teams as they trotted onto the field. Such courtesies did not prevent Ole Miss from running up the score on the hapless Baptists, however. Mississippi halfback Garland Mordecai Jones scored the first touchdown in school history a few minutes after kickoff. He and his teammates then proceeded to pile drive Union into the dirt, winning by a final score of 56–0. After the game, Bondurant, channeling Vice Admiral Horatio Nelson, wrote, "Every man did his duty and, for an opening game, the performance was rather unusual."[30]

The University of Texas also adopted football in the fall of 1893. On Thanksgiving Day, a group of UT students took on the Dallas Football Club at Fair Park in front of two thousand enthusiastic fans. "To a man who doesn't know a halfback from a tackle, the professional game of football looks very much like an Indian wrestling match with a lot of running thrown in," reported the *Dallas News*. Texas won the game 18–16.[31]

By the end of 1893, scientific football had become popular at colleges across the South, including at smaller institutions like Randolph-Macon College. Randolph-Macon sports received a shot in the arm when another Johns Hopkins PhD, Arthur Wightman, who had been hired to teach biology and physics, became president of the school's athletic association.

Randolph-Macon's football team subsequently played neighboring Hampden-Sydney College in what has since been dubbed "the oldest small-school rivalry in the South." In reality, that distinction belongs to VMI and Washington and Lee, who began playing each other in the early 1870s—albeit by a different set of rules.[32]

For students at Randolph-Macon and other southern colleges, football was intelligent, modern, and exciting. Their enthusiasm for the sport led to a decline of interest in other extracurricular activities including campus literary societies which had remained popular well into the 1880s. A unique football subculture developed among students who grew out their hair and wore ludicrously oversized clothing with chrysanthemums pinned to their lapels (the chrysanthemum corsage is still a common sight at some southern schools, especially during homecoming games). Football was also the sport of choice among their young professors, who were thought to be leading the South into a golden age of prosperity. In addition to being the father of Georgia football, Charles Herty was a gifted chemist who helped resurrect the naval stores industry in the Carolinas (the pine tar produced during this process is one of the more plausible explanations for the nickname "Tar Heels"). Herty also demonstrated that southern pine could be used as a substitute for Canadian spruce in the manufacture of paper and newsprint. Charles Coates dedicated himself to the success of Louisiana's sugar industry and received international praise for his research on the chemistry of sugar. George Petrie and Alexander Bondurant introduced modern scholarship methods to a generation of students who would go on to distinguished academic careers of their own.[33]

Youthful college administrators like John Franklin Crowell at Trinity College (today's Duke) were pleased by the attention and financial support their schools were receiving as a result of their successful football programs. Not everyone was a fan, however. Southern conservatives worried about the game's adverse effects on the health and morals of young men. "This new outbreak [of football] in the South, in contrast with the sturdy integrity of our past history, is but a natural result of lowering the standard of citizenship and manhood," complained the editors of the *Wesleyan Christian Advocate*. Their sentiments were shared by Warren Candler, president of Emory, who forbade students from participating in intercollegiate athletics out of concern that they promoted "gambling and other immoralities" and aroused "states of excitement absolutely subversive of habits of study."[34]

Colleges with a church affiliation, like Methodist Duke, were especially vulnerable to criticism. An education report produced by the Western North Carolina Methodist Conference in 1892 took aim at Crowell's support for intercollegiate athletics: "It is the decided opinion of your Board that while foot-ball and other such sports may perhaps be properly encouraged as means of exercise and of physical development on the college campus, yet match-games, in which teams from other colleges come to play with the young men of our schools, or teams from our schools go to play with those of other institutions, are a source of evil, and of no little evil, and ought to be stopped."[35]

According to Crowell, southern Methodists became hostile toward intercollegiate football after hearing reports from northern Methodists of wild parties hosted by football players. "Northern Methodist periodicals contained alarmist expositions," Crowell wrote, "and these were reprinted in Southern Methodist organs. Immediately [football] at [Duke] was condemned without further hearing."[36] The board's worst fears were realized when a keg of beer was discovered on a train filled with Duke students traveling from Charlottesville to Durham after a 30–0 loss to UVA.

Other faculty and trustees were opposed to football on the grounds that it distracted students from their studies. They tried to dampen enthusiasm for the sport by limiting the number of away games or banning them outright. There also was the question of money, or lack of it. Athletic associations often were unable to pay for equipment and team travel expenses, thus further deflating student interest in football.[37]

But the risk of player injury and death posed the biggest threat to college football's survival. During a board of trustees meeting in the early 1890s, University of North Carolina president Kemp Battle made a compelling case for why the game should be abolished: "Foot ball is brutal and dangerous in itself, as is shown by the breaking of the leg of one of our students, within a year the collar bone of another, and the wrist of a third . . . This brutality and danger are greatly increased under the furious rivalry engendered by contests in presence of numerous spectators, and especially in populous towns." Battle added that intercollegiate games encouraged fighting and cheating as well as "drinking and rowdyism." The board decided to steer a middle course: intercollegiate football games would no longer be allowed, but UNC students could continue playing one another within the safe confines of Chapel Hill. The board's decision irritated North Carolina fans. Their team had been on a winning streak ever since it had received training from Hector Cowan, a former Princeton tackle who had spent a week on campus in February 1889, drilling the Tar Heels in the fundamentals of the game.[38]

The problem of gridiron violence could not be swept under the rug, however, even by football's most ardent defenders. In 1893, a U.S. Naval Academy player named Joe Reeves received somber news from his doctor: repeated blows to the head were causing damage to Reeves's brain, so much so that one more blow could possibly kill him. Unwilling to abandon the sport he loved, Reeves hired an Annapolis shoemaker to construct a crude helmet made out of leather, one of the first ever seen on a playing field. Although helmets were rare, plenty of players were wearing nose guards and mouthpieces, undoubtedly spooked by the appearance of men like E. W. Sikes (the "Old War Horse"), who "wore a somewhat flattened nose through life" after playing football for Wake Forest.[39]

At the close of the 1893 season, the question of whether football would survive was still up in the air. On the plus side, public interest in the sport was at an all-time high. New teams were springing up at colleges and universities across the country. Amos Alonzo Stagg, a former Yale player who was being paid a full professor's salary to build a program at the University of Chicago, published *A Scientific and Practical Treatise on American Football*, to critical acclaim. "The game of football is fast becoming the national fall sport of the American youth," Stagg boasted. His boss, Chicago president William Harper, understood that universities with successful football programs raked in more money than those without a team—a lesson not lost on southern administrators who were doing their best to weather a severe economic depression. Big matchups, like the first game between Alabama and Auburn (which Auburn won 32–22) and the annual Virginia–North Carolina game (first played in October 1892 and thereafter referred to as the "South's oldest rivalry"), were drawing robust crowds and attracting media attention.[40]

But there were structural problems beneath the gilded exterior. The IFA, football's governing body, was in danger of disintegrating over the question of player eligibility. When Yale introduced a motion, in January

1893, to limit play to undergraduate students, the University of Pennsylvania strenuously objected. A few months later, Penn withdrew from the IFA over the eligibility rule change and was soon joined by Wesleyan. To make matters worse, reports of student deaths and injuries were fueling a growing antifootball movement, led by intellectual heavyweights such as Harvard president Charles Eliot. Within a few short years, the tragic death of a young Georgia player would bring college football in the South to the brink of extinction.[41]

Fig. 1. Homer Winslow's illustration of Civil War soldiers playing football appeared in the July 15, 1865, edition of *Harper's Weekly*. Mob football games were played by both Revolutionary War and Civil War troops. Soldiers fighting in Europe during World War I played "scientific" football, which by then had become firmly entrenched at America's colleges and universities. (Yale University Art Gallery.)

Fig. 2. Mob football games played in England were the progenitors of modern American football. One such game, Royal Shrovetide Football, has been an annual event in the town of Ashbourne, Derbyshire, for more than eight centuries. Here, Dr. Paul Kirtley initiates the 2012 contest by tossing out the ceremonial game ball to a crowd of enthusiastic participants. (Will De Freitas, public domain photograph, February 21, 2012.)

Fig. 3. Students at Washington & Lee University in Lexington, Virginia were among the first southern collegians to play football, scheduling games against intercollegiate rivals as early as 1869. Pictured here is the 1897–1898 Washington and Lee Football Team. (Calyx 1898, Special Collections and Archives, Washington and Lee University Library, Lexington, Virginia.)

Fig. 4. William Little learned how to play football while attending Phillips Academy in Massachusetts, and he introduced the sport to his classmates at the University of Alabama. Alabama's first game was played in November 1892 against a high school team coached by Professor Taylor. The Tide rolled their rivals 56–0. (University of Alabama Libraries Special Collections, Tuscaloosa, Alabama.)

Fig. 5. On December 27, 1892, Biddle University (now Johnson C. Smith) defeated Livingstone College 5–0 in the first football game between two historically black colleges. African Americans attending college during the Gilded Age, like their white counterparts, viewed football as a modern and exciting sport played by America's best and brightest. Here, players from the 1913 Biddle team pose for a photograph in front of the campus library. (Inez Moore Parker Archives and Research Center, Johnson C. Smith University, Charlotte, North Carolina.)

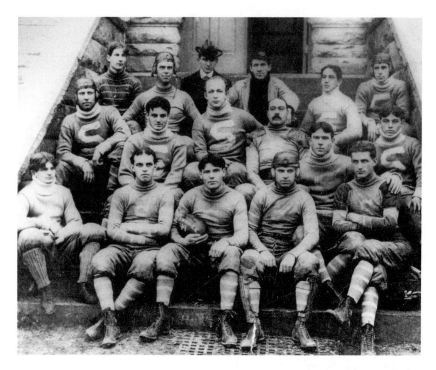

Fig. 6. The 1899 Sewanee Tigers won five away games in six days and finished the season with a perfect 12–0 record. Their achievement was largely ignored by a northern sports media fixated on Ivy League teams. College football fans in recent years have rediscovered the lost story of the Sewanee "Iron Men." In 2012, they were voted the top team in the College Football Hall of Fame's March of the Gridiron Champions online poll. (Courtesy of University Archives and Special Collections, University of the South, Sewanee, Tennessee.)

Fig. 7. In this photo, taken in June 1955, Henry Seibels chats with Sewanee's coaching staff after receiving an honorary doctorate from his alma mater. From left to
right are Bobby Parkes, captain of the 1954/1955 Sewanee Tigers; Seibels; Ernie
Williamson, Sewanee's head coach; and Mac Peebles, assistant coach. (Courtesy
of University Archives and Special Collections, University of the South, Sewanee,
Tennessee.)

Fig. 8. John Heisman (born Johann Wilheim Heisman) grew up playing "mob" football in his hometown of Titusville, Pennsylvania. Heisman played for Titusville High School, Brown University, and the University of Pennsylvania before embarking on a coaching career that would eventually bring him to Georgia Tech. In this photo, taken on November 11, 1910, Heisman poses on a Tech practice field while wearing a Penn sweater. Heisman's victory over Penn during the 1917 season bolstered Georgia Tech's credibility among northern sports journalists, which in turn helped the team secure the South's first undisputed national championship. (Permission of the Georgia Institute of Technology Library and Information Center, Archives and Records Management Department, Atlanta, Georgia.)

Fig. 9. Eugene Noble "Buck" Mayer played halfback for the University of Virginia from 1912 to 1915 and was the first southern player selected as a first-team All American. Mayer's statistics include 312 career points and forty-eight career touchdowns, twenty-one of which were scored in a single season. Tragically, Mayer contracted Spanish flu and died in 1918, while stationed at Camp Joseph E. Johnston in Jacksonville, Florida. (Holsinger Collection, Albert and Shirley Small Special Collections Library, University of Virginia, Charlottesville.)

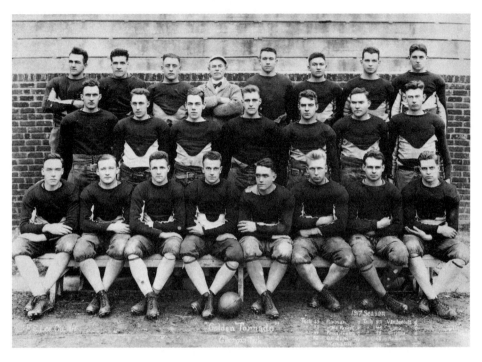

Fig. 10. The 1917 Georgia Tech Golden Tornado blew away the competition with a perfect 9–0 record and the South's first national championship. Georgia Tech's backfield was one of the best to ever play the game. Joe Guyon (top row, second from left), a Chippewa Indian, led the Tech rushing attack, along with fellow halfback Everett Strupper (bottom row, third from left), fullback Julian "Judy" Harlan (top row, second from right), and quarterback Albert Hill (bottom row, fourth from left). Tech's decision to continue playing football during World War I was criticized by University of Georgia students, who mocked the team during a postwar parade in Athens. (Permission of the Georgia Institute of Technology Library and Information Center, Archives and Records Management Department, Atlanta, Georgia.)

CHAPTER FIVE

ROUGH RIDERS AND
VON GAMMON'S MAMA

I t was the second year of the worst economic downturn anyone could remember. Thousands of unemployed men were roaming the countryside in search of food and shelter. A "let them eat cake" attitude prevailed inside the marbled halls and chandeliered conference rooms of Washington, DC, when Jacob Coxey and his five-hundred-man Army of the Commonwealth in Christ marched on the city in the spring of 1894, demanding the creation of a government work relief program. Instead of receiving a fair hearing, they were harassed and arrested by federal agents. President Grover Cleveland did not have time for disgruntled drifters; he had bigger fish to fry, like dispatching troops to end the Pullman Strike in Illinois.

George Pullman, the owner of a company that manufactured luxury railroad cars, had ignited a firestorm of controversy by slashing the wages of workers living in his eponymous factory town without offering them a corresponding break on company-controlled rents, utilities, or groceries. The American Railroad Union led a sympathy strike against the Pullman Company that paralyzed Midwestern rail traffic. Cleveland's decision to use troops as strikebreakers enraged labor activists, who responded in July 1894 by turning Chicago's rail yards into bloodstained battlefields. Thirty-four people were killed and millions of dollars' worth of railroad equipment went up in flames. Cleveland justified his use of force by invoking the Sherman Antitrust Act, arguing that the strike represented a conspiracy in restraint of trade. Originally intended to curb the power of corporations, the Sherman Antitrust Act was now a powerful weapon that could be used to control organized labor.[1]

Football supporters, meanwhile, were dealing with their own set of challenges. The pullout of Penn and Wesleyan from the Intercollegiate Football Association the previous year had knocked the organization back on its heels. There also was mounting public pressure to either minimize the risks of football or ban the sport altogether. In response, a group calling itself the Intercollegiate Rules Committee gathered at the University Athletic Club in New York City to mount a rescue effort. The IRC was composed of club members, former players, and representatives from Penn, Harvard, Yale, and Princeton. Paul Dashiell, a chemistry professor with a PhD from Johns Hopkins, also was invited to join the committee.

Dashiell had excelled in baseball, football, tennis, and gymnastics during his time at Hopkins and served as vice president of the school's athletic association. He and his fellow IRC members (a list that included Walter Camp) decided to sidestep the issue of player eligibility and to focus instead on making the game safer. The committee thus proceeded to enact a flurry of new safety-related rules. For instance, from now on, a player making a fair catch would be required to signal his intent by waving his hand and could not be tackled by the opposing team. A new official called a linesman would be added to the game to help his fellow officials keep an eye out for player infractions. As a way of limiting the damage caused by mass-momentum plays, no more than three offensive players would be allowed to go in motion prior to the snap. Other new safety regulations included reducing the length of the game from ninety minutes to seventy minutes and requiring that the ball travel at least ten yards on a kickoff.[2]

Critics derided the IRC's new rules as half measures, and during the 1894 season there was plenty of evidence to suggest that they might be right. The Harvard–Yale game that year produced so many injuries that it was forever after known as the "Hampden Park Blood Bath." Fred Murphy, a tackle for Yale, was knocked out cold and lay in a hospital bed for five agonizing hours before regaining consciousness. Rumors circulated that Murphy had died. A Harvard player named Edgar Wrightington had his collarbone broken by Yale tacklers. One of Wrightington's teammates, Charles Brewer, suffered a broken leg. Other players limped off the field with head injuries, black eyes, and strained backs. "The record of French duels for the last dozen years fails to show such a list of casualties as this one game of football produced," reported the *New York Times*. As a result of the high casualty rate, the annual contest was suspended for three years.[3]

Princeton and Penn severed ties for forty years after their 1894 game ended in a donnybrook involving students and townspeople. (Princeton fans were upset over their team's 0–12 loss.) An even worse tragedy occurred in Washington, DC, when Georgetown University quarterback George "Shorty" Bahen had his back broken by players from the Columbia Athletic Club, who were purposefully targeting him in order to knock him out of the game. Bahen died a few weeks later, prompting school officials to abolish football at Georgetown.

Against this backdrop of violence came a study trumpeting football's positive safety record. Commissioned by the Harvard Board of Overseers, the study concluded that the player injury problem was not as bad as the media were making it seem. The man who had been handed the task of producing the study was none other than Walter Camp, who later parlayed it into a published manuscript entitled *Football Facts and Figures.* By asking Camp to conduct the study, the Harvard board had made an end run around President Charles Eliot and other faculty members who were worried about football's deleterious effects on the health of students. Eliot refused to back down and published his own report the following year, which described football as a game "unfit for college use" that promoted "reckless violence."[4]

Southern football programs were also coming under fire for promoting violence and "professionalism." Several colleges, including Wake Forest and Duke, decided to abolish football and did not allow it to be played on campus again until the following century. In June 1894, the board of trustees at Washington and Lee University was asked to consider the following resolution: "That Foot-Ball playing should be discouraged in this University—; and that no leaves of absence should be allowed to students for the purpose of playing Foot-Ball with teams from other institutions, schools or towns." The board punted on the proposal by "recommending that no action be taken at present." Vanderbilt's board denounced intercollegiate sports in general terms and "mandated that the faculty enforce proper precautions and restrain all excesses."[5]

In response, Vanderbilt chemistry professor William Dudley put together a new-and-improved version of the Southern Intercollegiate Athletic Association, a multischool supervisory body that had been created two years earlier in Richmond, Virginia, but had since faded into obscurity. Dudley invited faculty representatives from Auburn, Georgia, Georgia Tech, Alabama, Sewanee, Johns Hopkins, and the University of North Carolina to attend the first meeting of the new SIAA at the Kimball House hotel in Atlanta. Charles Herty served as delegate for both Johns Hopkins and the University of Georgia. The group's lofty objective was no less than the "development and purification of college athletics throughout the South." To this end, a constitution was drafted, addressing what were thought to be the worst abuses of the system. First, those officiating a baseball or football game could no longer be a graduate of either school represented on the field. Second, professional athletes would no longer be allowed to play for teams that were part of the association. Instead, players would have to be "bona fide" students who were attending "at least five lectures or recitations a week, or their equivalent." A manager who suspected foul play could demand to see his opponent's player roster, which had to be certified in advanced by a college president or a secretary of the faculty. Any player whose eligibility was still in question after that would have to submit a sworn affidavit.[6]

These changes were part of a broader reform movement sweeping the nation known as progressivism. At its core, progressivism represented a backlash against the many problems caused by industrialization: immigrant slums, child labor, corporate monopolies, political corruption, and other social ills. It was also based on a belief in the human race's ability to solve its own problems. Although diverse in many respects, progressives tended to share a common view of bureaucracy—government bureaucracy, especially—as a force for good in a fallen world. If college football was too dangerous or too corrupt, then progressives believed it could be reformed through greater regulation and supervision by bureaucratic organizations such as the SIAA.

Some conservative college boards and community leaders disagreed and continued to call for the complete elimination of football. Southern evangelicals viewed football as a Trojan horse for a permissive northern theology that had already poisoned the minds of Ivy League students. The Apostle Paul had drawn a sharp distinction between body and soul, they reasoned, and called on believers to reject fleshly indulgences. Southern collegians were not just neglecting their studies in order to play football; the game was turning them into savages. The characteristics of traditional Christian masculinity—self-restraint, maturity, humble conviction—were being replaced by a pagan aggressiveness and impulsivity.[7]

In spite of these arguments, football's popularity on southern campuses continued to rise. On October 6, 1894, the Texas A&M Farmers, under the leadership of Coach F. D. Perkins, defeated the Galveston Sports Association in the school's first official game. A&M's only other game of the season was played against archrival Texas, which ended in a 38–0 loss for A&M. The University of Arkansas Cardinals (later renamed the Razorbacks in honor of the feral pigs that wander the Natural State) played in their first game the same season, trouncing an undersize team from Fort Smith High School 42–0. Arkansas whipped Fort Smith a second time before traveling to Austin to take on the University of Texas. Coach John Futrall, who taught Latin at Arkansas and would later serve as the university's president, watched in disgust as his defense crumpled under the weight of the beefy Texas offensive line. The Cardinals were soundly thrashed 54–0. Futrall had studied the finer points of football while attending the University of Virginia (both as an undergraduate and as a graduate student) and believed that the game would help Arkansas be seen as a more cosmopolitan place to live and study.[8]

On November 16, 1895, Mississippi A&M (today's Mississippi State University) played its first intercollegiate game in Jackson, Tennessee, against Southwestern Baptist University (Union). The Mississippi boys were coached and quarterbacked by a student named W. M. Matthews, who three years earlier had cut his teeth in a game against a faculty team led by Professor Frank Gulley. (Gulley's academic specialty was scientific and practical agriculture and horticulture.) The students lost by four touchdowns, but Matthews's reputation had survived unscathed. He was given the honor of choosing the school's team colors. Even though the Mississippi State baseball team was by this time already wearing handsome gray uniforms with black trim, Matthews selected maroon, a change his fellow students enthusiastically adopted. A new color scheme, though, was not enough to prevent Mississippi State from losing its inaugural game 21–0.[9]

During the same season, John Heisman was appointed head coach for the Agricultural and Mechanical College of Alabama (Auburn). Heisman had played as a student for Brown and then for Penn before briefly coaching at Oberlin College and at Buchtel College in Ohio (now the University of Akron). When Auburn officials found him, he was down on his luck and trying to make ends meet by growing tomatoes in East Texas. Heisman was nobody's fool, though, and he knew that a coaching gig at Auburn would be easier than picking produce in the blistering Texas heat.

On November 9, 1895, he lost his inaugural game to the Vanderbilt Commodores. Despite the loss, Heisman had demonstrated an obsessive commitment to winning when he directed Auburn quarterback Reynolds Tichenor to conceal the ball in his jersey while running a revolving wedge play. Tichenor's hidden ball trick completely fooled the Vandy defense, allowing him to scramble thirty-five yards for a touchdown. "In those days we were all enamored of the cleverness of tricks and plays of deception," Heisman recalled. "All's fair in war, and football comes close to being a war . . . The officials, the Vandy players and coaches, and their college paper . . . all thought the game most clever. They never dreamed of it as unsportsmanlike any more than we had."[10]

Two weeks later, Auburn traveled to Tuscaloosa and demolished the University of Alabama 48–0. The enmity that exists between the two teams today did not exist in 1895, and Alabama players were able to host a postgame party for their opponents, which included blue and orange decorations. On Thanksgiving Day, Heisman's team played archrival Georgia on a field in Atlanta that a few weeks earlier had hosted Buffalo Bill's Wild West show. The Bulldogs were coached by Glenn "Pop" Warner, who, like Heisman, was in his first year with a new school. (Warner was simultaneously coaching for Iowa State.) Warner had played for Cornell as a student and would eventually find fame mentoring Jim Thorpe and other talented Native American athletes at the Carlisle Indian Industrial School in Pennsylvania. But on that bleak Thursday in November 1895, his team lost by ten points.[11]

The following autumn, a football team was founded at the Clemson Agricultural College of South Carolina (today's Clemson University) by a former Auburn player named Walter Riggs. Clemson students accepted Riggs's suggestion that they adopt his alma mater's mascot name and color scheme. In October 1896, the Tigers won their debut game against Furman, only to lose a bigger matchup a few weeks later against archrival South Carolina. Hatred between the two schools stemmed in part from Clemson fans' perception of South Carolina as a playground for the idle rich. Benjamin Ryan "Pitchfork Ben" Tillman, a populist politician who would win both the governorship of South Carolina and a U.S. Senate seat, contributed to this stereotype through his unabashed support for Clemson and his harsh criticism of blue-blood Brahmins from South Carolina's Lowcountry region.

The game was played on the state fairgrounds in Columbia, in front of two thousand fans. It was the beginning of a "Big Thursday" tradition that would last until the 1950s. Clemson players were "dressed in orange sweaters" with "orange and blue stockings" and had the support of a bevy of southern beauties from nearby Winthrop College. A contingent of women from Methodist College cheered for South Carolina. In the first half of the game, N. W. Booker scored a touchdown for Carolina after his team recovered a Clemson fumble on the Tigers' fifteen-yard line. C. H. McLaurin drop-kicked the ball through the uprights, giving Carolina a 6–0 lead. Clemson responded early in the second half with a sixty-yard touchdown run by J. A. Stone; another two-point conversion kick made it a 6–6 tie. Cansen Foster scored the game-winning touchdown for Carolina. The final score was South Carolina 12, Clemson 6.[12]

As South Carolina students celebrated their victory, several students at Auburn were pulling a prank that would bring them everlasting notoriety. On the night before a home game against Georgia Tech, they snuck out of their dorms and greased the tracks in front of the Auburn railroad station. When a train carrying the Tech team arrived the next day, it skidded five miles beyond its stop, forcing Tech players to walk back to town. Adding insult to injury, the Tigers blanked the visiting team 45–0.[13]

That same month, Americans elected Republican William McKinley as their twenty-fifth president. McKinley's opponent was a silver-tongued congressman from Nebraska named William Jennings Bryan, who had secured the Democratic nomination by denouncing the gold standard for the nation's currency. "You shall not press down upon the brow of labor this crown of thorns," Bryan told his fellow delegates attending the 1896 Democratic convention. "You shall not crucify mankind upon a cross of gold."

Bryan's speech made him an instant celebrity. During the campaign season, he embarked on an eighteen-thousand-mile whistle-stop tour, giving as many as thirty speeches a day. In contrast, McKinley spent most of his time at home in Canton, Ohio, delivering carefully prepared remarks that were reprinted in national newspapers. McKinley's campaign manager, Mark Hanna, did a masterful job of portraying Bryan as a loose cannon whose fiscal policies would further damage an economy already in shambles. The strategy worked. On Election Day, McKinley won 51 percent of the popular vote and 60 percent of the electoral vote.[14]

McKinley inherited a country sharply divided along racial lines. Earlier in the year, the U.S. Supreme Court had decided, in the *Plessy vs. Ferguson* case, that "separate but equal" facilities for blacks and whites were constitutional. Homer Plessy's arrest for riding in a whites-only train car in Louisiana had been part of a well-orchestrated campaign by black leaders in New Orleans, who were hoping to derail their state's unjust "Separate Car Act" (1890). Instead, the case became a golden spike for de jure segregation across the South, thus widening the gap between black and white southerners.[15]

Seven months after McKinley took the oath of office, a tragedy in Georgia brought southern college football to the brink of extinction. On October 30, 1897, a group of UGA fans, including Georgia governor William Atkinson and his wife, Susie, arrived in Atlanta's Brisbane Park to watch the Bulldogs play the Virginia Cavaliers. Although Virginia was considered one of the top programs in Dixie at the time, Pop Warner's coaching replacement, Charles McCarthy, felt confident his boys could hold their own against the Wahoos. They had gone undefeated the previous season under the steady leadership of quarterback Richard Vonalbade "Von" Gammon. At the beginning of the 1897 season, though, McCarthy had decided to move Gammon to the fullback position, hoping to take advantage of the young man's intense "driving power."[16]

At halftime, the Cavaliers were leading 11–4. The Bulldogs knew they would have to play twice as hard in the second half to make up the deficit. Early in the third quarter, the Virginia offense gave the ball to halfback Julien Hill, who slammed into Georgia's defensive line like a runaway freight train. The details of what happened next are unclear. According to one newspaper account, Gammon attempted to tackle Hill but "missed his mark and fell heavily on his head, his chin striking the ground first." Another report claimed that the young Georgian had "bowled head-over-heels, and in some manner the heel of his shoe struck his skull violently." What we do know is that Gammon lay motionless on the turf after the play ended. His teammates gently carried him to the sidelines, where he was examined by doctors before being rushed to Grady Hospital. Gammon's parents were notified of their son's condition and immediately left their home in Rome, Georgia, to be at his side. Shortly after his father arrived at the hospital, Von Gammon passed away. Although it is impossible to determine the precise cause of death without medical records (which have long since vanished), it seems likely Gammon died from complications caused by a concussion and skull fracture.[17]

Von Gammon's death instantly became national news and unleashed a tidal wave of antifootball sentiment. A number of Georgia players, including star halfback J. T. Moore, resigned from the team. Georgia Tech and Mercer College suspended their seasons. The media ran bombastic op-eds that further fanned the flames of controversy. The *Athens Banner* declared "unrelenting war on football." A headline in Gammon's hometown newspaper, the *Rome Tribune*, screamed "'Football Must Go,' Stop the Deadly Game." The *Atlanta Constitution* heralded the "Death Knell of Football." Southern preachers and politicians were equally histrionic. Reverend Warren Candler, president of Emory College, denounced football games as "worse than slugging matches" and encouraged southerners to reject the "demoralizing, second-hand English sport" before it obtained "a permanent footing in our colleges." A group of Baptist ministers in Atlanta also issued a statement condemning football. They were joined by a group of women in Virginia known as the City Union of King's Daughters, who drafted a petition calling on the Virginia General Assembly to ban the sport.[18]

While the Virginia assembly refused to take any precipitate action, the Georgia General Assembly rushed through a bill abolishing football. The bill required the governor's signature to become law, however, and Atkinson was unsure what he should do. On the one hand, he knew there was strong support for college football among his constituents (including Charles Herty, who was actively defending the sport in the press) and that influential northern opinion makers were ridiculing Georgians for even considering a ban. Moreover, Atkinson had openly expressed his support for football in the past, going so far as to say he hoped his son would take up the sport. On the other hand, he had already publicly stated that he did not consider a bill abolishing football to be "of sufficient importance for a veto or to raise a row about," hinting that he would sign it. It was a tough call, but Atkinson ultimately decided to exercise his veto power. The tipping point may have been when he learned of a letter written by Von Gammon's mother, Rosalind, to her representative in the Georgia assembly:

It would be the greatest favor to the family of Von Gammon if your influence could prevent his death from being used as an argument detrimental to the athletic cause and its advancement at the university. His love for his college and his interest in all manly sports, without which he deemed the highest type of manhood impossible, is well known by his classmates and friends, and it would be inexpressibly sad to have the cause he held so dear injured by his sacrifice. Grant me the right to request that my boy's death should not be used to defeat the most cherished object of his life.[19]

For a generation that had witnessed countless mothers grieving for sons lost in the Civil War, Rosalind Gammon's letter struck a nerve. She has since become the Holy Mother of college football, a southern heroine who bravely sacrificed her child for a noble cause. In 1921, the University of Virginia presented UGA with a bronze plaque commemorating the Gammon family's sacrifice. Resembling Michelangelo's *Pietà* in Rome, it shows Rosalind cradling her dying boy with one arm and holding a shield with the other. The inscription reads "The Cause Shall Live In Which His Life Was Given" and "A Mothers [*sic*] Strength Prevailed." The plaque is currently on display at Georgia's Butts-Mehre Heritage Hall.[20]

Rosalind Gammon's letter may have saved football in Georgia, but general support for the sport waned during the 1897 and 1898 seasons. Yellow fever was partly to blame. Outbreaks flared up along the Gulf Coast and elsewhere, killing more than five hundred people and terrifying millions more. LSU decided to delay its first game of the 1897 season until December, when it was normally cold enough to check the spread of the disease (the mosquitoes that carry yellow fever are inactive during the winter months). Ole Miss did not even bother fielding a team. The University of the South (Sewanee) was forced to abandon football halfway through the 1898 season, due to yellow fever and other threats. Faculty and boards of trustees at many schools were growing fed up with the violence and corruption associated with football. Washington and Lee administrators disbanded the football team after it was discovered that a ringer had been used during a game in Kentucky. Wake Forest administrators banned intercollegiate games in order to dampen student enthusiasm for the sport. Alabama administrators abolished road games for the same reason. At other universities, such as Mississippi State and Tennessee, students struggled to come up with enough money to cover team expenses.[21]

A far more severe disruption occurred on April 25, 1898, when the United States declared war on Spain. The nation ostensibly went to war over the sinking of the USS *Maine* in Havana Harbor, an event blamed on Spanish saboteurs, which in reality may have been caused by an accidental explosion (or by clever Cuban revolutionaries attempting to frame the Spanish). In any case, the American people were already frustrated with Spain when the *Maine* exploded. Stories of atrocities suffered by innocent Cubans at the hands of depraved Spanish troops (Cuba at the time was a Spanish colony) had been circulating for months in newspapers such as the *New York World* and the *New York Journal.*

Joseph Pulitzer, owner of the *World,* and William Randolph Hearst, owner of the *Journal,* both were shrewd businessmen who knew how to sell newspapers. One of their more effective marketing tactics was to whip readers into a frenzy through a sensationalist style of reporting known as yellow journalism. Not coincidentally, Pulitzer was the first newspaperman to create a sports department, while Hearst was the first to create a permanent sports section in his paper. Football's meteoric rise in the 1890s was in part attributable to their sensationalist coverage of games.[22]

The college football community made a significant contribution to the war effort. Colonel Leonard Wood—a former ringer, captain, and coach for Georgia Tech—became commander of the First U.S. Volunteer Cavalry, the Rough Riders. Wood's second-in-command was Theodore Roosevelt, a New York Knickerbocker who had resigned his position as assistant secretary of the navy in order to join the regiment. Among the volunteers recruited by Wood and Roosevelt was a group of East Coast footballers, men like Dudley Dean, a one-time All-American whom Roosevelt described as "perhaps the best quarterback who ever played on a Harvard eleven," and Dr. Robb Church, a former Princeton player who served as the regiment's surgeon. There was also John Greenway, a Huntsville, Alabama, native who had once played football for Yale and whose father had served in the Confederate army.[23]

These men and their fellow Rough Riders—southwestern cowboys, Indians, and a handful of Hispanics and "ethnic" European Americans—made a name for themselves by capturing the high ground surrounding Santiago, Cuba. Their charge up Kettle Hill, in particular, brought them national attention—Roosevelt especially. Missing from the story was the role played by the "Buffalo Soldiers" of the Ninth and Tenth Negro Cavalry regiments, who helped to clear Spanish fortifications from Kettle Hill before the Rough

Riders launched their glorious assault. Roughly one-quarter of the soldiers who participated in the invasion of Cuba were black, in part due to the government's belief that African Americans possessed a greater immunity to tropical diseases such as yellow fever.[24]

Also forgotten were volunteers from southern colleges and universities. The Virginia Tech Corps of Cadets tendered its services to Governor James Tyler immediately after the war started. When Tyler graciously declined their offer, a number of cadets dropped out of school in order to join the Second Regiment of Virginia Volunteers, a unit that was mustered into federal service in May 1898. Texans, too, rallied around the Stars and Stripes. A memorial at Texas A&M pays tribute to the roughly eighty-nine Aggies who participated in the Spanish–American War. The University of Tennessee suspended its football program during the 1898 season so that players and fans could focus all of their energies on the war effort. The Volunteer State produced four volunteer infantry regiments, which were led by officers from southern military schools such as the Citadel and the Virginia Military Institute.[25]

Collegians also were serving with Commodore George Dewey's fleet when it destroyed a rival Spanish fleet in the Philippines, another of Spain's colonies. By the summer of 1898, Spain could see the writing on the wall and sued for peace. Under the terms of the Treaty of Paris (1898), Spain was forced to recognize Cuban independence and to cede Guam, Puerto Rico, and the Philippines to the United States. The terms of the treaty touched off a heated political debate in Washington between those who thought colonies violated the nation's founding principles and their opponents, who believed an American empire would make the world a safer place.

The chief spokesman for the anti-imperialist faction was former presidential candidate William Jennings Bryan, who insisted that he would never trade "the glory of [the American] Republic for the glory of all the empires that have risen and fallen since time began." Teddy Roosevelt led the charge for the imperialists by linking the acquisition of colonies with what he called the "strenuous life." "If we are to be a really great people, we must strive in good faith to play a great part in the world," he told an audience in Chicago. "We cannot avoid meeting great issues." Like a coach giving a pep talk before a big game, T.R. exhorted the American people to meet global challenges head-on: "Let us therefore boldly face the life of strife, resolute to do our duty well and manfully; resolute to uphold righteousness by deed and by word; resolute to be both honest and brave, to serve high ideals, yet to use practical methods."[26]

One of the nation's first big challenges was a rebellion in the Philippines. The enemy this time was not dastardly Spaniards but Filipinos who were dismayed at seeing one colonial master from Europe replaced by another from America. The Filipino–American War would wind up costing taxpayers $160 million and claiming the lives of more than 4,200 U.S. servicemen. Somewhere between fifty thousand and two hundred thousand Filipinos also died during the conflict, from disease, starvation, and combat-related injuries.

The nation's aggressive foreign policy, worries over the decline of American masculinity, and the Darwinian ethos of the era fueled an enthusiasm for football among southern college students that could not be curbed by warnings about the sport's dangers. Most shared Von Gammon's belief that "manly sports" strengthened a man's virility by testing the upper limits of his physical and mental endurance. Their fathers, grandfathers, and uncles had fought bravely during the Civil War and had held their heads high in spite of a humiliating defeat. There was also the media coverage and positive attention from women that accompanied success on the gridiron. Football made southern men feel like men in a way few other sports could. And self-help books that were popular during the Gilded Age drove home the message that men could find success and happiness only through self-reliance and constant struggle, both of which were hallmarks of scientific football.[27]

CHAPTER SIX

IRON MEN

A s fighting raged in the Philippines in the autumn of 1899, students from Baylor University in Waco, Texas, participated in their very first football game, against a team from Toby's Practical Business College. Edward Toby expected the young men under his tutelage to refrain from drinking, smoking, and immoral behavior while learning bookkeeping, penmanship, and other skills in high demand in America's new industrial economy. Football, it seems, was less of a priority for Toby, whose squad of teetotalers fell to Baylor 20–0. Baylor played Texas A&M the same season, as well as AddRan Male and Female College (today's Texas Christian University), which had also selected Toby for its inaugural game. Addison Clark Jr., the son of an AddRan founding father, had been "bitten by the football bug" while visiting friends in Michigan and had returned to Texas to spread the contagion.[1]

The Sewanee Tigers, meanwhile, were beginning a journey that would earn them a place in the annals of southern gridiron glory. Their trek began on October 21, with a game against the University of Georgia. UGA fans dressed in red and black, including a "number of the fair sex," crowded into bleachers in Atlanta's Piedmont Park, where a cool autumn breeze made it feel more like game day in Massachusetts than in Georgia. Sewanee's sponsors—Miss Laura Johnson and Miss Myrtice Scott—arrived in a horse-drawn carriage, waving a purple banner. Historian Andrew Doyle says female sponsorship of southern football teams—a common practice during the game's early years—added an air of medieval pageantry to the region's gridiron matches. Like damsels at a jousting tournament, sponsors bestowed "a pregame benediction on the young warriors poised to do battle in their honor." Female sponsorship helped to legitimize football in the South by linking the modern sport with the chivalry of antebellum planters and their cavalier customs.[2]

Sewanee players were quick to accuse their opponents of behaving in an unchivalrous manner. A Georgia player named Finnegan, they said, had taught physical education at the college level and was therefore ineligible to play as an amateur athlete. Finnegan admitted to teaching P.E. but insisted he had never been paid for the gig. Game officials decided to let him play. The Bulldogs won the coin toss and elected to receive. Their kick returner was tackled at the Georgia ten-yard line by Tiger defenders. Three plays later, Sewanee recovered a Bulldog fumble. Henry "Diddy" Seibels then found a hole "big enough for a wagon to drive through" and picked up twelve yards for Sewanee before fumbling the ball himself. Georgia recovered the fumble, but the Tiger defense kept them in a box, forcing a turnover on downs. Seibels dropped the ball again on his next carry. Additional fumbles occurred on both sides until Ormond Simkins, Sewanee's fullback, found the end zone on a twelve-yard run and then kicked his own point after touchdown.[3] During the second half, after a prolonged stalemate against a stubborn Bulldog defense, halfback Rex Kilpatrick found an opening at left tackle and scored a second Tiger touchdown. Simkins again kicked the extra point. The final score was Sewanee 12, Georgia 0.[4]

Two days later, the Sewanee team returned to Piedmont Park to play Georgia Tech. The result was a lopsided 32–0 Tiger victory. Less than two minutes into the game, Sewanee blocked a Tech punt that was picked up and planted in the end zone by Charles Gray. Gray, an Ocala, Florida, native who played cello with the Sewanee orchestra when he was not playing football, scored a second touchdown seven minutes later "on a right end run for 25 yards." Diddy Seibels added four touchdowns of his own in the time remaining.[5]

Like Gray, Seibels stayed busy off the field. He was a member of the Sewanee board of editors, the Kappa Alpha Order fraternity, the law club, and the German club, and he served as president of the athletic association. His school had been founded forty-two years earlier by Leonidas Polk (the "Fighting Bishop") and a group of like-minded Episcopalians who believed that the South needed its own center of learning to preserve the southern way of life and guard against radical Yankee ideas like abolitionism. To this end, a semester system with a unique three-month winter break was established so that each student would be able to go home and "engage in the sports which make him a true Southern man, hunting, shooting, riding."

A number of Seibels's teammates were the sons of prominent Confederate leaders. Ormond Simkins's dad had participated in the bombardment of Fort Sumter. Joseph Lee Kirby-Smith was the son of General Edmund Kirby Smith, who had continued battling Yankees in Texas two months after Lee surrendered at Appomattox and then fled the country to avoid charges of treason. Smith later returned to the United States and taught mathematics at Sewanee until his death in 1893. Preston Smith Brooks Jr. was the grandson of Congressman Preston Brooks, a hot-tempered South Carolinian who had used a gutta-percha cane to beat Massachusetts Senator Charles Sumner senseless inside the Senate chamber after Sumner gave a speech criticizing the Palmetto State, slavery, and Brooks's cousin, Senator Andrew Butler (South Carolina).[6]

The team played Tennessee on October 28 in a rainstorm that turned each five-yard line on Sewanee's home field into a "miniature stream." Coach Henry Suter, a one-time Princeton Tiger, watched from the sidelines, dressed in a raincoat, as his team cut through the Vols' defensive line like a hot knife through butter. Two minutes into the game, Rex Kilpatrick scored the first touchdown for the Tigers; the rest of the game was a rout. According to the *Sewanee Purple,* the university's student newspaper, "Touchdown followed touchdown, until finally Sewanee stopped scoring from sheer exhaustion, and allowed the Knoxville boys to handle the mudspattered ball." Accounts of the final score varied. The *Purple* recorded it as a 46–0 victory for the Tigers. The editorial staff of the *Volunteer,* Tennessee's yearbook, believed it had been a 47–0 shutout. Their peers at the *Sewanee Cap and Gown* were sure the final score had been 51–0.[7]

It was a shutout, in any case, and the Tigers were brimming with confidence when a squad from Southwestern Presbyterian University (today's Rhodes College) arrived on campus the following week. Sewanee tossed the Rhodes players around like rag dolls, winning 54–0.[8]

As events would show, however, the games against Georgia, Georgia Tech, Tennessee, and Rhodes were merely the preliminary winds of a Category 5 hurricane. Prior to the start of the season, Sewanee's team manager, Luke Lea (who would later get elected to the U.S. Senate before participating in a daring raid to capture the Kaiser during World War I), had scheduled five consecutive away games that were to be played over the course of six days. No college athletic director in his right mind would contemplate such a thing today. But for Lea and many of the men attending Sewanee in 1899, it seemed like a neat idea. "All the boys seemed to feel it was a great lark and lots of fun," recalled one player who participated in the road trip. "There certainly was no thought of criticizing Luke Lea for making the schedule." J. G. de Roulhac Hamilton, a center for the Sewanee scrub team, had a slightly different recollection: "There was considerable criticism of Luke Lea's schedule, but as time passed, he was highly praised for it."[9]

Lea was less concerned with winning the hearts and minds of his players than with making sure Sewanee turned a profit during the trip. He needed to replace revenue he had lost by canceling a game against Vanderbilt over Vandy's refusal to fork over a larger share of the gate receipts. Road games brought in much-needed cash; the pair in Georgia had netted the team more than one hundred dollars.[10]

Lea also knew his team had a decent chance of winning all five games. The Tigers had gone undefeated the previous year, until a yellow fever epidemic brought their season to a premature end. Quarterback William Blackburn "Warbler" Wilson was a rising star whom Lea had personally recruited from Rock Hill, South Carolina, to play for Sewanee. He had also helped persuade Suter to coach the team. Finally, thanks to Sewanee's unusual academic schedule, which kept students on campus during the summer months, Lea knew his boys would be in good shape and ready to play when the 1899 football season unfolded. Their opponents, on the other hand, would likely still be sluggish and unfocused after the long summer hiatus.[11]

The scheme had the support of Sewanee administrators, who agreed to buy the team new uniforms and equipment. In order to keep his players healthy during the trip, Lea filled two big barrels with water drawn from a spring near campus. At a time when Americans were still at risk of contracting waterborne diseases such as typhoid fever, Lea's decision made sense. He also chartered a private Pullman train car so that his players could travel in style. The car featured luxurious sleeping berths and plenty of room for studying and relaxing between games. Finally, Lea hired two "big, husky" trainers to provide rubdowns for players with sore muscles. With plenty of clean water, brand-new equipment, comfortable accommodations, and a team of skilled massage therapists, the Sewanee Tigers were ready to go on the offensive.[12]

On November 8, the team arrived in Austin to play the University of Texas. It was the first game of what would turn out to be the greatest college football road show in history. Austin in the late 1890s was still a frontier town with a libertine attitude. According to the *Austin Daily Statesman,* Sewanee players went straight from their train to their hotel rooms, thus avoiding the town's saloons, brothels, gambling parlors, and other dens of iniquity.[13]

The next day, a well-rested Tiger squad slugged it out against a stubborn Texas defense. With nine minutes left to play in the first half, Diddy Seibels scored a touchdown on a seven-yard carry. Hugh "Bunny" Pearce's follow-up kick put Sewanee on top 6–0. Although Seibels sustained a head injury that left him bleeding "like a hog," he refused to hit the benches. The rules of the era stipulated that players who left the field for any reason were not allowed to return. Seibels's decision paid off for his team in the second half, when he scored another touchdown, this time on a nine-yard carry. The Sewanee defense held its own by stopping UT in a first and goal situation. "Thrice did Texas hurl her backs against that purple wall, and thrice did Sewanee repel the onslaughts," beamed the *Sewanee Purple.* The final score was Sewanee 12, Texas 0.[14]

After spinning a few "beautiful Texas gals" at a postgame party, the Sewanee team climbed back into their Pullman for the 165-mile ride to Houston and a November 10 showdown with the Texas A&M Farmers. The Farmers were led by an intimidating group of backfielders known as the "four horsemen"—halfbacks Charley Johnson and Frank Dwyer, fullback Dutch Schultz, and quarterback O. M. Simpson. Twenty-five years later, sportswriter Grantland Rice—who played football for Vanderbilt in 1899 and knew Coach Suter—would use the same nickname to describe a Notre Dame quarterback, fullback, and two halfbacks who led the Fighting Irish to a national championship.[15]

William Claiborne, an Amherst County, Virginia, native who played right guard for Sewanee, liked to try to get inside the heads of his opponents in order to throw them off balance. Claiborne had suffered a serious eye injury years before he began playing football, and he made sure A&M players noticed the damaged eye a few minutes before kickoff. "See this?" he said. "I lost it yesterday in Austin. This afternoon I'm getting a new one!" Claiborne also liked to pinch noseguards on the back of the arm before the snap, causing them to lunge angrily at him instead of at the Sewanee center. When questioned about the fairness of such tactics, the big guard bellowed, "Hell, this is no parlor game!"[16]

Finding the center of A&M's line "practically impregnable," the Tigers adjusted by running outside. John William Jones, a theology student with a penchant for swearing, returned a punt from midfield to the A&M five-yard line, setting up an easy Sewanee touchdown. Bunny Pearce missed the extra point. Warbler Wilson added another touchdown in the second half, but Pearce shanked a second extra point attempt, making the final score Sewanee 10, Texas A&M 0.[17]

Sewanee's next stop was New Orleans, for a Saturday matchup against Tulane. Rex Kilpatrick scored the first touchdown for Sewanee, six minutes into the game. Charles Gray found the end zone two more times for the Tigers before being injured and replaced by Daniel Hull, a five-foot-ten 160-pounder from Savannah, Georgia. Kilpatrick punched in a final touchdown for his team "before darkness finally set in and time was called." Sewanee won 23–0. The *New Orleans Times-Picayune* heaped praise upon the Tennesseans: "The big fellows in purple, although well trained and experienced men, accomplished more than an ordinary victory in defeating Tulane . . . They traveled all Friday night to keep their engagement with Tulane, and came into the city tired and out of sorts, as athletes will become on railroad journeys. Without much rest they again went on the field, and again scored a victory."[18]

With no game scheduled for Sunday, the team took advantage of its time off and went on a sightseeing tour of southern Louisiana. A wealthy Sewanee alumnus named John Shaffer invited them to his plantation, Ellendale, in Houma, Louisiana, for a hearty meal and a healthy dose of southern hospitality. Another of Shaffer's plantations, Ardoyne, was as an important sugar manufacturing center during the Gilded Age. The German, Italian, and African immigrants who worked there were paid in company scrip (Ardoyne "plantation tokens"), which could be redeemed only at stores owned by Shaffer. This was a common practice in coal mining and other industries, and it gave company owners nearly unlimited control over their workers' lives.[19]

The team also went on a boat ride across Lake Pontchartrain before taking in a play—Anthony Hope's *Rupert of Hentzau,* the sequel to his smash hit *The Prisoner of Zenda.* When an actor appeared on stage dressed in a purple costume, the players "burst into a whooping rendition of the Sewanee yell, mystifying actors and audience alike."[20]

On Monday, Sewanee humiliated the LSU Tigers 34–0 at home in Baton Rouge. A Tennessee journalist penned a glowing recap of the game:

> The game was a repetition of Sewanee's work all season, a continuance of their beautiful team work along with the splendid plunging of the backs. In spite of their long, tiresome trip, the Sewanee men were lively as school boys out for a day off, and they seemed to grow more eager for the fray as the game advanced. Sewanee scored seventeen points in each half, and during the game six substitutes were in the team's make-up. Louisiana was never able to gain enough ground to hold the ball for a first down. In spite of having traveled over 2,000 miles and played four hard games in five days, the Sewanee players are in good condition owing to the rigid way in which they have been training.[21]

On Tuesday, the Tigers ended their grueling road trip in Memphis with a sloppy victory over Ole Miss. Sewanee players fumbled and were called for holding multiple times, but it didn't matter. Seibels found the end zone on a ten-yard carry in the first half, and Kilpatrick scored another touchdown moments before the game ended. The final score was Sewanee 12, Ole Miss 0. Their train then headed home. It was met at the Sewanee station by a jubilant crowd of students, faculty, and townspeople. The sound of a ten-piece fife and drum corps could be heard above boisterous cheering. Countless torches, Japanese lanterns, and bonfires lit up the Sewanee campus like a giant lightning bug. The players were placed in carriages and paraded through the streets like triumphant Roman generals. Fireworks crackled in the night sky. Lea, Seibels, and Suter gave brief speeches thanking the students and faculty for their support. "No other team in the country since the history of football was written ever played five games in six days and won them all, and all with zeros at the right end," proclaimed the *Sewanee Purple*.

The praise was deserved: five away games over the course of six days, with five shutout victories (figure 6). No football team before or since has equaled Sewanee's remarkable feat. The Iron Men of 1899 had traveled more than two thousand miles through the heart of Dixie and vanquished every foe they faced. They had also shown uncommon courage, camaraderie, and sportsmanship—the same virtues that would enable Americans to build an empire in the next century (for better or worse) and to transform their sparsely populated, rural country into a global powerhouse.[22]

As much fun as it was celebrating with their fellow students, the Sewanee Iron Men refused to rest on their laurels when they returned home. They still had games to play. On November 20, they crushed Cumberland University 71–0 at Hardee Field (today's McGee Field) in front of an enthusiastic home crowd. The *Sewanee Purple* considered it "no game at all," but rather "a foot race" to see which Tiger player could score the most points. Ten days later, the team traveled to Montgomery, Alabama, for a Thanksgiving Day game against Auburn. It was the biggest matchup of the season. Both teams were coming into the game undefeated. Four thousand people turned out to see what would happen when an unstoppable force collided with an immovable object. Southern football historian Fuzzy Woodruff recorded the Victorian-era excitement on the sidelines: "Auburn's entire student body came over to Montgomery for the game and Sewanee also boasted a horde of partisans . . . On every side of the roped off field were gay traps and carriages and feverishly excited college boys with their chrysanthemum hair cuts." Kickoff was at 2:55 p.m. By 3:15, Auburn's Franklin Bivings had found his way into the Sewanee end zone. Sewanee's fans were gobsmacked. No one had scored on their team all season![23]

An enraged Henry Suter blew a fuse. "Are you fellows going to be run over like this all afternoon?" he asked one of his injured players.

"Coach," came the feeble reply, "we just can't stand this stuff. We've never seen anything like it."

Turning to John Heisman, who happened to be standing nearby, Suter muttered, "Can you beat that?" Heisman kept his mouth shut. His team was winning, and that was all that mattered to him.[24]

A short time later, Ed Huguley, Auburn's quarterback, got loose and scrambled forty yards before being tackled by Seibels. But the play was overturned by the officials, who insisted they had blown it dead. Auburn players howled in protest. It was one of a number of questionable calls that would go against them that afternoon.[25]

Sewanee players also were upset with the officiating, which they believed was being influenced by rowdy Auburn fans. With spectators gradually encroaching on the field and no police on hand to stop them, referees were nervous that a riot might ensue if they made too many calls against Auburn. According to several Sewanee sources, John Heisman took advantage of the chaos by putting twelve men on the field, a barefaced violation of the rules. The *Sewanee Purple* reported that Auburn players on the benches were jumping into the game at will and throwing blocks. (Alabama's Tommy Lewis would pull a similar stunt during the 1954 Cotton Bowl, when he left the sidelines to tackle Dicky Moegle, a Rice halfback.) "Sewanee has never before played an opponent who used such un-sportsmanlike methods," the paper complained. Suter's blood boiled. When Heisman approached him to ask a question, the Sewanee coach supposedly snarled, "Shut up, goddamn you, I'll spit down your throat!" The animosity spilled over into the following season, when Sewanee refused to play Clemson because Heisman had accepted a coaching position there.[26]

In spite of the challenges, Sewanee managed to stay in the game, thanks to an eight-yard touchdown carry by Kilpatrick, making it a 5–5 tie. Auburn responded with a punishing counteroffensive. Huguley struck first, with a big twenty yard gain; then Bivings, for seven; Arthur Feagin, for four; Feagin again, for ten; Bivings, for five; Huguley again . . . touchdown! Cheers erupted from the sidelines. "War Eagle!" Fortunately for Sewanee, William Claiborne managed to throw up one of his big paws and block Auburn's extra point attempt, holding the Tigers to a 10–5 lead.[27]

The most exciting play of the game occurred toward the end of the first half, on an Auburn fumble. Auburn's right guard, Dan Martin, spotted the loose ball and fell on it . . . or so it seemed to a number of eyewitnesses. Fuzzy Woodruff explained what happened next: "For some reason, never explained . . . [the referee] gave the ball to Sewanee on Auburn's one-yard line. Simkins went over for the touchdown and kicked [the extra point]. The score was 11–10 and Sewanee had won the game." Auburn fans were furious. A newspaper article the following day described the contest as "a game for blood" that had caused "a good deal of wrangling," especially from Auburn fans, who were convinced their team had been robbed of a victory by lousy officiating.[28]

A Sewanee alumnus named James Young remembered seeing fights in the stands and on the field between players and fans after the game ended. The fighting supposedly continued for years afterward, whenever anyone took "a strong position on either side of the argument."[29]

As a result of their razor-thin victory over Auburn, the Iron Men were named 1899 SIAA champions. The "championship of the South," however, was still up for grabs and could only be captured by winning one more game: a December 2 showdown in Atlanta against the North Carolina Tar Heels. UNC and UVA were the dominant southern programs of the era. North Carolina had gone undefeated the previous season and had won six straight games during the 1899 season before falling to Navy. John Heisman, still bitter over his team's loss, made a hundred-dollar bet with Sewanee players that they would lose to the Tar Heels. Ralph Black and his fellow teammates emptied their pockets of "dimes and dollars" to cover the wager. "We had fun over this for we knew we would win," Black recalled.[30]

The game turned out to be a defensive grudge match. Neither team could find a way to score. At one point, the Tar Heels managed to claw their way inside of Sewanee's five-yard line and, as result of back-to-back Tiger penalties, were given eight chances to find the end zone; eight times the UNC offense broke against Sewanee's defensive line like waves crashing on a rocky coast.[31] Sewanee finally got the ball back on downs and punted it out of danger. Rex Kilpatrick won the game for the Tigers on a field goal. Warbler Wilson described Kilpatrick's heroic kick in a letter he wrote in 1954: "I was playing the back-field, as I always did, and North Carolina kicked, it was a high spiral. I signaled for a fair catch on the 42 yard line and was tackled, which gave us fifteen yards and the choice of play. We were about ten yards from the left side line, I called Kilpatrick and held the place kick. He kicked it six or eight feet above the cross bars for the five points and 5 to 0 was the final score in the game." The Sewanee Tigers were the undisputed champions of the South. "We feel that the whole South should join us in our exultation," wrote the editors of the *Sewanee Purple*. "If our sister colleges have met defeat, it has been to a college which is working hand in hand with them to bring fame to Southern teams, to raise our younger athletics to the standard of the East. It is a glorious record."[32]

Sadly, few outside of the South seemed to care about Sewanee's remarkable season. The national sports media were far more interested in covering northeastern teams like Harvard, Yale, Penn, and Princeton. The 1899 All-America team did not feature a single southern player. Instead, southerners were relegated to a separate All-Southern team that included a number of Sewanee players. For all that it had accomplished since the end of the Civil War, the New South was still viewed as a provincial backwater with inferior universities, ignorant people, and second-rate football teams. Southerners themselves were guilty of perpetuating these stereotypes through their hostility toward outsiders, pathological racism, and disenfranchisement of poor black and white voters. The South had briefly won the praise of a grateful nation by sending a disproportionate number of its sons to fight in the Spanish–American War. But wartime heroics could not disguise the region's many problems, including illiteracy and hookworm, which non-southerners viewed with a mixture of loathing and compassion.[33]

This sanctimonious view of the South applied to the world of college football as well. Sewanee may have vanquished a dozen or so southern teams, but it could hardly be expected to slay a northern giant like Harvard. Even southerners thought so. Princeton's 115–0 drubbing of UVA in 1890 haunted the South for twenty years before Vanderbilt broke the curse by holding Yale to a 0–0 tie. Memories of the 1899 Sewanee team gradually faded as its members moved on with their lives. Diddy Seibels founded a successful insurance company in Birmingham, Alabama, after college (figure 7). Ringland "Rex" Kilpatrick moved to New York City to sell real estate. Warbler Wilson earned a law degree and won a seat in the South Carolina legislature. Bunny Pearce became a chaplain for the navy. William "Wild Bill" Claiborne also became a chaplain and founded the St. Andrew's School for boys in Sewanee. Claiborne was affectionately known as the "Archdeacon of Sewanee" for his charity work and humanitarian deeds. Ormond Simkins spent his career in Washington, DC, working as an attorney for the federal government. Tragically, Simkins died in 1921 while having a leg amputated at Georgetown University Hospital—a consequence, his relatives said, of his football career at Sewanee. "The arteries in his legs were so badly bruised that he developed Raynaud's disease and suffered fourteen years or more," his sister Helen complained. Raynaud's restricts the blood flow to a person's limbs, causing a tingling sensation, numbness, and pain. In extreme cases, amputations are required. Simkins was having his second leg amputated when he died.[34]

In October 1961, America rediscovered the lost story of the Sewanee Iron Men when an article entitled "The Miracle of Sewanee" appeared in a new magazine called *Sports Illustrated.* Twelve years later, Henry Seibels was posthumously inducted into the National Football Hall of Fame. By then, southern football was walking in tall cotton, thanks to the success of teams from Alabama, Ole Miss, and other big-time state schools. During a special halftime ceremony at Sewanee, in 1973, Seibels's son H. Kelly Seibels accepted a Hall of Fame award on behalf of his father. The award was presented by Bill Spears, a former Vanderbilt quarterback, who had been inducted into the Hall of Fame a decade earlier. In 2012, the College Football Hall of Fame created a Facebook poll that asked fans to choose the greatest college football team of all time. Sewanee won, hands down, in a sixteen-team playoff over other legendary teams such as the 1947 Notre Dame Fighting Irish, the 1961 Alabama Crimson Tide, the 1971 Nebraska Cornhuskers, and the 1974 Oklahoma Sooners.[35]

Such lavish praise and attention likely would have amused the Sewanee Iron Men. In their day, college football was a controversial sport played by rowdy young amateurs with something to prove. None of them could have imagined that the game would survive the next century—or that it would redefine what it meant to be a southerner.

CHAPTER SEVEN

"WHY SHOULD BETTER CARE BE TAKEN OF A GAME CHICKEN THAN A SCHOOL BOY?"

On September 6, 1901, a mentally disturbed anarchist named Leon Czolgosz shot the president of the United States at a reception in Buffalo, New York. William McKinley died eight days later, leaving the presidency in the hands of his forty-two-year-old vice president, Theodore Roosevelt. The scion of a well-heeled New York family, Roosevelt had never used his privileged upbringing as an excuse for idleness. As a child, he had overcome asthma and other bodily infirmities through rigorous exercise, and he studied harder than most of his peers at school. As an adult, he hunted grizzly bears in the American West before hunting Spaniards in Cuba with his fellow Rough Riders. His career in politics had been a dizzying ride to the top—New York State assemblyman, U.S. Civil Service commissioner, New York City Police commissioner, assistant secretary of the navy, and governor of New York—before becoming McKinley's vice president. "It is a dreadful thing to come into the Presidency this way," Roosevelt told a friend, after learning that McKinley had not survived the shooting. "But it would be a far worse thing to be morbid about it. Here is the task, and I have got to do it to the best of my ability; and that is all there is about it."[1]

T.R. got off on the wrong foot with many southerners when, shortly after becoming president, he invited Booker T. Washington to dine at the White House. Washington's reputation as a gentleman and political moderate allowed him to move with ease in both black and white social circles. During the 1895 Cotton States Exhibition in Atlanta, he had assuaged the guilty consciences of many white segregationists by assuring them that "the wisest among my race understands that the agitation of questions of social equality is the extremest folly, and that progress in the enjoyment of all the privileges that will come to us must be the result of severe and constant struggle rather than of artificial forcing. The opportunity to earn a dollar in a factory just now is worth infinitely more than the opportunity to spend a dollar in an opera house." Washington's apparent willingness to surrender African American political and social equality in exchange for greater economic and educational opportunities drew criticism from some of his fellow black leaders. "Mr. Washington represents in Negro thought the old attitude of adjustment and submission," W. E. B. Du Bois wrote pungently. "By every civilized and peaceful method we must strive for the rights which the world accords to men."[2]

Although popular in the South, Washington was still expected to abide by the region's social conventions. When word leaked that he had been invited to dine at the president's table, the southern press blew a gasket. "It means that the President is willing that negroes shall mingle freely with whites in the social circle," griped the *Richmond Times*. "White men of the South, how do you like it?" asked the editors of the *New Orleans Times-Democrat,* before revealing the true source of their outrage: "White women of the South, how do YOU like it?" The *Memphis Scimitar* described the dinner as "the most damnable outrage ever perpetrated by any citizen of the United States."

Roosevelt was caught off guard by the South's hostile reaction, and he punched back, albeit behind closed doors: "The idiot or vicious Bourbon element of the South is crazy because I have had Booker T. Washington to dine. I shall have him to dine just as often as I please." In fact, Washington was never invited back to the White House and Roosevelt publicly downplayed the significance of their meeting, describing it as an impromptu affair devoid of any real meaning or motives. Whatever his personal views, T.R. the politician understood that alienating the white South would make it difficult—if not impossible—to govern the nation.[3]

The primary topic of conversation in Starkville, Mississippi, that fall was not politics but the return of Mississippi A&M (Mississippi State) football after a four-year hiatus. Interest in the sport had fizzled after only two seasons (1895 and 1896), as the result of a prolonged losing streak and yellow fever. The hiring of Irwin Sessums as athletic director brought Mississippi State football back from the dead. Sessums, who had enjoyed watching Bulldog practices as a student, fought hard for funding and faculty approval of a team. He also convinced L. B. Harvey, a star halfback from Georgetown College in Kentucky, to coach and play in Starkville. Sessums's efforts paid off handsomely when Mississippi State thumped in-state rival Ole Miss 17–0 in Mississippi's very first Egg Bowl game. Harvey contributed two touchdowns and two extra points to the victory and was carried back to campus on the shoulders of grateful Mississippi State cadets.[4]

In neighboring Louisiana, students at the Louisiana Industrial Institute (today's Louisiana Tech) played LSU in their first intercollegiate varsity game, losing 57–0. In September, the Southwestern Louisiana Industrial Institute (now the University of Louisiana at Lafayette) opened its doors to students, who formed a football team shortly afterwards.[5]

University of Virginia players proclaimed themselves "champions of the South," after beating Sewanee 23–5 on Thanksgiving Day. During the same season, work began on Lambeth Field, named after William A. Lambeth, the "father of athletics" at UVA. It would serve as the Cavaliers' home field until the 1930s, when the team relocated to a new facility on grounds named Scott Stadium, in honor of its benefactor, Frederic William Scott, the wealthy cofounder of a Richmond-based brokerage firm called Scott & Stringfellow (now BB&T Scott & Stringfellow).[6]

The Vanderbilt Commodores were also dubbed "champions of the South," after defeating the University of Nashville 10–0 on Thanksgiving Day. Vanderbilt ended the season first in the Southern Intercollegiate Athletic Association, with a 6–1–1 record.[7]

Not that the SIAA title really mattered. At the association's December meeting in Chapel Hill, delegates were preoccupied with the problem of corruption at member schools. Both Sewanee and the University of Nashville had been suspended for poaching players from other SIAA colleges and allowing them to play before a year had elapsed, a direct violation of article 9, section 13 of the governing body's constitution.[8] Other programs were in hot water for more serious offenses. Tulane had been caught red-handed using a ringer in a game against LSU (a conviction stemming from charges brought by Tiger players). As punishment, Tulane was forced to forfeit its 22–0 victory and the game was recorded as an 11–0 LSU victory instead. The Georgia Tech baseball team also was facing ringer-related charges. In response, the SIAA appointed a special committee headed by William Dudley to amend the constitution in order to make it harder for teams to cheat. In the meantime, the charges against Sewanee and other member schools were to be quietly swept under the rug.[9]

The big news from up north was Coach Fielding Yost's "hurry up" offense at the University of Michigan and his team's 11–0 season. One of the stars of Yost's "Point-a-Minute" squad was a Michigan law student named Dan McGugin, who had played tackle for Drake University in Iowa before moving to Ann Arbor. On New Year's Day 1902, McGugin and his fellow Wolverines crushed Stanford 49–0 in the nation's first Rose Bowl game.[10]

In February, Roosevelt's justice department filed an antitrust lawsuit against the Northern Securities Company, a "holding company" that belonged to John Pierpont Morgan and several business allies, who were using it to monopolize railroad business in the northwest. When Morgan learned of the lawsuit, he called a meeting with Roosevelt and offered a compromise: "If we have done anything wrong, send your man to my man and they can fix it up." Morgan's cavalier attitude irritated the president. The federal government was not a rival corporation that could be bribed and browbeaten into submission. The antitrust suit against the Northern Securities Company would proceed as planned. After years of siding with big business, the federal government was finally using the Sherman Antitrust Act for its intended purpose: to blitz monopolies and contain the activities of unscrupulous corporations.[11]

Roosevelt also went after a group of mine owners who were treating their workers like dirt. Miners toiling in the anthracite coalfields of Eastern Pennsylvania had called a strike after their demands for better pay, shorter hours, and union membership were rejected. In October, T.R. invited John Mitchell, president of the United Mine Workers, and several mine owners—including George Baer, who controlled the Reading Railroad—to the White House for a conference. Baer's jaw dropped when the president announced his support for Mitchell's idea of an arbitrated settlement and threatened to seize the mines of any owner who did not cooperate. With support from the White House, the miners successfully negotiated a 10 percent wage increase, a nine-hour workday, and membership in the United Mine Workers.

In August 1903, the senate of Colombia rejected a deal that would have allowed the United States to build a canal across Colombia's Panamanian territory in exchange for a one-time payment of $10 million plus $250,000 a year in rent. Roosevelt was furious. In his eyes, the veto represented a dirty trick by ungrateful Colombians who were simply trying to squeeze more money from their rich Uncle Sam. Colombia's foreign minister had already approved the Hay–Herrán Treaty, and the U.S. Senate had ratified it. On November 4, Americans awoke to news that rebels in Panama had declared their independence from Columbia and were being supported by U.S. gunboats. Two weeks later, the newly independent republic of Panama ceded ownership of the Panama Canal Zone to the United States.[12]

On November 26, South Carolina pummeled Georgia Tech 16–0 at Piedmont Park in Atlanta. It was the fifth loss of the season for a struggling Tech team with a seven-game schedule. Oddly enough, Tech fans appeared unfazed by the loss. The reason why became clear only at the end of the fourth quarter, when a group of students rushed the field carrying a banner that read, "Tech gets Heisman for 1904." John Heisman, whose Clemson team had crushed Georgia Tech 73–0 a month earlier, had been hired to turn things around in Atlanta.

As events would show, it was the beginning of a golden age for Tech football. It was also an indication of the growing importance of professional coaches. Previously, coaching duties often had been fobbed off on players or faculty who possessed a limited understanding of football. Men like Heisman represented a new class of coaches with specialized knowledge and skills that were in high demand on campuses across the country.

Heisman, an experienced actor, called a team meeting before the start of the 1904 season. "What is this?" he asked, cradling a football as if it were a prop skull from a production of *Hamlet*. "It is a prolate spheroid, an elongated sphere in which the outer casing is drawn tightly over a somewhat smaller rubber tubing." Heisman then paused for dramatic effect before delivering a line that must have sent chills down the spines of his rookie players: "Better to have died as a small boy than to fumble this football."

Heisman's theatrical coaching style paid dividends right away. Georgia Tech whipped Fort McPherson 11–5 in the 1904 season opener and then went on to win its next four games before losing to Auburn. It was the sole loss of the season for a Heisman team that finished 8–1–1, a record that included wins against Georgia, Tennessee, and Florida and a tie with Clemson, Heisman's former employer.[13]

Vanderbilt ended the 1904 season with a perfect 9–0 record under its new head coach, Dan McGugin. After finishing law school at the University of Michigan, McGugin had received two coaching offers, one from Western Reserve University in Cleveland (now Case Western Reserve) and the other from Vandy. Although the Western Reserve job paid more, McGugin decided to "come South and see and know the people." Before long, he was engaged to Virginia Fite, the daughter of a wealthy Nashville businessman. Fielding Yost served as best man at the couple's wedding and fell in love with Virginia's sister, Eunice, whom he later married.[14]

Auburn also hired a new coach in 1904, who led the Tigers to a perfect 5–0 record. Michael Donahue, a native of County Kerry, Ireland, had lettered in football, basketball, track, and cross country at Yale before heading south to pursue a career in coaching. Donahue's happy-go-lucky attitude and incandescent wit endeared him to his players, who also knew he could get hot under the collar if they made too many mistakes on game day.[15]

Students at Southwest Texas State Normal School (today's Texas State) began playing football in the fall of 1904, with victories over St. Edward's College, West Texas Military Academy, the Texas Deaf and Dumb Asylum (now the Texas School for the Deaf), and Austin College. Texas State played the Texas School for the Deaf twice, losing once, and finished the season with a respectable 5–1 record. Decades before Lyndon Baines Johnson became a student there, Texas State was considered an up-and-coming college with a formidable football program.[16]

As talented as they were, however, the coaches at Texas State were not in the same league as Heisman, McGugin, and Donahue, whose career stats qualify them as southern coaching legends. Between 1904 and 1919, Heisman racked up 102 wins, 29 losses, and 7 ties, including Georgia Tech's (and the South's) first undisputed national championship (figure 8). McGugin went 197–55–19 during his thirty-year career at Vanderbilt. And in twenty-three seasons at Auburn and LSU, Donahue amassed an overall record of 122–54–8. These numbers forced the national media to take notice of southern football and instilled a sense of pride among rank-and-file southerners. Southern collegians might not have access to the same fancy book learning as their peers at Ivy League universities, but they could hit just as hard on the gridiron.[17]

While Heisman, McGugin, and Donahue were still getting settled in their new coaching jobs, southern cotton farmers were losing sleep over the boll weevil, a Central American beetle that had crawled over the border into Texas in the 1890s and spread north like a virus. Boll weevils feed on cotton leaves and deposit their eggs in the plant's buds, or "squares." A female boll weevil can lay one hundred to three hundred eggs at a time and produce as many as eight broods per year. The insect wreaked havoc in cotton-producing regions across the South, prompting a mass exodus of black and white southerners who suddenly found themselves unable to make a living in their home communities. The boll weevil invasion even caught the attention of the president of the United States, who referenced it in his 1904 State of the Union Address. "The boll weevil is a serious menace to the cotton crop," Roosevelt warned. "A scientist of the Department of Agriculture has found the weevil at home in Guatemala being kept in check by an ant, which has been brought to our cotton fields for observation. It is hoped that it may serve a good purpose." Unfortunately, the Guatemalan ant fix proved to be a failed Hail Mary pass, and the boll weevil would continue its devastating march across Dixie for another three decades.[18]

Cotton-munching insects, however, were not enough to prevent voters from electing Theodore Roosevelt to a full term as president. They were impressed with the way T.R. had handled himself since McKinley's assassination and appreciated his promise of a "square deal" for every citizen. Progressives were especially happy with his efforts to eradicate corporate malfeasance and political corruption. On Election Day 1904, Roosevelt captured 56 percent of the popular vote and 336 electoral votes; his Democratic challenger, Alton Parker, finished second, with 140 electoral votes and 37 percent of the popular vote. T.R. interpreted the victory as a mandate for reform and began searching for other things in need of fixing.[19]

In 1905, his steely gaze fell on college football. For Roosevelt and other like-minded progressives, the sport was a savage beast in need of taming. According to the *Washington Post*, "at least 45 football players died from 1900 to October 1905, many from internal injuries, broken necks, concussions or broken backs." Worse yet, a majority had supposedly been killed as a result of cheap shots like illegal kicks to the head and stomach. Something had to be done. Not that T.R. objected to rough-and-tumble sports. "I believe in outdoor games," he told a group of Harvard alumni. "And I do not mind in the least that they are rough games, or that those who take part in them are occasionally injured . . . But when these injuries are inflicted by others, either wantonly or of set design, we are confronted by the question, not of damage to one man's body, but damage to the other man's character."

In other words, dirty plays not only were destroying bodies but also were putting young men's souls at risk.[20]

Roosevelt's appetite for reform had been whetted by a series of articles published in *McClure's Magazine,* in the summer of 1905, by his friend Henry Beach Needham. Football, Needham argued, had turned colleges into rival corporations that were using ringers to win games and pad their bottom lines. Faculty and administrators might profess support for the amateur ideal, but they were not practicing what they preached. Even worse, players were being encouraged to target their opponent's star athletes, a cruel practice that often resulted in broken bones and shattered dreams.[21]

In October 1905, T.R. summoned representatives from Harvard, Princeton, and Yale to the White House to discuss ways the game could be reformed. Among those present at the meeting were Walter Camp, who was reluctant to make any changes to a sport he had practically invented on his own, and T.R.'s secretary of state, Elihu Root. Roosevelt began by striking a conciliatory tone, asking how they could all work together to ensure that the existing rules of football were enforced and that players practiced good sportsmanship. While expressing broad support for the president's views, the group did not commit itself to any specific changes, and they issued a perfunctory statement after the meeting, pledging to follow "in letter and spirit the rules of the game."[22]

A month later, a Union College player named Harold Moore died from a brain injury after receiving a kick in the head during a game against New York University. Moore's death shocked the public. The *Cincinnati Commercial Tribune* published a cartoon of a smiling Grim Reaper perched on top of a football goalpost. The same year, Roosevelt's own son, Theodore Jr., a guard for the Harvard Crimson, suffered a broken nose during a game against Yale and had to be helped off the field. The 1905 season would be remembered as one of the bloodiest on record. Eighteen deaths and 149 serious injuries were reported. In response, Duke, Northwestern, South Carolina, Columbia, and other schools banned football, while students at Stanford and the University of California switched to rugby, a sport that some considered less dangerous. Harvard's program appeared to be next on the chopping block, with President Charles Eliot, a well-known football foe, eagerly awaiting an opportunity to drop the ax. But Eliot's views were not shared by the president of the United States, who, under pressure from

Harvard alumni and himself a die-hard Crimson fan, once again used his presidential bully pulpit to issue a call for reforms.[23]

A new rules committee was hastily assembled at the end of the 1905 season. The lion's share of its members were men from eastern schools, like Walter Camp, Harvard coach William T. Reid Jr., and Paul Dashiell, who by this time was coaching at Navy. A rival committee with a more diverse regional membership met separately during the same period. The two committees merged the following year to form the Intercollegiate Athletic Association (ICAA), a forerunner of the NCAA, the organization currently responsible for governing college sports.[24]

The ICAA's greatest achievement was the legalization of the forward pass. The play had been around for years but was rarely used because of its questionable legal standing. John Heisman credited the North Carolina Tar Heels with executing the first pass play in history, in 1895, during a game against the University of Georgia. Under pressure from the Bulldog defense, Carolina's punter had supposedly made a snap decision to throw the ball instead of kicking it. The pass was caught by George Stephens, who ran seventy yards for a touchdown. Or that was how Heisman remembered it, anyway. During an interview long after his football career had ended, Stephens confessed that he had no recollection of the play. Heisman insisted that he had witnessed it from the sidelines and remembered seeing Pop Warner, UGA's coach at the time, argue with officials for not calling a penalty.[25]

By legalizing the forward pass, the ICAA hoped to open up the game and reduce the player injury rate. Fans loved it for a different reason: the forward pass added a dazzling air show to a game that frequently became bogged down in the trenches. With the new rule in place, a player could gain twenty yards—or score a touchdown—in the blink of an eye. A number of old dog coaches, however, refused to learn the new trick and continued to focus on improving their ground games. Other safety-related changes enacted by the ICAA included establishing a neutral zone at the line of scrimmage, raising from five to ten the number of yards required for a first down (Camp believed this would force teams to run outside more often), shortening each half to thirty minutes, and cracking down on penalties and unsportsmanlike conduct.[26]

In February 1906, Upton Sinclair published *The Jungle,* a fictional account of immigrant life in the United States, which the author hoped would persuade people to become socialists. It turned their stomachs, instead, with nauseating accounts of the unsanitary conditions inside America's meatpacking plants. The ensuing public outcry goaded Congress into passing the Meat Inspection Act and the Pure Food and Drug Act.

In June, Roosevelt signed into law the Act for the Preservation of American Antiquities (also known as the National Monuments Act). The law empowered the president to "declare by public proclamation historic landmarks, historic and prehistoric structures, and other objects of historic and scientific interest . . . to be National Monuments." Roosevelt wasted no time in exercising his new authority; he designated Devil's Tower in Wyoming, the Petrified Forest and Montezuma Castle in Arizona, and El Morro in New Mexico as national monuments. This was part of a broader effort by progressives to preserve natural spaces for future generations. Roosevelt's decision to set aside millions of acres of national forest reserves—an idea encouraged by his close friend and chief of the Forest Service, Gifford Pinchot—angered many old guard Republicans, who considered it unconstitutional and antithetical to free market principles.[27]

In September, a race riot engulfed Atlanta, a city Henry Grady had hoped would be the New Jerusalem of the New South. Newspapers in Atlanta had for some time been publishing lurid tales of black men's insolence, murder, rape, and debauchery, especially in the "vice district," where a handful of white women had allegedly been assaulted. Despite pleas from Atlanta's mayor and police commissioner to exercise restraint, a mob of more than ten thousand angry whites went on a violent rampage, indiscriminately attacking black citizens—both men and women—in the streets. Although precise figures are unknowable, it is estimated that around twenty-five African Americans and one white person were killed in the melee, along with dozens of others who sustained serious injuries.[28]

In November, Roosevelt traveled to Panama on an inspection tour of the canal construction project—the first official trip abroad ever taken by a sitting president. On his second day in the country, T.R. was photographed wearing a white suit and a Panama hat while sitting behind the controls of a ninety-five-ton steam shovel. It has since become an iconic image, a glimpse of an American president at the height of his power, driving his country toward a more active role in world affairs.[29]

In Nashville, meanwhile, the Vanderbilt Commodores stunned college football fans by beating the Carlisle Indians, an elite squad that had earned a reputation for manhandling opponents, even Ivy League teams. Bob Blake, whom John Heisman would later describe as one of the South's "very best drop and place kickers," won the game for Vandy on a thirty-eight-yard field goal.[30]

The University of Florida's inaugural season ended in 1906 with a 5–3 record. Florida's coach at the time was James "Pee Wee" Forsythe, a North Carolina native who had played football at Clemson during the Heisman era. Legend has it that the team was christened the Alligators the following year by Austin Miller, a UVA student originally from the Sunshine State. The story goes that Miller and his father, a merchant who owned a novelty shop and soda fountain in Gainesville, were in a Charlottesville print shop one day, placing an order for UF pennants, which the elder Miller hoped to sell in his store. When the manager of the print shop asked whether Florida had a mascot, Austin suggested the alligator, because of the animal's connection to the state and because no other school had claimed it. The blue pennants with orange alligators on them were an immediate hit with Florida students, and the name Alligators—or "Gators," for short—stuck.[31] That is how Miller remembered the story, anyway, when he shared it with a reporter for the *Florida Times-Union* in the 1940s. Carl Van Ness, curator of manuscripts and archives for the University of Florida libraries, is doubtful that Miller came up with the team name, but he does believe Florida blue and orange could be a variation of Virginia's blue and orange. "I think there is a strong possibility that Miller simply confused the colors with the mascot," he told me.

Van Ness's own research into the origins of the Gator nickname led him to the story of Neal "Bo Gator" Storter, an engineering student from Everglades City, who captained the 1911 football team and founded a student group called the Bo Gators, which some say was the true inspiration for the Florida mascot name. Storter himself credited a Georgia journalist with creating it, in 1910, when the football team traveled to Macon to play Mercer College. In all likelihood, the truth is lurking just below the surface of one or more of these murky tales.[32]

In December 1906, Roosevelt received a Nobel Prize for brokering a peace deal between Russia and Japan. The two colonial powers had gone to war in 1904 over rival territorial claims in Asia. Western observers were shocked when Japan's military got the better of Tsar Nicholas II's forces, since it was assumed that no Asian military power could ever defeat a European one. Roosevelt was humbled by the award. "I am profoundly moved and touched," he wrote to the Nobel committee. "What I did I was able to accomplish only as the representative of the Nation of which for the time being I am President." He donated the cash prize—nearly $37,000—to a foundation committed to advancing international peace.[33]

Football's popularity steadily climbed during the 1907 and 1908 seasons, thanks in part to the new rules created by the ICAA. Most people felt that the new-and-improved version of the game was safer and more fun to watch. In November 1907, Alabama and Auburn butted heads on neutral ground in Birmingham (an annual game dubbed the "Iron Bowl" because of the city's ties to the steel and iron industries) for state bragging rights. The game ended in a 6–6 tie. An ensuing argument over money and alleged improprieties prevented the two teams from playing each other again until 1948.[34]

The LSU Tigers played in the first international exhibition game in Cuba, on Christmas Day 1907, against a team from the University of Havana. Football had been brought to Cuba by U.S. troops occupying the country at the end of the Spanish–American War and by Cuban men who had attended American colleges such as the Audubon Park Sugar School and Experiment Station at LSU. (Charles Coates, the founding father of LSU football, was the first dean of the Sugar School.) On game day, Coach Edgar Wingard's Tigers crushed Havana 56–0. The Cubans took it all in stride. George E. "Doc" Fenton's sensational open-field runs earned him the nickname "el Rubio Vaselino," or "the Greased Blond," in the Cuban press. Unfortunately, a number of U.S. servicemen who showed up at the game proved far less charitable toward their hosts and taunted the Havana team with racist jeers such as "Lick the spicks, kill the spicks . . . Rah! Rah! Rah! Louisiana!"[35]

Racism was pervasive in both the United States and Europe in the early twentieth century. During a debate on the floor of Congress over America's occupation of the Philippines, Senator Albert Beveridge (R-IN) claimed that Filipinos were incapable of managing their own affairs because they were "Orientals, Malays, instructed by Spaniards in the latter's worst estate." Beveridge and others believed that English-speaking whites had been specially chosen by God to "administer government among savage and senile peoples." "Were it not for such a force as this the world would relapse into barbarism and night," the Indiana senator insisted. Plenty of other Occidentals agreed. Rudyard Kipling, author of *The Jungle Book*, published an ode to imperialism he called "The White Man's Burden." Many white southerners believed they had a God-given right to rule over their black neighbors, just as white U.S. servicemen stationed in Cuba regarded themselves as racially superior to the island's brown and black inhabitants.[36]

The West's obsession with race during the Progressive Era contributed to the creation of a new science, eugenics (from the Greek word *eugenes*, meaning "good stock"). Eugenicists believed that the health of any society could be improved through selective breeding and that those with undesirable traits, such as "feeblemindedness" or "criminality," should not be allowed to have children. In 1907, Indiana became the first state in the nation to enact a sterilization law. Other states soon followed suit. Eugenicists held conferences, printed pamphlets, and showcased exhibits at state and county fairs in order to promulgate their pseudoscientific ideas. "How long are we Americans to be so careful for the pedigree of our pigs and chickens and cattle—and then leave the ancestry of our children to chance, or to 'blind' sentiment?" read one typical eugenics poster on display at a Kansas fair. Another exhibit showed three pairs of male and female guinea pigs and their offspring—one "pure" white family, one "pure" black family, and one mixed family. The racial message was obvious. Eugenics was taken seriously in academic and scientific circles, until its hideous repercussions became apparent in the aftermath of World War II. Even so, states such as Virginia continued to carry out forced sterilizations well into the late twentieth century.[37]

The LSU Tigers capped the 1908 football season with a perfect 10–0 record. Unfortunately, accusations of jiggery-pokery cast a cloud of suspicion over the program. The controversy began when Grantland Rice published an article in the *Nashville Tennessean* accusing Coach Wingard of fielding ringers. John Seip, the Smith brothers (Clarence and "Bull"), "Doc" Fenton, Mike Lally, and Marshall Gandy all were being paid to play in Baton Rouge, Rice insisted. Tulane supporters, still smarting from the accusations made by LSU seven years earlier, which had cost them a 22–0 win over the Tigers, piled on the accusations. Charles Bauer, an LSU halfback from the 1907 season, they said, was actually a former Wabash College player named Charles Buser, whom Wingard had recruited despite knowing Buser was ineligible. Tulane also backed Rice's claim that other Tigers, including Seip and the Smiths, were ringers.

At its December meeting in Knoxville, the SIAA appointed a special three-man committee composed of Sewanee's vice-chancellor, a professor from Alabama, and another from Ole Miss to investigate the charges. The committee discovered that Mike Lally had compromised his amateur status by playing minor league baseball over the summer, a common infraction among college athletes in need of money. (Jim Thorpe was forced to leave Carlisle after he was caught playing summer ball for a bush league team in North Carolina.) Despite the charges against their team, Tigers fans celebrated the championship season with a banquet, a pep rally, and a nighttime parade in Baton Rouge that was attended by Governor Jared Sanders and other dignitaries. Lally was quietly dropped from the team at the end of the 1908 season (but later reinstated), and Coach Wingard left to go work as an assistant for Pop Warner at Carlisle; he was banned from ever coaching again in the SIAA.[38]

Auburn lost only one game during the 1908 season, a 10–2 heartbreaker against LSU. Auburn fans were furious that their team's perfect season had been spoiled by a team of alleged cheaters. LSU fans dismissed the complaints as sour grapes and continued celebrating their championship. The southern media sided with Auburn and named Mike Donahue's squad as SIAA champions. The controversy continues to this day.[39]

In November 1908, Republican William Howard Taft became the nation's twenty-seventh president. Taft easily defeated his Democratic opponent, William Jennings Bryan (this was Bryan's third and final run for the White House), with 52 percent of the popular vote and 67 percent of the electoral vote. Taft had distinguished himself as the first American governor-general of the Philippines, before becoming Roosevelt's secretary of war. T.R. had high hopes for his handpicked successor, but he worried that Taft might not be tough enough to handle the bare-knuckle politics of Washington. "He's all right. But he's weak," Roosevelt told a journalist on Inauguration Day. "They'll get around him. They'll lean against him." Roosevelt and Taft would have a falling out a few years later.[40]

Ten days before Taft's inauguration, the U.S. Navy's "Great White Fleet" (a nickname derived from the ships' distinctive white hulls) arrived in Hampton Roads, Virginia, after a fourteen-month voyage around the world. Roosevelt had commissioned the voyage in order to test his fleet's battle readiness and to project American strength overseas. Fourteen thousand sailors and marines participated in the trip, which included twenty ports of call on six continents.[41]

In the autumn of 1909, a brand-new team representing Troy State Normal College (today's Troy University) in Alabama played a three-game schedule against local high school teams. Professor Vergil Parks McKinley coached the Teachers to a 1–2–0 record. McKinley, a graduate of the University of Alabama, had been handed the task of building a football program by Troy's president, Edwin Eldridge.[42]

In October, President Taft traveled to New Orleans to deliver a speech on federal funding for waterway improvements and to shore up his political alliances in the Pelican State. He also planned to make an appearance at an LSU–Sewanee game, despite objections from his Secret Service detail. A delegation from Tulane buttonholed the president at his hotel and asked if he would also be willing to attend a Tulane–Mississippi State game scheduled for the same day. "It would be a rank shame, they said, if the president saw the other game and not theirs. Besides, they had sold ten thousand tickets on the report that he would be on the field." Taft agreed to show up at both games. His private car drove along LSU's sidelines first, and the president witnessed a Sewanee touchdown during his five-minute stay. Next, he headed over to the Tulane game and stayed "just long enough to allow the management to make good with the crowd."[43]

Tragedy struck the University of Virginia in November, when halfback Archer Christian died from injuries he received during a game against Georgetown. Although the precise cause of death was undetermined, the general consensus was that Christian had not been the victim of a controversial "mass play" but rather had been cleanly tackled after breaking through Georgetown's defensive line. The story was picked up by the *New York Times,* which listed the cause of death as a "cerebral hemorrhage following concussion." Christian's parents and his brother were by his side when he passed away. His mother had insisted that the family attend the game, based on a hunch that something dreadful was going to happen to her child. Christian's father refused to blame anyone for the tragedy, acknowledging that "his son had been killed by accident in fair play." Students gathered in the UVA chapel to pray "for the repose of the soul of young Christian." Both Georgetown and Virginia canceled their remaining games.[44]

UVA's president, Edwin Alderman, immediately came under pressure to abolish football at the university. Alderman chose instead to pursue rule changes that he hoped would make the game safer. He asked William Lambeth, head of the university's Department of Physical Education, to accompany him to New York to address the ICAA. Lambeth accepted and was invited to join the association's rules committee, where he proposed (among other things) subdividing future games into four quarters so that players would have more time to rest.[45]

One of Alderman's harshest critics was the legendary "gray ghost of the Confederacy," John Singleton Mosby. Mosby, who had sent countless young men to their graves as commander of a notorious Confederate guerilla unit operating in Northern Virginia, was appalled by Archer Christian's death and the health risks associated with playing football. In December 1909, he penned a letter sharing his disgust over UVA's sufferance of the game:

> I do not think foot-ball should be tolerated where the youth of the country are supposed to be sent to be taught literature [and] science. The game seems to over shadow every thing else at the University. I believe that cock-fighting is unlawful in Virginia: Why should better care be taken of a game chicken than a school boy? The amusement is a renaisance [*sic*] of the worst days of the Caesars. You say that fox hunting is as dangerous as foot-ball but there is no public protest against it. The difference is a Hunt Club is not a public institution supported by the State like the University where the youth are sent to learn not only the Classics and Mathematics but principles of Ethics . . . It has been said that the athletic training that Wellington's soldiers got at the English schools won Waterloo; *per contra,* I say that [Stonewall] Jackson's men won their victories without any such nursing.

In Mosby's eyes, college football was nothing more than a crass moneymaking scheme. "It is notorious that foot-ball teams are largely composed of professional mercenaries who are hired to advertise colleges," he complained. "Gate money is the valuable consideration. There is no sentiment of Romance or Chivalry about them."[46]

Mosby's denunciation of the violence associated with football is remarkable when one considers his own violent past, both as a Confederate officer and as a UVA undergraduate. In the spring of 1851, as a first-year student, Mosby had been fined ten dollars for breaking a gun stock over the head of a Charlottesville police officer who was trying to break up a street brawl between students and townies. Two years later, Mosby shot a man named George Turpin in the mouth after Turpin threatened to pummel him. Mosby was convicted of "unlawful shooting" and sentenced to one year in jail. He was released after seven months, for good behavior.[47]

Mosby's views became public knowledge when a letter he had written to the UVA Board of Visitors, "condemning the connection of foot-ball games with the University and other schools," was intercepted by the press. Mosby welcomed the publicity: "I hope it will do some good in arousing public attention to a great nuisance." Other members of the Civil War generation shared his bleak view of football. "I have read your letter on the brutality and criminality of Foot ball and agree with every word of it," wrote Robert Waterman Hunter, former chief of staff to John B. Gordon, one of Lee's favorite generals. "There can be no doubt that Athletics as now allowed & encouraged at our colleges has lowered the standard of scholarship & set up false Gods for the worship of young men. The inevitable tendency is to make brutes instead of gentlemen."[48]

Mosby and Hunter were not alone. When a navy cadet was paralyzed while playing Villanova and an army cadet was subsequently killed in a game against Harvard, the critics pounced. The rule changes of 1906, they insisted, were a complete farce. Football was still murdering and maiming young men in the prime of their lives. "We have certainly got to do something Walter, for the season has been a mighty bad one for a number of individuals as well as for the game," Amos Alonzo Stagg warned Camp.[49]

In response, the ICAA issued a new set of regulations, in 1910, the same year that the group changed its name to the National Collegiate Athletic Association. The new rules required seven men on the line of scrimmage during a snap; banned the practice of pulling and pushing a ballcarrier to help him gain extra yards; barred blockers from linking arms and hands; repealed an old rule restricting the horizontal movement of ballcarriers (checkerboard lines on football fields would disappear, as a result); limited passes to twenty yards beyond the line of scrimmage and forced quarterbacks to throw from a minimum of five yards behind the line; subdivided games into four fifteen-minute quarters (Lambeth's proposal); and allowed only one man in motion prior to the snap, who could not advance toward the line of scrimmage.

The new rules were a reflection of the age in which they were written. Football might have been conceived in the laissez-faire climate of the Gilded Age, but progressives were determined to make the sport safer for future generations. The same men and women who were building settlement houses for immigrants, sterilizing the mentally ill, halting the exploitation of child labor, and changing society in countless other ways were confident they could improve football through greater regulation and bureaucratization. Nothing, it seemed, was impossible for them. That is, until war and disease shattered their faith in man's ability to control his destiny.

CHAPTER EIGHT

WAR, PESTILENCE, AND THE
GOLDEN TORNADO

I n the fall of 1910, the Vanderbilt Commodores were considered the golden boys of southern college football. No team below the Mason–Dixon Line wanted to take the field against them. They were too tough and too clever, especially the team's star quarterback, Ray Morrison. Born in Indiana in 1885, Morrison had spent most of his childhood on a farm near McKenzie, Tennessee, and worked on a dredge boat on the Mississippi River before enrolling in college. Weighing a scant 155 pounds his freshman year, Morrison had hit the gym and bulked up after joining the Commodore football team. In October 1910, he and his teammates traveled to Connecticut to play the defending national champion Yale Bulldogs. The Bulldogs had run the table the previous year with ten straight shutout victories, including an 8–0 win over Harvard. Their game against Vandy was supposed to be a walk in the park, just as every other Ivy League contest against a southern team had been since the nineteenth century.[1]

And then the unthinkable happened. The undersize Commodores tore into their opponents like a pack of wild dogs with their tails on fire. According to one newspaper account, Vanderbilt's defense swarmed "the man with the ball, rolling back the attack with a power hardly to be expected from [a team] fifteen pounds lighter to the man." Heavy rains muddied the playing field, causing both teams to fumble and miss field goals. But without sending in a single substitute, the Commodores accomplished what no one had previously thought possible: they held Yale to a scoreless tie.[2]

"Every man on the squad simply went in like a tiger, and there was no let-up," Coach Dan McGugin proudly explained after the game. "They put every ounce of fighting strength they had into every play." News of the tie reached Tennessee in the middle of the night. Overjoyed Vanderbilt students jumped out of bed and held an impromptu "victory" parade in downtown Nashville, dressed in their pajamas. Afterwards, they headed over to the Belmont College for Young Women before gathering on Dudley Field for a bonfire party that lasted into the wee hours of the morning.[3]

Students at Randolph-Macon College in Ashland, Virginia, were equally jubilant when their football team defeated archrival Hampden-Sydney College 10–3. The victory meant the Yellow Jackets would be able to play Richmond College (today's University of Richmond) for the 1910 Virginia Eastern Collegiate Championship. Randy Mac's faculty, however, was anything but pleased. They had granted the entire student body a half day of leave for the Hampden-Sydney game but were annoyed to learn the football team had stayed off campus the entire day. The faculty initially disbanded the team as punishment, but backpedaled in the face of widespread student protests. Instead, only those who were actually playing in the championship game would be allowed to travel to Richmond. No one else, not even team managers, would be excused from classes. And anyone caught violating the order would be subject to expulsion.[4]

Team manager E. Barrett Prettyman took the news hard. He had worked all season to put Randolph-Macon on top, and he did not want to miss the championship game. With the help of a fellow student, nineteen-year-old Marion Fisher, Prettyman hatched a bold plan: he would ask the president of the United States to pressure Randy Mac's faculty into repealing the travel ban.

Prettyman had learned that Taft would be in Richmond prior to the game, and he considered the visit a favorable omen. He and Fisher knocked on the front door of the Virginia Governor's Mansion on the morning of the visit and were immediately ushered in to see Governor William Mann. (Mann, a staunch prohibitionist, would turn out to be the last Confederate veteran to serve in Virginia's highest office.) The governor agreed to allow Prettyman and Fisher to meet with the president, who arrived a short time later, escorted by an honor guard of Virginia Tech cadets.

"How may I serve you?" Taft asked, placing his hand on Prettyman's shoulder. When the pair explained their dilemma, the president was seized with laughter. "It began with a low chuckle and exploded into an infectious laugh that shook the ample presidential frame." After regaining his composure, Taft promised to do all he could to help—as long as it was okay with Charles Norton, his private secretary. Norton, who was equally amused by the boys' capering, told them they needed to find a way to get the presidential train to stop at the college. Prettyman and Fisher knew just what to do. They called in a favor with a Randolph-Macon alumnus named William White, who happened to be president of the Richmond, Fredericksburg, and Potomac Railroad. When White heard the plan, he agreed to divert Taft's train.[5]

A large crowd was on hand to greet the president's train when it arrived in Ashland. Shortly after six p.m., Taft began speaking.

> Now about this football situation. If you boys were all locked up in the federal penitentiary, over which I have some authority, I would not hesitate a moment about issuing an order that you should be released to see this game. But the trouble is that I have no authority to issue an order to the faculty. However, Dr. Blackwell [president of Randolph-Macon] has been on the train all the way from Richmond, and I have argued with him all the way as to why you should be allowed to see the game. I have pleaded your case with all the power I have and with all the arguments I can think of. I don't know what the faculty will do about it, but I assure you boys that I have done everything that is within my authority to persuade them to rescind their order.[6]

Realizing they had been outwitted by a pair of clever undergraduates, Randy Mac's faculty threw in the towel; the travel ban would be lifted. Prettyman and Fisher were overjoyed—and even happier still when their beloved Yellow Jackets stung the Richmond Spiders 11–6, making them the undisputed football champions of Eastern Virginia.

Although he was popular in Ashland, Taft was fighting for his political life elsewhere. His decision to fire Gifford Pinchot, Roosevelt's chief of the Forest Service, had infuriated the progressive wing of the Republican Party. The president's feud with Pinchot had started when Richard Ballinger, Taft's secretary of the interior, decided to release a number of federally protected lands for commercial development. Pinchot protested the decision and accused Ballinger of trying to personally profit from the sale of some land in Alaska that J. P. Morgan and the mining tycoon David Guggenheim had been coveting. When Taft rallied to Ballinger's defense instead of reprimanding him, Pinchot leaked the story to the press and was summarily dismissed.

Teddy Roosevelt, returning from safari in Africa, was told that Taft had gone rogue and could no longer be trusted. In September, the former president gave a speech in Osawatomie, Kansas, outlining his plan for a "new nationalism" that would use the power of the federal government to protect the vulnerable and check the influence of corporations. The speech marked his formal return to the political arena and, with it, a split in the Republican Party.

Americans shared T.R.'s unease with the growing power of corporations. A series of articles written for *McClure's Magazine* by a journalist named Ida Tarbell had alerted readers to the shady business practices of Standard Oil. Tarbell portrayed Standard as a company that would stop at nothing to destroy competitors and gain control over every aspect of the oil production process—even if that meant skirting the edges of ethical and legal behavior. Railroad companies were jawboned into paying kickbacks ("rebates") or financial penalties, called drawbacks, for shipping competitors' products. A Standard Oil trust was established to bypass antimonopoly laws. Stockholders surrendered their stock in return for trust certificates, which gave the "trustees" absolute control over an unlimited number of companies. For John D. Rockefeller, founder of Standard Oil, such practices were the warp and woof of capitalism. He had to seize every opportunity that came along, or one of his competitors surely would.[7]

John W. Heisman felt the same way about football. College teams, in his mind, were rival companies engaged in a life-or-death struggle; only the strongest could survive in an era of social Darwinism. To make his teams more competitive, Heisman would sometimes employ questionable tactics, such as having football-shaped patches sewn onto his players' uniforms, to confuse tacklers, or attaching straps to the pants of his running backs so they could be more easily tossed over the line of scrimmage. At Georgia Tech, he introduced his own version of the jump shift (or "Heisman shift"), a play that would baffle defenses for years. A classic Heisman shift consisted of the quarterback, fullback, and halfbacks lining up in a basic I formation. A split second before the ball was snapped, one or more of these players would suddenly "jump" to the right, throwing the defense for a loop. Heisman's great-nephew John M. Heisman described it as a "chickadee hop" that "entailed strong but fluid jumps forward, laterally, and diagonally to assigned positions that disguised where and to whom the center snap was going."[8]

The Heisman shift helped Georgia Tech finish the 1911 season with a respectable 6–2–1 record. Vanderbilt remained the top dog in Dixie, however, with an 8–1 record and the SIAA conference title. McGugin's sole loss was a 9–8 heartbreaker against his brother-in-law's team from Ann Arbor. Despite the loss, McGugin and Yost remained close friends and continued playing each other in the years that followed. Legend has it that prior to the 1922 Michigan-Vanderbilt game, McGugin pointed to a military cemetery near Dudley Field and told his players, "In that cemetery sleep your grandfathers. And down on that field are the grandsons of the damn Yankees who put them there." Understandably, McGugin failed to mention that his own father had been an officer in the Union army. Whether it is true or not, the story illustrates how far he would go to motivate his team.[9]

Students at Middle Tennessee State Normal School (today's Middle Tennessee State University) in Murfreesboro and the First District Agricultural School (now Arkansas State) in Jonesboro, Arkansas, were motivated enough in the fall of 1911 to form their own football teams. Middle Tennessee, coached by L. E. "Mutt" Weber, lost its one and only game to Fitzgerald-Clarke School 6–0. Arkansas State fared slightly better, losing one game and winning another against Paragould High School.[10]

In the business world, there were plenty of supervisors who preferred to micromanage their employees rather than search for ways to motivate them. On March 25, 1911, a fire broke out on the upper floors of the Triangle Shirtwaist Company building in New York City, trapping Triangle employees, many of whom were young Jewish and Italian women, in smoke and flames. The interior doors of the workers' offices had been locked in order to keep them from leaving early or taking unauthorized breaks. Rather than endure the agony of being burned to death, a number of women chose to leap from their office windows. By the time the fire was brought under control, dozens of lifeless bodies lay on the sidewalk in front of the Triangle building.[11]

Tragedies such as the Triangle Shirtwaist fire kindled workers' wrath and drove them to join unions. Those who were unwilling (or unable) to join mainstream unions like the American Federation of Labor gravitated toward more radical organizations like the Industrial Workers of the World ("Wobblies"). Wobblies rejected traditional collective bargaining tactics in favor of what they called "direct action": "Direct action means industrial action directly by, for, and of the workers themselves, without the treacherous aid of labor misleaders or scheming politicians. A strike that is initiated, controlled, and settled by the workers directly affected is direct action . . . Direct action is industrial democracy."[12]

The Wobblies were allied with the socialists, a group that worked hard to cultivate a more wholesome public image. Led by the charismatic Eugene Debs (who had spent time in jail for his role in the Pullman Strike), the Socialist Party adopted many of the ideas espoused by the old Populist Party, including public ownership of railroads, high taxes on the rich, and government-owned grain elevators. The socialists took it a step further, however, by declaring the capitalist system an utter failure "incapable of meeting the problems now confronting society." At least 900,743 Americans agreed and cast their ballots for Debs during the 1912 presidential election, handing him 6 percent of the popular vote.[13]

Debs received only 50,020 votes in the former Confederate states, half of which were cast by Texans. Most southerners were blue dog Democrats who supported free market capitalism. They rolled out the red carpet for companies that promised jobs for the unemployed and tax revenue for empty state coffers. The textile industry, once the pride of New England, relocated to the South in search of cheap labor. In 1880, there were seventeen thousand southerners working in textile mills; ten years later there were thirty-six thousand; by 1900 the number had increased to ninety-eight thousand (a majority worked in mills in the Carolinas). Coal companies carved up the hills of Kentucky, West Virginia, Virginia, and Tennessee. Iron production boomed in Alabama. Lumber, too, had become big business. By 1910, the South accounted for 45 percent of the nation's lumber production.[14]

Although supportive of free markets, most southerners were savvy enough to realize that corporations needed to be regulated by the state. Thus, they responded favorably to Democratic presidential candidate Woodrow Wilson's call for a "new freedom" that would use the power of the federal government to dismantle trusts rather than simply police them, as Roosevelt wanted to do under his New Nationalism plan. Wilson, a southerner and the son of a Presbyterian minister, believed that unrestricted capitalism posed a threat to the nation's Christian moral order. His candidacy came as a surprise to many people. After a lifetime in academia, including a stint as president of Princeton University, Wilson had run for governor of New Jersey in 1910 as a political novice, and won.

Wilson's main challenger during the race was Roosevelt, who had formed his own party—the Progressive, or "Bull Moose," Party—after his split with Taft, a decision that signed the Republican Party's death warrant. Many of the progressives who had voted for Taft four years earlier transferred their support to Roosevelt. Taft was so certain of defeat that he barely campaigned. On Election Day, he carried just two states—Vermont and Utah—and received 23 percent of the popular vote. Roosevelt came in second, with 4,121,609 popular votes (27 percent) and 88 electoral votes. Wilson easily won the White House, with 6,294,384 popular votes (42 percent) and 435 electoral votes.[15]

The NCAA also voted for change in 1912. New rules were enacted, which promised to improve player safety while simultaneously boosting football's popularity. It was decided that the length of a field should be reduced from 110 yards to 100, with two ten-yard end zones tacked on to both ends of the field (end zones were necessary to accommodate the new forward pass play). Touchdowns would now be worth six points instead of five. Kickoffs would henceforth be from the kicking team's forty-yard line instead of midfield. And offenses would be given four chances instead of three to advance the ball ten yards. The most exciting change of 1912 concerned the size of the ball, which was reduced from roughly 27 inches in circumference to a more aerodynamic 22.5 to 23 inches, with tapered ends, making it easier for quarterbacks to throw tight spirals.[16]

The William M. Rice Institute for the Advancement of Literature, Science and Art (Rice University), the Mississippi Normal College (today's Southern Mississippi), and the West Tennessee Normal School (now the University of Memphis) all began playing football the same year. The Southern Mississippi team was coached by R. G. Slay, a professor of science and modern languages who agreed to serve as the school's athletic director. Slay's squad finished 2–1–0 with victories over the Mobile Military Academy and a team of Boy Scouts from Hattiesburg and a loss to the Gulf Coast Military Academy. Slay was replaced after a single season by M. J. "Blondie" Williams, a star athlete and recent graduate of Mississippi State. Phil Arbuckle, Rice's first coach, was able to hold on to his job for eleven seasons. Arbuckle beat Houston High School, Orange High School, and Sam Houston State during his first year as head coach, while falling to Southwestern University and Austin College. The University of Memphis Blue and Gray (renamed the Tigers in 1939) tied the Memphis University School and won its first game against a team from the Bolton Agricultural College. The final score was Memphis 13, Bolton 0.[17]

In Washington, DC, representatives from southern black colleges and universities incorporated the Colored Intercollegiate Athletic Association. Football's popularity on African American campuses had been steadily climbing ever since Johnson C. Smith (Biddle) defeated Livingstone. Southern blacks, like southern whites, wanted their schools to measure up to northern universities, where football was considered part of an elite education. They wanted their sons and daughters to be part of the American mainstream.[18]

Hatred stood in their way. Between 1901 and 1914, approximately one thousand black people were lynched by white vigilante mobs. In response, African American leaders such as W. E. B. Du Bois and Ida B. Wells sharpened their criticism of Booker T. Washington, whose strategy of accommodation, they argued, had failed the black community. Du Bois also founded a new progressive organization dedicated to fighting racism, the National Association for the Advancement of Colored People. The NAACP spread awareness of hate crimes through its magazine *The Crisis* and filed lawsuits on behalf of victims of racial discrimination. The founding of the NAACP marked the beginning of the modern civil rights movement, which would ultimately lead to a "second reconstruction," in the 1950s and 1960s. By 1913, NAACP branch offices were popping up in Boston, Baltimore, Detroit, St. Louis, Kansas City, and other cities.

In Alabama, meanwhile, Mike Donahue's Auburn Tigers were running roughshod over their opponents. Led by halfback Kirk "the Runt" Newell (a Tallapoosa County, Alabama, native who would go on to become a war hero), the Tigers mauled Mercer, Florida, Mississippi State, Clemson, LSU, and Georgia Tech in the run-up to a game against Vanderbilt, on November 15, that was hyped as the biggest southern matchup of the season. Auburn led 7–6 at halftime. In the fourth quarter, quarterback Ted Arnold found the end zone for the Tigers and then kicked his own extra point. The final score was Auburn 14, Vanderbilt 6.

It was the first time in two decades that the Tigers had beaten a team from Nashville. James Chappell, a sports reporter for the *Birmingham News,* got swept up in the excitement and penned a recap of the game that sounded as if it might have been ripped from the pages of a dime novel: "The lean, lank Tiger of the Plains, held back from his prey for twenty tedious years, feasts at last upon the life-blood of the Commodores. Years of waiting had but added to his appetite until Saturday it was well-nigh insatiable." A week later, the Tigers won the SIAA championship by beating Georgia 21–7 in front of twelve thousand fans at Ponce de Leon Park in Atlanta.[19]

There were "no professors, no departments, just teachers—and only about sixteen of them" at the North Texas State Normal College (University of North Texas) when J. W. Pender began putting together a program there, in 1913. Students had to clear the playing field of burrs before they could practice. North Texas played only one game during its inaugural season, a 0–13 loss to Texas Christian University. Football began catching on at other Texas schools during the same period. Tom Dwyer became head coach of the State School of Mines and Metallurgy (today's University of Texas at El Paso) a year after the North Texas debut; former Vanderbilt star Ray Morrison moved to Dallas to launch a program at Southern Methodist University. Morrison, who also coached SMU's basketball, baseball, and track teams, would return to Vanderbilt during World War I to fill in for his old coach Dan McGugin, who took a leave of absence to serve in the military.[20]

The NCAA formally recognizes three national champions from the 1913 season—Harvard, the University of Chicago, and Auburn. Richard Billingsley, a college football historian and founder of the College Football Research Center, believes Auburn deserves the national championship more than the other two schools. "In my mind, Auburn played a harder schedule and performed above expectations," Billingsley says. "There was a mentality [in 1913] that no football was played outside the East or Midwest. If you didn't play in the Big Ten or Ivy League, you weren't considered a good team. I think Auburn completely dispelled that because you know what? My computer doesn't give a darn if you're playing in the Ivy League or Big Ten." Billingsley's computational research is the main reason the NCAA now recognizes the 1913 Tigers as national champions. Previously, the Tigers were forced to settle for the lesser honorific "Champions of the South." In 1913, sports journalists and NCAA officials were skeptical that southern programs could compete against northern powerhouses like Chicago and Harvard.[21]

Donahue's 1914 team also turned out to be one of the best in Auburn's history. The Tigers finished 8–0–1, thanks to a dominant defense that prevented opponents from scoring a single point all season (Georgia held Auburn to a 0–0 tie on November 21). The biggest game of the year was against Pop Warner's Carlisle Indians, which Auburn narrowly won 7–0. Legare "Lucy" Hairston scored the game-winning touchdown in the fourth quarter on a six-yard carry.[22]

Although talented, Auburn was forced to share the 1914 SIAA championship with the undefeated Tennessee Volunteers. The Vols were coached by Zora "Z. G." Clevenger, a thirty-two-year-old Indiana native who had played halfback and coached at the University of Indiana before accepting a job at UT. Clevenger's recruiting methods included pulling out of the stands Tennessee students he thought looked big enough to play football. He assembled an offensive line that was formidable by the standards of the era. Alonzo "Goat" Carroll and Graham Vowell, the two ends, weighed in at 168 and 178 pounds, respectively. The left and right tackles—S. D. Bayer and Farmer Kelly—weighed 180 and 198. Guards Robert "Mush" Kerr and Bob Taylor tipped the scales at 185 and 183, while the center, Evan McLean, weighed 170 pounds soaking wet.[23]

The Volunteers annihilated Carson-Newman College 89–0 in their September 26 season opener. A week later, they swatted another flyweight Tennessee team, King College, 55–3. Their first real test came on October 10, in a game against Clemson. Quarterback Bill May electrified Vols fans by throwing two touchdown passes to Goat Carroll, lifting Tennessee to a 27–0 victory. Because the forward pass was still considered a novelty play in 1914, an account of the game appearing in the *Atlanta Constitution* the following day drew a distinction between May's passes and "straight football." Tennessee outscored its next three opponents—Louisville, Alabama, and Chattanooga—by a total of 143 points. The highly anticipated matchup with Vanderbilt, Tennessee's in-state rival, took place on November 7, in Nashville. Tennessee students with tickets to the game were issued orange and white felt hats adorned with the initials U.T. The Southern Railway put together a special $6.75 round-trip fare between Knoxville and Nashville. And those who could not make it to the game had the option of receiving play-by-play telegraph updates, at Knoxville's Grand Theatre, delivered by a sportscaster perched on stage, who shouted them through a megaphone.[24]

Goat Carroll was the game's Most Valuable Player. He caught two touchdown passes from May and kicked an extra point as well as a fifteen-yard field goal. The final score was Tennessee 16, Vanderbilt 14. It was the first time the Volunteers had ever beaten Vanderbilt. "For twenty years Tennessee football teams have been trying to accomplish what many thought was the impossible," crowed the *Knoxville Journal*. "For twenty years Volunteer teams have been marching up the hill, only to turn around and march right down again, but today, they pulled the hill down with them." Tennessee faculty canceled classes to give students a chance to paint the town orange. The Tennessee football team celebrated by dining with Goat Carroll's family, who lived only a short distance from the Vanderbilt campus.[25]

As Vol fans were celebrating their historic win, men in other parts of the world were butchering each other like hogs. The "war to end all wars" had begun in the summer of 1914, following the assassination of Archduke Franz Ferdinand, heir to the Austro-Hungarian throne, and his wife, Sophie. The assassin, a nineteen-year-old radical named Gavrilo Princip, belonged to a group linked to a Serbian terror organization known as the Black Hand. The murder prompted Austria-Hungary to declare war on Serbia, which in turn triggered a series of complicated, prearranged treaty agreements—Russia sided with Serbia, Germany sided with Austria-Hungary and declared war on Russia's ally France, the Ottoman Empire and Bulgaria sided with Germany, and the British sided with the French and Russians after Germany invaded neutral Belgium. Japan, Romania, and Italy also sided with Britain, France, and Russia (the Allied nations) in a war against Germany and Austria-Hungary (the Central Powers). The slaughter of the First World War was under way.

President Woodrow Wilson encouraged Americans to be "impartial in thought as well as in action." If Europeans wanted war, then that was their business; the United States would remain on the sidelines. But remaining impartial in thought as well as in deed was easier said than done. America's history, institutions, culture, and language made her a natural ally of Great Britain. Shared commercial interests also linked the two countries. Between 1914 and 1916, U.S. trade with the Allies rose from $800 million to $3 billion, while trade with the Central Powers dropped from $170 million to a paltry $1 million. (Britain's navy ruled the waves at the time.)

The Allies also had the upper hand when it came to wartime propaganda. In May 1915, a German submarine sank the British passenger liner *Lusitania,* killing 1,198 people, including 128 U.S. citizens. Americans were outraged, in part because they were never told the ship had been carrying munitions and was therefore a legitimate military target. Although the sinking of the *Lusitania* generated a public outcry for war, Wilson chose to work through diplomatic channels instead and successfully pressured Germany into agreeing not to attack citizens of neutral nations, even when they were traveling aboard Allied vessels.[26]

In Tennessee, meanwhile, the Vanderbilt Commodores were struggling to recover from a lackluster 2–8 season. Coach McGugin was counting on his 130-pound quarterback, Irby "Rabbit" Curry, to turn things around. Curry, a Marlin, Texas, native who would later be killed in an aerial dogfight over France, did not disappoint. He was a straight shooter who, according to McGugin, never uttered "a word his mother might not hear and approve." He also was a ferocious competitor. Under Curry's leadership, the Commodores scored 514 points in 510 minutes of playing time, making them a true "point-a-minute" squad. The speed and raw power of Vanderbilt's offense stunned observers. The Commodores shut out their first seven opponents by a total of 459 points, including a 35–0 rout of the Tennessee Volunteers during a game played in Nashville, on October 30, 1915.[27]

Vanderbilt's hopes for an undefeated season were crushed in November by the University of Virginia. The Cavalier offense was led by one of the greatest halfbacks to ever play the game, Eugene "Buck" Mayer, a Norfolk, Virginia, native who also ran track for UVA. Claude Moore was a starting lineman for Virginia during the 1914 and 1915 seasons and remembered Mayer as "the best football player I ever saw . . . ever. . . . When he got down inside that ten-yard line, nothing would keep him from scoring," Moore recalled during a 1988 interview. "He had it all. He used to tell me, 'Claude, I'm coming through. Have a hole for me.' And boy, I would." Mayer posted forty-eight career touchdowns, including twenty-one in a single season, and scored 312 career points. As a result, he became the first southern player to win first-team All-America honors (figure 9).[28]

The 1915 Cavaliers were a cut above every other football team in the South. They made history on October 2 as the first southern team to beat Yale. UVA shut out the Bulldogs 10–0 at home in New Haven. "We beat them by playing straight up football," Moore remembered. "We went there with that intention. We were driven." The victory turned Moore and his teammates into instant celebrities in the Commonwealth of Virginia. "For years, I was pointed out," said the lineman. "They'd say, 'Oh, he played on the team that beat Yale.'"[29]

Expectations were running high, two weeks later, when UVA returned to New England for a matchup against Harvard. This time, however, it was the Puritans who managed to get the upper hand over the prideful Cavaliers. Edward "Eddie" Mahan, Harvard's captain (whom Jim Thorpe would later describe as the greatest football player he ever saw), kicked three field goals—including one from forty-five yards out—to give the Crimson a 9–0 win in front of fifteen thousand fans.[30]

Bent but not broken, the Wahoos returned to Charlottesville to begin preparing for their next game, a matchup in Athens against the University of Georgia. It was a strange contest. UGA was ahead 7–6 late in the fourth quarter, as the sun began sinking on the Georgia horizon. Believing the game was over and that their team had won, jubilant Bulldog fans swarmed the field to perform a celebratory snake dance. The officiating crew insisted there were still eight seconds left on the clock, however, and gave the Cavs the ball on UGA's fifteen-yard line. Buck Mayer was forced out of bounds on a subsequent running play. The ball then went to R. E. Tippett, who drop-kicked a field goal from the Georgia twenty as time expired. UGA fans sat in stunned silence, their mouths agape. How had the Cavaliers managed to run two plays in eight seconds? Virginia's 8–1 record at the end of the 1915 season drew national attention and put the team on top in the newly created South Atlantic Intercollegiate Athletic Association.[31]

In February 1916, an increasingly desperate Germany declared unrestricted submarine warfare on all armed merchant ships, including those from neutral nations. A month later, the French passenger ship *Sussex* was torpedoed in the English Channel by a German submarine commander who mistook it for a mine layer. Several Americans were injured during the attack. In response, Wilson issued an ultimatum: if the sinking of nonmilitary vessels continued, then the United States would break off diplomatic relations with Germany, a precursor to war. Worried that America's entry into the conflict might tip the balance of power in favor of the Allies, Germany agreed to Wilson's terms but warned that unrestricted submarine warfare could resume if Britain's navy continued stopping neutral vessels bound for German ports. The Sussex Pledge boosted Wilson's popularity at home. He was reelected in November 1916 under the slogan "He kept us out of war."

That same autumn, students at the University of Texas acquired a Longhorn steer they nicknamed "Bevo." When students at Texas A&M learned about their archrivals' mascot, they surreptitiously branded the animal with a large "13–0," the final score of A&M's win over Texas the previous season. UT students took it all in stride and later barbecued Bevo at a cookout attended by the pranksters, who received the "13–0" hide as a souvenir.[32]

On the other side of the Mississippi River, the Tennessee Volunteers and the Georgia Tech Golden Tornado (later renamed the Yellow Jackets) were gunning for the top spot in the SIAA. John Heisman's squad crushed lowly Cumberland College in what would turn out to be the most lopsided victory in the history of college football. Earlier that spring, Heisman's baseball team had been thrashed 22–0 by a Cumberland team made up of ringers from Nashville. Eager for revenge, Heisman continued running up the score on his opponents even after it became clear that Cumberland's ragtag band of law students and fraternity boys was no match for Tech. At halftime, the score was 126–0. "You're doing all right," Heisman told his players with an impish grin, "But you just can't tell what those Cumberland players have up their sleeves."

The final score was Georgia Tech 222, Cumberland 0. Heisman had not only exacted revenge for his baseball team's loss but also sent a message to sportswriters who liked to compare the strength of teams based on the total number of points they scored each week, an evaluation method the coach considered "useless." "Still the writers persisted and some at each season's end would still presume to hang an argument on what they claimed it showed," Heisman explained. "So, finding that folks are determined to take the crazy thing into consideration, we at Tech determined this year . . . to show folks that it was no very difficult thing to run up a score in one easy game, from which it might perhaps be seen that it could be done in other easy games as well."[33]

Washington and Lee spoiled Georgia Tech's undefeated season by holding them to a 7–7 tie on October 28. Tech's wins against Mercer, Cumberland, Davidson, North Carolina, Tulane, Alabama, Georgia, and Auburn, however, were enough to make them cochampions of the SIAA, along with Tennessee. The 1916 Volunteers had earned their top spot by beating Tusculum, Maryville, Clemson, South Carolina, Florida, Chattanooga,

Vanderbilt, and Sewanee. On November 30, the University of Kentucky tied Tennessee 0–0, leaving the team with a final record of 8–0–1, the same as Georgia Tech. In a remarkable display of good sportsmanship, UT fans conceded the SIAA championship. "Kentucky did well," opined the editors of the *Volunteer*, Tennessee's student yearbook. "She fought as wild cats are capable of fighting, and while neither side scored, Kentucky won and the Vols lost—not the game, but a right to claim the Southern laurels with Georgia Tech. Tech had a great team. She went through her season without being tied or defeated by a S. I. A. A. team. So we hand it to you Tech-nically." The Tennessee Athletic Council agreed. "I think it will show the proper sportsmanship on our part to concede to Georgia Tech immediately," advised one council member. "We do not want to take a position that will bring us into ridicule and make us the objects of uncomplimentary remarks." In an odd twist, despite Tennessee's public concession, both schools recorded the other as SIAA cochampion. Tennessee has since renounced its claim, leaving Tech to bask in the limelight alone, as Volunteer fans had originally intended.[34]

As Georgia Tech and Tennessee were climbing to the top of the SIAA, U.S. troops were hunting Pancho Villa, a notorious Mexican revolutionary-cum-outlaw accused of killing American civilians and launching raids on U.S. soil. (Villa was upset over Washington's withdrawal of support for his army.) General John J. Pershing commanded the American expeditionary force that chased Villa into the bowels of Mexico, but the wily guerrilla fighter managed to elude capture. By February 1917, with war in Europe looming on the horizon, Wilson abandoned the chase and called his troops back home.

On January 31, 1917, Germany's ambassador to the United States announced that unrestricted submarine warfare would resume the following day. It was a last-ditch effort to starve the Allies into submission by cutting off their supply lines. Wilson immediately broke off diplomatic relations with Germany, but he clung to a straw of hope that war could somehow be avoided. By March, that hope was gone. Not only were German U-boats actively sinking American vessels but also British intelligence had intercepted a telegram sent by Germany's foreign minister, Arthur Zimmermann, to his attaché in Mexico, proposing a military alliance between the two countries. In return for assisting the Central Powers in their fight against the United States, Mexico would be given guns, money, and the lost territories of Texas, New Mexico, and Arizona. The American people were outraged when they learned of the Zimmermann proposal, and on April 6, Congress declared war on Germany.

Life in the United States changed overnight. Massive government bureaucracies were put in charge of the nation's food production, transportation networks, and manufacturing facilities. A boom in industry prompted tens of thousands of black and white southerners to abandon their homes for high-paying jobs in Cleveland, Philadelphia, Chicago, New York, Detroit, and other northern cities. The Selective Service Act of 1917 empowered the federal government to draft millions of men for military service. The Espionage Act (1917) and the Sedition Act (1918) gave it the authority to arrest anyone considered a spy or who criticized the war effort, the Constitution, or even the flag.

The war also affected the 1917 college football season. Some universities, such as North Carolina, Virginia, Georgia, and Tennessee, suspended their varsity football programs. Others, including Auburn, Clemson, and Georgia Tech, plowed ahead in spite of player losses caused by the draft. On a majority of campuses, faculty and students were united in their commitment to the war effort. "A college cannot but be proud of its sons who have responded so readily to their country's call," wrote the editors of UGA's yearbook. "And though we missed football this year, yet we gave it up gladly to enlarge our military activities and as a further step toward economizing expenses." At the University of Texas, home to a combat pilot training center, students bragged about the Longhorns' high rate of military service. "Varsity's athletes, like the University students in general, volunteered for the service in far greater numbers than all the other college athletes in the State combined . . . Let us not forget that Texas' weakness on the football field was due to her strength on the battle field."[35]

John Heisman was not about to let a war in Europe spoil his season. He had already invested considerable time and effort in assembling a roster of dominant players. On the line, there were the two big ends, R. S. "Cy" Bell and Ray Ulrich; center G. M. "Pup" Phillips; guards J. H. "Ham" Dowling and Dan Welchel; and the two tackles, Walker "Big Six" Carpenter and Bill Fincher (who had a glass eye that he liked to remove to spook opponents). Heisman's backfield was even more talented than his offensive line. Halfback Joseph Napoleon "Indian Joe" Guyon would later be described by a sportswriter for the *Atlanta Constitution* as "the greatest player the South ever saw." Born on a Chippewa Indian reservation in Minnesota, in 1892, Guyon possessed a self-deprecating sense of humor that put people at ease: "When I was a kid, I heard a man say the only good Indian was a dead Indian, and from then on I was a pretty fast Indian." Before enrolling at Tech, Guyon had played football with Jim Thorpe at the Carlisle Indian School. The other big guns in Heisman's backfield were halfback George Everett "Strup" Strupper, who would be posthumously inducted into the College Football Hall of Fame, freshman fullback J. W. "Judy" Harlan, and quarterback Albert Hill.[36]

Georgia Tech opened the 1917 season with an unusual doubleheader. Heisman had arranged to play Furman and Wake Forest on the same day in order to make room on his schedule for the University of Pennsylvania, Heisman's alma mater. He knew that a big win over an Ivy League team like Penn would force the media to pay attention to Tech. The Golden Tornado first shut out Furman 25–0 before pummeling Wake Forest 33–0 on a soggy, rain-soaked field. The Quakers were in Atlanta the following week.

Newspapers across the region picked up an Associated Press story that referred to the Tech–Penn matchup as "one of the most important intersectional games ever played in the South." Penn had previously won six national titles, and its 1917 roster included one of the best players in the country, All-America halfback Howard Berry. On game day, thousands of fans descended on Grant Field—the South's first major venue—to watch the Golden Tornado defend Georgia's honor.

The game turned into a rout almost immediately. Within minutes, Everett Strupper, who had been injured in a car accident earlier in the day, broke loose and dashed seventy yards for a touchdown. More touchdowns rapidly followed, as Guyon, Strupper, and Hill (figure 10) "smashed through the Pennsylvania line at will." Heisman was able to baffle the Quaker defense by running conventional plays rather than the infamous "Heisman shift" that Penn players had been expecting. The final score was Georgia Tech 41, Penn 0. "Vanderbilt held Yale to a tie score several seasons ago and boosted southern football stock considerably in the eyes of the eastern and western critics," reported the *Atlanta Constitution,* evidently ignoring or forgetting UVA's 1915 win over Yale. "The Tech victory should further emphasize the fact that southern elevens have made wonderful strides in the great college sport and should receive the credit that is their due."[37]

Tech's blowout victory over Penn did help to change public perceptions of southern football, just as Heisman had intended. Conventional wisdom had long held that southern teams were no match for Ivy League ones such as Harvard and Yale, a canard that had carried down from the Gilded Age. But the strength and raw talent of Heisman's eleven defied stereotypes. "Penn's Invasion of Southern Gridiron Results in Rout," reported the *Philadelphia Inquirer,* one day after the Golden Tornado's victory. In a larger sense, southerners were being accepted back into the national fold after a half century of second-class citizenship. For the first time since Andrew Johnson's failed presidency, a southerner occupied the White House. Southerners were disproportionately represented in the armed forces fighting in Europe. And the South's economy was healthier and more diverse than at any time in its history.[38]

At the same time, southerners were promoting a sanitized version of their region's history and doubling down on segregation, with help from Hollywood, academia, churches, veterans' groups, and other civic organizations. D. W. Griffith's *The Birth of a Nation*—released in 1915—thrilled audiences with its heroic portrayal of the Ku Klux Klan and white resistance to race mixing. John Burgess and William Dunning, two influential historians at Columbia University, began the scholarly study of Reconstruction, an era they regarded as a historical calamity. Southern whites had been victimized by Radical Republicans, the professors said, who had turned over control of the South to ignorant freedpeople and unscrupulous carpetbaggers. Eventually, the white South had risen up and restored "home rule," a euphemism for white supremacy. As Burgess and Dunning's ideas spread, private organizations such as the United Daughters of the Confederacy were helping to perpetuate the myth of the "Lost Cause" by erecting statues of Confederate leaders in public spaces. Their efforts contributed to what one historian has aptly described as the South's post-war "dream of a cohesive Southern people with a separate cultural identity." The Confederacy might have died in 1865, but its traditions and values would live on with support from true southerners.[39]

On October 13, the Davidson College Wildcats made history as the only squad able to score more than seven points on Heisman's 1917 team (the final score was 32–10). Davidson's scrappy performance impressed Atlanta sports journalists, who dubbed the team "the light-weight champions of the U.S." Davidson would finish the season with six victories, including wins over Clemson and Auburn, based largely on the strength of its passing game.[40]

Georgia Tech got back on track the following week by demolishing the Washington and Lee Generals 63–0. Washington and Lee students took solace in the fact that their outmatched team had put up a valiant fight. A postgame comment attributed to Heisman gave them ample reason to feel proud: "Although Tech won by a big score, the hard fighting of the Virginians caused as many injuries as a close encounter."[41]

Tech's next game was against Vanderbilt. The 1917 Commodores were not as physical as previous Vandy squads. The school yearbook described them as a "bunch of youngsters and light-weights" compared to Vanderbilt's best players, all of whom were in Europe carrying "the Gold and Black banner into Berlin." Georgia Tech humiliated the Commodores 83–0.[42]

Tech also embarrassed Tulane, on November 10, inside of its fancy new concrete stadium in New Orleans. The Olive and Blue were not at full strength. Two of their marquee players were unable to play and a third had to leave the game early due to an injury. The final score was Tech 48, Tulane 0.[43]

Tech's final two games of the season were against Carlisle and Auburn. If Joe Guyon had any qualms about playing against his fellow Indians, he did not show it on the gridiron. Guyon performed "up to his usual high standard" before being pulled in the second quarter due to a rib injury. He and his teammates obliterated Carlisle 98–0.[44] The game against Auburn was also one-sided. Coach Donahue's defense proved unable to stop the run, allowing Tech to glide to an easy 68–7 victory.

Georgia Tech finished the 1917 season with a perfect 9–0 record and in the process scored 491 points against teams that could only muster seventeen points in response. Newspapers across the country rushed to name the Golden Tornado the undisputed national champions. "Football, once an eastern specialty, now is a national sport, and in recognition of that fact we are glad to acclaim Georgia Tech the greatest eleven in the country," the *New York Sun* reported. "Georgia Tech stands revealed as the most sensational football eleven of the year," added the *New York Evening Mail.* "There is no question about it. The University of Pittsburgh, Ohio State and

Minnesota have great football teams this year. But the record of the Golden Tornado of Atlanta is a bit beyond that of all of them."

Nine years before Alabama defeated the University of Washington on New Year's Day in what some football historians have dubbed "the game that changed the South," the Georgia Tech Golden Tornado demonstrated the power and legitimacy of southern college football. In the same way that Knute Rockne's teams of the 1920s helped Catholics achieve mainstream acceptance, John Heisman's Georgians forced the nation to take seriously southerners and southern sports. "Such a feat [as a national championship] has never been approached before in the annals of Southern football," crowed the editors of the *Blue Print,* Georgia Tech's yearbook. "And such recognition brings credit to Tech, to Georgia and to the SOUTH."[45]

On December 8, a banquet was held at the Druid Hills Golf Club in Atlanta to honor the South's gridiron heroes. Each player received a gold football bearing the inscription "National Champions, 1917." Walker "Big Six" Carpenter was presented with a captain's ring. G. M. "Pup" Phillips received the Hal Nowell trophy for "the most efficient play during the season." Additional "letters, medals, shingles, and trophies of all descriptions" were handed out to team members. They laughed and joked and feasted, realizing it would probably be their final time together. Five players—William Mathes, Dan Welchel, William Thweatt, Theodore Shaver, and William Higgins—had already enlisted in the Marine Corps. Four other players—Robert Bell, Jim Fellers, Pup Phillips, and Charles Johnson—would enlist a week later.[46]

War began in earnest for the United States in the spring of 1918, when the American Expeditionary Force halted a German army threatening Paris. A few months later, more than a million U.S. troops participated in an Allied counterattack that moved east through France's Argonne forest, toward the German border. College campuses, meanwhile, were being transformed by the federal government into military camps. Students and nonstudents alike enlisted in the Student Army Training Corps, which was open to all physically fit males eighteen years and older. College life quickly became a drag for those accustomed to the peacetime status quo.

At Washington and Lee, 60 percent of the people who showed up for the first day of classes were "new men, but not Freshmen, since in 'Uncle Sam's' army of students there was to be no class distinction." Housing was in short supply. New arrivals were squeezed into dorm rooms or assigned a cot in the school's gymnasium. At Ole Miss, men were also quartered in dorms, four to a room, with the doors removed and with no furniture except for army cots and a single chest of drawers. Privates were under strict orders not to leave campus without a pass from their commanding officers.

The regimentation of military life depressed and frustrated many students. Undergraduates at the University of Texas attributed the widespread unhappiness on campus to a "lack of co-operation between the military and academic authorities." At Vanderbilt, discontentment among medical and dental students in the Student Army Training Corps was so severe that it "rose almost to the point of rebellion."[47]

And just when it seemed as though things could not get any worse, a mysterious and deadly virus—the so-called Spanish flu—appeared out of thin air. Unlike other flu strains, which ravage the old and the infirm, this one targeted people in the prime of their lives—men and women between the ages of sixteen and forty. As many as 100 million people worldwide would lose their lives to the virus. According to John Barry, author of *The Great Influenza,* the 1918 flu pandemic "killed more people in a year than the Black Death of the Middle Ages killed in a century" and more "in twenty-four weeks than AIDS has killed in twenty-four years."[48]

College campuses were not immune to the pandemic. At the University of Virginia, students wore masks to class in order to avoid breathing in deadly pathogens. They were shocked by news that Buck Mayer—who had joined the military after earning a law degree from UVA—had died from flu complications while stationed at Camp Johnston in Jacksonville, Florida. Student Army Training Corps soldiers at the University of North Carolina were quarantined, causing restlessness, anxiety, and low morale. Vanderbilt did not have adequate facilities to deal with the approximately one hundred students who contracted influenza. Although a new hospital in Wesley Hall was under construction, it was not completed in time to help Vandy's flu victims. Auburn experienced similar problems. A shortage of medical staff meant that untrained Auburn students had to nurse the sick.[49]

Miraculously, college football survived at most schools. The Golden Tornado came close to winning a second consecutive national championship but were defeated by Pop Warner's Pittsburgh Panthers. Tech's decision to field a team during the war annoyed some students at the University of Georgia, where varsity football had been suspended. They organized a parade in Athens after the war, which included a tank-shaped float with a sign reading "Georgia in Argonne." Trailing behind the float was a small car (some claim it was a donkey) with a snarky message for the GT faithful: "1917 Tech in Atlanta." The "clean, old-fashioned hate" generated by this prank kept the two teams apart until 1925.[50]

On the eleventh hour of the eleventh day of the eleventh month of 1918, the war in Europe came to an end. The German government, facing an imminent invasion of its territory and antiwar protests at home, asked for a cease-fire. This was to be followed by negotiations for a permanent peace settlement based on Woodrow Wilson's Fourteen Points, a series of initiatives designed to prevent future wars. The death toll from World War I was sobering: 112,000 Americans, 900,000 British, 1.4 million French, 1.7 million Russians, and 2 million Germans.

The horror of seeing so many of their comrades killed in action prompted soldiers to seek out diversions. Homesick American troops had formed football teams and fashioned makeshift uniforms from Red Cross sweaters, leather aviator caps, and army uniforms. They had even improvised an American Expeditionary Force championship series that drew the attention of General John Pershing and other high-ranking military officials. Between 1917 and 1919, an estimated 1.3 million U.S. servicemen played football. For some, it was their first exposure to the sport, and they returned home eager to learn more. A surge of men enrolled in college after the war, influenced by mass-circulation magazines that depicted higher education as a pathway to prosperity. Colleges were no longer the exclusive haunts of upper-class snobs studying Greek and Latin; they also became training centers for aspiring midlevel business managers. Enrollment numbers increased, and so did the number of men playing football.[51]

The game that had started out as a crude pastime during the Gilded Age was, by 1918, an essential part of the college experience. In the South, a successful football program was evidence of a successful modern university, like Yale or Harvard, where men were taught how to be physically tough as well as to think critically. Football also threaded seamlessly into the South's culture of violence and respect for martial displays. A man who could prove himself on a football field was a man indeed. And, in the years following the Civil War, southern men were anxious to demonstrate their worth to a skeptical nation. Success on the gridiron gave them something to be proud of, in a region that was often labeled as parochial and impoverished.

The 1899 Sewanee Tigers had been the first truly great team to emerge below the Mason–Dixon Line, but their exploits were largely ignored by a northern media fixated on Ivy League programs. By the time the Georgia Tech Golden Tornado began flexing its muscles, southerners were being welcomed back into the American family as full-fledged citizens, after a fifty-year stint as second-stringers. College football would eventually help other marginalized groups become part of the American mainstream, but, for southerners, the game carried with it a special tide of cathartic emotions—restored pride, joy, excitement, and nostalgia for a mythical past when the fair flower of youth had blossomed beneath a warm southern sun.

EPILOGUE

When I was a kid, my grandfather used to talk about the time his football team held the University of Virginia Cavaliers to a scoreless tie. I knew he had attended Hampden-Sydney College, an all-male liberal arts school located in Prince Edward County, Virginia, but not much else; he never told me which position he played on the football team there or when the David versus Goliath slugfest with UVA had taken place. He only said that in those days (whenever they were), every man had to play both offense and defense for the duration of the game, and no one was allowed to drink water because their coaches thought it would make them cramp up. I could see from the twinkle in his eye, however, that in spite of these hardships, my grandfather considered the game one of the greatest moments of his life.

Years after my grandfather passed away, I tracked down a copy of the 1927 Hampden-Sydney yearbook. In the athletics section, I found a photo of him, standing alongside three of his teammates, dressed in a college sweater and football pants. He looked like a pip-squeak compared to the other guys. I learned from the yearbook that he had played center, but there was no information on which defensive position he had played. I also discovered that the legendary game against the Cavaliers had occurred on a hot and humid day in September 1926, in Charlottesville, and that the "Tigers gave a wonderful exhibition of defensive power, turning back the proud Cavaliers time after time." The editors of the *Kaleidoscope* also took note of my grandfather's heroic on-field performance, which made me feel proud: "Outstanding in this game was Ex-Captain [Alfred "Dickie"] Dudley who played the most brilliant game of his colorful career." I imagined my grandfather smashing into Virginia players twice his size and grinding them into the dirt. He and his generation were tough as leather, smart as whips, and as sober as Presbyterians. The Tigers finished the 1926 season 5-2-3, an impressive record which included a tie game against the Florida Gators in Tampa before a crowd of ten thousand.[1]

My grandfather was almost certainly aware of another game that had occurred earlier that year, one that sent the popularity of southern college football soaring to new heights: the 1926 Rose Bowl. When the Rose Bowl committee began searching for an opponent that could put up a decent fight against the undefeated University of Washington Huskies, southern teams were not on their radar screen. Even Georgia Tech's 1917 national championship was apparently not enough to convince them that southern programs were on par with their northeastern, Midwestern, or western counterparts. The committee reached out to Dartmouth, Colgate, Michigan, and Princeton in short order, but none could participate in the game. Reluctantly, they took a look at the Alabama Crimson Tide. Under the leadership of Coach Wallace Wade, a former assistant to the legendary Vanderbilt coach Dan McGugin, the Tide had amassed a perfect record during the 1925 season, which included eight shutout victories. "I've never heard of Alabama as a football team," one Rose Bowl official supposedly sniffed. Nevertheless, Bama was invited to play in Pasadena on New Year's Day.[2]

With most of the national media predicting an easy win for the Huskies, southerners closed ranks. For many, it had become a question of defending the South's honor. Students at other southern universities who normally criticized the Crimson Tide began cheering for them instead. Southern newspapers framed the contest as an opportunity to put smart-mouthed Yankees in their place. Southern politicians fired off telegrams of support to Wade and his team of underdogs.

On game day, it initially looked as if Bama's detractors might be right. The Huskies, led by their All-America halfback George "Wildcat" Wilson, came down on the Alabamians like a ton of bricks. At halftime they were up by a score of 12–0. Wallace Wade shared his disgust with his players in the locker room: "And they told me southern boys would fight."[3]

Perhaps as a result of their coach's censure, or perhaps because they were simply tired of being a national laughingstock, the Tide returned to the playing field born again hard. They put up twenty unanswered points in the third quarter, largely on the strength of Johnny "Mack" Brown's balletic performance, which included a thrilling fifty-yard touchdown catch. (Brown would later parlay his gridiron success into a lucrative acting career in Hollywood.) The Huskies fought back in the fourth quarter, but Bama's

defense was able to hold them to a single touchdown, giving the Tide a razor-thin 20–19 victory.

It was the shot heard round the world of college football. Southerners
hugged each other, jumped for joy, and heaped praise on Coach Wade's team.
The *Atlanta Georgian* described it as "the greatest victory for the South
since the first battle of Bull Run." Tony Brandino, a Woodlawn, Alabama, native who was ten years old at the time, remembered listening to the game on
the radio with his older brother and a group of neighborhood kids. "Everyone
started screaming and hollering," he told Warren St. John, author of the best
seller *Rammer Jammer Yellow Hammer*. "That's when the Bama bug bit me."[4]

The outsize impact of Alabama's Rose Bowl victory was made possible
by cultural and technological changes that were sweeping the United States
in the 1920s. A new class of marketing professionals had discovered that
sporting events attracted large audiences, both in person and through the
power of radio. Almost no one owned a radio in 1920, but by the end of the
decade, nearly a third of American homes had one. The growth of radio,
along with an expansion of advertising and magazine publishing, fueled the
development of a national cult of celebrity. The celebrities of the Roaring
Twenties were movie stars like Charlie Chaplin and Mary Pickford, as well
as sports icons like George Herman "Babe" Ruth, who hit sixty home runs in
1927, and Knute Rockne, who led his Notre Dame Fighting Irish to national
championships in 1924 and 1929. The 1899 Sewanee Tigers and the 1917
Georgia Tech Golden Tornado may have been just as talented as the 1925
Alabama Crimson Tide, but they appeared on the historical timeline too
early to take advantage of the overblown media hype and celebrity worship
that emerged during the postwar period.

Southerners in the 1920s were especially hungry for homegrown celebrities they could idolize and brag about to the rest of the country. The myth
of the ignorant southern clay eater had once again reared its ugly head,
nurtured in part by a resurgence of the Ku Klux Klan and embarrassing ep-
isodes such as the Scopes Monkey Trial. By beating a top-tier program from
outside the South in the biggest game of the year, Alabama drove home the
message that Dixie deserved respect. In the years following Bama's upset
victory, southern teams were invited to play in fourteen out of twenty-one
Rose Bowl games, prompting historians to dub the 1926 Rose Bowl "the
game that changed the South."[5]

A stock market crash followed by an economic depression and a war on two fronts were not enough to dampen public enthusiasm for southern college football. In Atlanta, African Americans struggling to cope with the devastating effects of the Great Depression still found enough money to attend weekly games at Clark, Morehouse, and Morris Brown colleges. Whites attended games in Austin, Tuscaloosa, Baton Rouge, Oxford, and other college towns, despite the fact that many had no affiliation with the schools there. One reason was the South's lack of professional teams. The National Football League, founded in Ohio, in 1920, had little incentive to expand into a poor and mostly rural region with only a handful of medium-size cities. (After World War II, the NFL reversed course and granted franchises to the growing Sunbelt cities of Dallas, Houston, New Orleans, Atlanta, and Miami.)

More important, showing support for the local college team had, by the early twentieth century, become a southern tradition. Each team had its own quirky rituals and unique backstory that made area fans, whether college-educated or not, feel a stronger connection to their communities. And the "us versus them" mentality that had defined southern culture for centuries found new expression in the rivalries between in-state and out-of-state programs.[6]

The civil rights movement of the 1950s and 1960s presented a new challenge for southern college football. With "Dixiecrat" governors like Mississippi's Ross Barnett and George Wallace in Alabama preventing African Americans from attending public universities, southern coaches continued their long-standing practice of recruiting white players exclusively. In an attempt to keep the peace in Oxford, Mississippi, after a federal court ordered Ole Miss to admit an African American air force veteran named James Meredith, President John F. Kennedy spoke directly to the Rebel faithful during a 1962 nationally televised address: "You have a great tradition to uphold, a tradition of honor and courage won on the field of battle and on the gridiron as well as the University campus . . . The honor of your University and State are in the balance. I am certain that the great majority of the students will uphold that honor." Unfortunately, many did not, and on September 30, 1962, an angry mob threw bricks and bottles and fired guns at Meredith's dormitory. Two people died and hundreds more were injured. The Ole Miss football team managed to go undefeated in spite of the violence, and it laid claim to the 1962 national championship after beating Arkansas in the Sugar Bowl (though the University of Southern California Trojans were named champions, instead, by the Associated Press and Coaches Polls).[7]

The Southeastern Conference remained segregated until 1967, when an African American named Nathaniel Northington broke the color barrier by suiting up for the Kentucky Wildcats. Two years later, Auburn, Mississippi State, and Florida began recruiting black players. In 1970, the Crimson Tide were crushed by a team from the University of Southern California that included a black fullback named Sam "Bam" Cunningham, who rushed for 135 yards and scored two touchdowns on twelve carries. Cunningham's role in convincing the Alabama faithful to accept African American players has been exaggerated over the years. Legend has it that Coach Paul "Bear" Bryant, or possibly one of his assistants, said, "Sam Cunningham did more to integrate Alabama in sixty minutes that night than Martin Luther King had accomplished in twenty years."[8]

Although it is doubtful that either Bryant or one of his coaches uttered this remark (they were already recruiting black athletes prior to the game against USC), it underlines an important truth: integrated football teams have contributed to a general improvement in race relations in the South since the 1960s. I witnessed this firsthand in the 1990s, when I was an undergraduate student at Alabama. During Crimson Tide football games, I saw black fans and white fans who likely would never be caught dead together at a political rally or a church picnic high-five each other and embrace like long-lost family members. This is when I realized that sports provide our culture with something more than just entertainment; they also convey an awareness of our shared history and humanity and our limited time together in this life.

Nowhere is this more conspicuous than on any given Saturday in the South during football season. In his book *Sports in America,* James Michener observed that, "Most of life is a falling-away, a gradual surrender of the dream. The reason sports provide such dramatic material is that the climax comes so early in a man's life, the decline so swiftly."[9] I think Michener was on to something. Part of the reason college football remains popular is that it reminds us of our own fleeting youth and vitality, even as it allows us to live vicariously—if only for sixty minutes—through eleven men who are in the prime of their lives. And in the South, the rituals, the pageantry, the *rat-a-tat-tat* of tight snare drums, the *clack* of colliding shoulder pads, the smell of freshly turned turf—all of these things add a special poignancy and magic to the mix. We remember generations past, including departed friends and relatives who shared our love of college football and would enjoy seeing a modern game if they could somehow be here with us again.

In the final years of his life, as his mind deteriorated, my grandfather became confused at much of the world around him. "Do you understand any of this?" he asked my mother one day, while watching television from a hospital bed.

"No," she replied, in an attempt to ease his anxiety.

On another occasion, Mom managed to get him out of bed and over to an athletic field where a local high school football team was practicing. The synapses in my grandfather's brain crackled to life the moment he saw the action on the field. "Watch," he said. "The fullback is going to hit the gap between the right guard and tackle." The play unfolded just as he had predicted.

NOTES

INTRODUCTION

1. Emily Caron, "Highest-Paid NCAA Football Coaches: Nick Saban, Urban Meyer . . . and Lovie Smith?" *Sports Illustrated,* October 3, 2018, https://www.si.com/college-football/2018/10/03/nick-saban-urban-meyer-jim-harbaugh-jimbo-fisher-highest-paid-football-coaches-2018; Jason Alsher, "5 College Conferences That Bring in over $250 Million," *Sports Cheat Sheet,* February 15, 2017, https://www.cheatsheet.com/sports/the-5-most-valuable-conferences-in-college-sports.html/?a=viewall; "College Football's Top 10 . . . According to Walmart," AL.com, October 4, 2017, http://www.al.com/news/index.ssf/2017/10/college_footballs_top_10accord.html?utm_source=bustedcoverage.com&utm_medium=referral&utm_campaign=bustedcoverage; Dennis Dodd, "Why an Eight-Team College Football Playoff Could Come to Pass Sooner Than We Expect," CBS Sports, January 3, 2018, https://www.cbssports.com/college-football/news/why-an-eight-team-college-football-playoff-could-come-to-pass-sooner-than-we-expect.

2. Taylor Branch, "The Shame of College Sports," *The Atlantic,* October 2011, https://www.theatlantic.com/magazine/archive/2011/10/the-shame-of-college-sports/308643.

3. Leo Andrew Doyle, "Causes Won, Not Lost: Football and Southern Culture, 1892–1983" (PhD diss., Emory University, 1998), 129.

4. Susan Reyburn, *Football Nation: Four Hundred Years of America's Game* (New York: Harry N. Abrams, 2013), 17–20.

5. "History of Football—The Global Growth," FIFA.com, https://www.fifa.com/about-fifa/who-we-are/the-game/global-growth.html; Samuel Luckhurst, "The FA Turns 149, Here Are Football's Rules from 1863," *Huffington Post UK,* October 26, 2012, http://www.huffingtonpost.co.uk/2012/10/26/the-fa-149_n_2021717.html.

6. David M. Nelson, *The Anatomy of a Game: Football, the Rules, and the Men Who Made the Game* (Newark: University of Delaware Press, 1994), 25; Reyburn, *Football Nation,* 25; Bob Holmes, "Remembering the First High School Football Games," *Boston Globe,* November 21, 2012, https://www.bostonglobe.com/sports/2012/11/21/oneida-football-club-first-team-play-high-school-football/OBtaKz79JZcmtxkm5WQ40M/story.html; Ronald A. Smith, *Sports and Freedom: The Rise of Big-Time College Athletics* (New York: Oxford University Press, 1988), 20.

7. Melvin I. Smith, *Evolvements of Early American Foot Ball: Through the 1890/91 Season* (Bloomington, IN: AuthorHouse, 2008), 204; Jerry Ratcliffe, e-mail to author, February 19, 2018.

8. R. G. Collingwood, *The Idea of History* (London: Clarendon, 1946), 215.

9. Doyle, "Causes Won, Not Lost," 20.

10. Mark Edmundson, "Football Is America's War Game," *Los Angeles Times,* August 23, 2014.

CHAPTER ONE

1. *Southern Collegian* 5, no. 2 (October 26, 1872), Washington and Lee University, Lexington, VA.

2. Luckhurst, "The FA Turns 149; Sam Lawson, "How the Other Half Play," *Nouse,* May 25, 2010, http://www.nouse.co.uk/2010/05/25/how-the-other-half-play.

3. See Matthew James Harrison and Matt Fidler, "Ashbourne's Royal Shrovetide Football Match," *Guardian,* February 11, 2016, https://www.theguardian.com/uk-news/ng-interactive/2016/feb/11/ashbournes-royal-shrovetide-football-match-photo-essay.

4. Thomas Hughes, *Tom Brown's School Days* (London: Longmans, Green, 1913), 17.

5. Reyburn, *Football Nation,* 31.

6. "The First Game: Nov. 6, 1869," Rutgers University Athletics, https://scarletknights.com/sports/2017/6/11/sports-m-footbl-archive-first-game-html.aspx.

7. Philip Alexander Bruce, *History of the University of Virginia,* vol. 4 (New York: Macmillan, 1921), 140.

8. John M. Heisman with Mark Schlabach, *Heisman: The Man Behind the Trophy* (New York: Howard, 2012), 16.

9. Robert H. Wiebe, *The Search for Order, 1877–1920* (New York: Hill and Wang, 1967), 4.

10. "Robert E. Lee, President, Washington College, 1865–1870," Washington and Lee University, http://www.wlu.edu/presidents-office/about-the-presidents-office/history-and-governance/past-presidents/robert-e-lee; "Battle of New Market," Virginia Military Institute, https://www.vmi.edu/archives/civil-war-and-new-market/battle-of-new-market.

11. *Southern Collegian* 6, no. 3 (November 8, 1873).

12. Margaret Humphreys, *Yellow Fever and the South* (Baltimore: Johns Hopkins University Press, 1992), 5; David Herbert Donald, Jean Harvey Baker, and Michael F. Holt, *The Civil War and Reconstruction* (New York: W. W. Norton, 2001), 623.

13. Donald, Baker, and Holt, *Civil War,* 591–592.

14. During the elections of 1865, southerners chose four former Confederate generals, six former members of Jefferson Davis's cabinet, and fifty-eight men who had served as senators and congressmen in the Confederate government to represent them in Washington. Other controversies soon followed. Mississippi refused to repudiate its Confederate wartime debt. South Carolina, while acknowledging Washington's legal authority over slavery, nevertheless kept its state slave codes on the books. Georgia approved the Thirteenth Amendment contingent upon former masters receiving compensation for lost slaves. These and other ham-fisted gestures convinced Congress that more radical reforms were necessary before the southern states could be safely readmitted to the Union.

15. Donald, Baker, and Holt, *Civil War,* 524–525; Joseph A. Waddell, *Annals of Augusta County, Virginia, from 1726 to 1871* (Bridgewater, VA: C. J. Carrier, 1902), 515.

16. Robert W. Johannsen, ed., *Reconstruction, 1865–1877* (New York: The Free Press, 1970), 90–100; Eric Foner, *A Short History of Reconstruction, 1863–1877* (New York: Harper & Row, 1990), 137.

17. *Richmond Enquirer,* November 1, 1867; Donna L. Dickerson, *The Reconstruction Era: Primary Documents on Events From 1865 to 1877* (Westport, CT: Greenwood, 2003), 153.

18. Eric Foner, *Reconstruction: American's Unfinished Revolution, 1863–1877* (New York: Harper & Row, 1988), 138–139.

19. Thomas J. Schlereth, *Victorian America: Transformation in Everyday Life* (New York: HarperPerennial, 1991), 249; *Southern Collegian* 5, no. 2 (October 26, 1872), and 10, no. 11 (March 2, 1878); Matthew Frye Jacobson, "Becoming Caucasian: Vicissitudes of Whiteness in American Politics and Culture," *Identities: Global Studies in Culture and Power* 8 (March 2001): 83–104.

20. John Hope Franklin, "Slavery and the Martial South," *Journal of Negro History* 37 (January 1952): 36–53.

21. Rex Bowman and Carlos Santos, *Rot, Riot, and Rebellion: Mr. Jefferson's Struggle to Save the University That Changed America* (Charlottesville: University of Virginia Press, 2013); Jerry Ratcliffe, *The University of Virginia Football Vault: The History of the Cavaliers* (Atlanta: Whitman, 2008), 7.

22. See Joanne B. Freeman, *Affairs of Honor: National Politics in the New Republic* (New Haven, CT: Yale University Press, 2001). Leo Andrew Doyle, a football historian who teaches at Winthrop University in South Carolina, believes that the Old South's code of honor impeded the spread of football due to its obsession with class distinctions. A man of honor at the top of southern society, says Doyle, would never stoop to engaging in a physical contest with a social inferior, even on a football field. See Doyle, "Causes Won, Not Lost." While I fully appreciate the nuances of Doyle's argument, which I think focuses on an older, genuine code of honor rather than bourgeois *notions* of honor, my own research has led me closer to Patrick B. Miller's view that "a richly textured tradition of southern honor that had long animated the region . . . facilitated the rise of intercollegiate athletics." See Miller, ed., "The Manly, the Moral, and the Proficient: College Sport in the New South," in *The Sporting World of the Modern South* (Urbana: University of Illinois Press, 2002), 17–51.

23. Jim Webb, *Born Fighting: How the Scots-Irish Shaped America* (New York: Broadway, 2004), 10–19.

24. *Southern Collegian* 4, no. 13 (April 4, 1874).

25. Edward L. Ayers, *The Promise of the New South: Life After Reconstruction* (New York: Oxford University Press, 1992), 160–167; Edward R. Crowther, "Holy Honor: Sacred and Secular in the Old South," *Journal of Southern History* 58, no. 4 (November 1992): 619–636.

26. Ollinger Crenshaw, *General Lee's College: The Rise and Growth of Washington and Lee University* (New York: Random House, 1969), 196.

27. Roger Pielke Jr., "Why Are College Football Games on Saturdays?," The Least Thing

blog, February 19, 2012, http://leastthing.blogspot.com/2012/02/why-are-college-football-games-on.html.

28. *Southern Collegian* 7, no. 1 (October 10, 1874).

29. Mark Wahlgren Summers, *The Era of Good Stealings* (New York: Oxford University Press, 1993). For a recent take on William Tweed's notorious career, see Kenneth D. Ackerman, *Boss Tweed: The Rise and Fall of the Corrupt Pol Who Conceived the Soul of Modern New York* (New York: Carroll and Graf, 2005).

30. Donald, Baker, and Holt, *Civil War,* 606–607.

31. Foner, *Reconstruction,* 165–167.

32. Donald, Baker, and Holt, *Civil War,* 623; David W. Blight, *Race and Reunion: The Civil War in American Memory* (Cambridge, MA: The Belknap Press of Harvard University Press, 2001), 130.

33. Thomas B. Alexander, "Persistent Whiggery in the Confederate South, 1860–1877," *Journal of Southern History* 27, no. 3 (August 1961): 305–329; Blight, *Race and Reunion,* 130; William Gillette, *Retreat from Reconstruction, 1869–1879* (Baton Rouge: Louisiana State University Press, 1979), 150–165.

34. Donald, Baker, and Holt, *Civil War,* 624.

35. Blight, *Race and Reunion,* 131.

36. James S. Pike, "Society Turned Bottom-Side Up (1874)," in *The Civil War and Reconstruction: A Documentary Collection,* ed. William E. Gienapp (New York: W. W. Norton, 2001), 395–397.

37. *The Nation,* "This Is Socialism (1874)," in Gienapp, *Civil War and Reconstruction,* 397–400.

38. *Southern Collegian* 7, no. 1 (October 10, 1874). In 1872, the Washington and Lee student body consisted of eighty-one men from Virginia, thirty-one from Texas, twenty-four from Kentucky, twenty-three from Tennessee, twenty-two from Louisiana, seventeen from Mississippi, sixteen from Alabama, fifteen from South Carolina, fifteen from Arkansas, ten from West Virginia, ten from Missouri, eleven from Georgia, nine from North Carolina, five from Maryland, five from New York, two from Illinois, one from Florida, one from Ohio, one from Iowa, and one from Idaho Territory. See *Catalogue of Washington and Lee University, Virginia, for the Year Ending June, 1872* (Baltimore: John Murphy, 1872), Washington and Lee University Special Collections and Archives Department.

39. *Southern Collegian* 4, no. 11 (March 9, 1872). For more information on boating and baseball at Washington and Lee, see *Southern Collegian* 4, no. 12 (March 23, 1872), no. 14 (April 20, 1872), no. 15 (May 4, 1872), and no. 18 (June 15, 1872); and 9, no. 14 (April 21, 1877).

40. Ayers, *Promise of the New South,* 26–28.

41. "Henry W. Grady Heralds the New South, 1886," in *Major Problems in the Gilded Age and Progressive Era,* ed. Leon Fink (Lexington, MA: D. C. Heath, 1993), 104–107; Ayers, *Promise of the New South,* 26–28.

42. Reyburn, *Football Nation,* 33.

43. *Southern Collegian* 10, no. 8 (February 10, 1877).

CHAPTER TWO

1. Nelson, *Anatomy of a Game*, 33; William J. Baker, *Sports in the Western World* (Totowa, NJ: Rowman and Littlefield, 1982), 128–129.

2. Holmes, "Remembering the First High School Football Games"; Allison Danzig, *The History of American Football: Its Great Teams, Players, and Coaches* (Englewood Cliffs, NJ: Prentice-Hall, 1956), 9; Reyburn, *Football Nation*, 31–32.

3. Nell Irvin Painter, *Standing at Armageddon: The United States, 1877–1919* (New York: W. W. Norton, 1987), 15–18.

4. Painter, *Standing at Armageddon*, 3.

5. Baker, *Sports in the Western World*, 129. See also "The History of Rugby at Yale," Yale University Rugby Football Club, http://www.yalerfc.com/history; and John Sayle Watterson, *College Football: History, Spectacle, Controversy* (Baltimore: Johns Hopkins University Press, 2000), 19.

6. Andrew McIlwaine Bell, *Mosquito Soldiers: Malaria, Yellow Fever, and the Course of the American Civil War* (Baton Rouge: Louisiana State University Press, 2010), 15, 117; Humphreys, *Yellow Fever and the South*, 5, 60–61; "The Great Fever," *American Experience*, PBS, September 29, 2006, http://www.shoppbs.pbs.org/wgbh/amex/fever/peopleevents/e_1878.html.

7. Walter Camp, *American Football* (1891; repr. New York: Arno Press, 1974), 8–9.

8. Nelson, *Anatomy of a Game*, 44; Ivan N. Kaye, *Good Clean Violence: A History of College Football* (Philadelphia: J. B. Lippincott, 1973), 22.

9. Baker, *Sports in the Western World*, 129–130.

10. See Tony Barnhart, *Southern Fried Football (Revised): The History, Passion, and Glory of the Great Southern Game* (Chicago: Triumph, 2008); Alexander M. Weyand, *The Saga of American Football* (New York: Macmillan, 1955), 113; and "Kentucky Football History," in *2017 Kentucky Football Media Guide*, 136, https://ukathletics.com/documents/2017/8/24/1718_FB_MediaGuide_WEB.pdf.

11. "The Electric Light," *Wabash Weekly Plain Dealer*, April 9, 1880; "Wabash, Indiana: First Electrically Lighted City in the World," RoadsideAmerica.com, http://www.roadside-america.com/tip/10495; James Rodger Fleming, "Science and Technology in the Second Half of the Nineteenth Century," in *The Gilded Age: Essays on the Origins of Modern America*, ed. Charles W. Calhoun (Wilmington, DE: SR Books, 1996), 31.

12. Lawrence Goodwyn, *The Populist Moment: A Short History of the Agrarian Revolt in America* (Oxford: Oxford University Press, 1978), 20–22.

13. Painter, *Standing at Armageddon*, 60–61. The National Grange of the Order of Patrons of Husbandry existed before any of the Alliance groups. The Grange was politically active in the 1860s and 1870s and championed a number of progressive ideas that were later adopted by the Farmers' Alliance.

14. C. Vann Woodward, *Origins of the New South, 1877–1913* (Baton Rouge: Louisiana State University Press, 1951), 440.

15. "Dr. Edward Renouf, Chemist, Dies at 88," *New York Times,* November 14, 1934; Lenore O'Boyle, "Learning for Its Own Sake: The German University as Nineteenth-Century Model," *Comparative Studies in Society and History* 25 (January 1983): 3–25; Carl Diehl, "Innocents Abroad: American Students in German Universities, 1810–1870," *History of Education Quarterly* 16 (Autumn 1976): 321–341.

16. Frederick H. Getman, *The Life of Ira Remsen* (Easton, PA: Journal of Chemical Education, 1940), 41–46; Germaine M. Reed, *Crusading for Chemistry: The Professional Career of Charles Holmes Herty* (Athens: University of Georgia Press, 1995), 4; *Debutante* (1889), 63, and *Hullabaloo* (1895), 19, Special Collections Library, Johns Hopkins University, Baltimore, Maryland.

17. "A Century of Football," Johns Hopkins University Archives, Department of Physical Education and Athletics, Records of Department of Physical Education and Athletics 1889–1993, record group number 13.020, box 3, folder: Programs, Tickets, and Announcements: Football, 1924–81, Johns Hopkins University, Baltimore, Maryland; *Hullabaloo* (1895); John Wendell Bailey, *Football at the University of Richmond, 1878–1948* (Richmond, VA: John Wendell Bailey, 1949), 20–21. Today, Randolph-Macon plays the College of William & Mary each year for the Capital Cup (previously known as the I-64 Bowl). The annual contest is sometimes erroneously referred to as the South's "oldest rivalry." In truth, Randolph-Macon began playing William & Mary in 1898, seventeen years after the Yellow Jackets played Richmond College and long after other southern schools were playing annual games against one another.

18. See Barbara Welter, "The Cult of True Womanhood: 1820–1860," *American Quarterly* 18 (Summer 1966): 151–174; Nancy F. Cott, *The Bonds of Womanhood: "Woman's Sphere" in New England, 1780–1835* (New Haven, CT: Yale University Press, 1977); and Christine Stansell, *City of Women: Sex and Class in New York, 1789–1860* (Urbana: University of Illinois Press, 1987).

19. Drew R. McCoy, *The Elusive Republic: Political Economy in Jeffersonian America* (New York: W. W. Norton, 1982), 21–24; Kristin L. Hoganson, *Fighting for American Manhood: How Gender Politics Provoked the Spanish–American and Philippine–American Wars* (New Haven, CT: Yale University Press, 1998), 12.

20. Ayers, *Promise of the New South*, 314.

21. *Hullabaloo* (1895).

22. Camp's original plan was to make a touchdown worth two points, a goal-after-touchdown worth four, a safety worth one, and a field goal worth five.

23. Fleming, "Science and Technology," 31; "Railroads Create the First Time Zones," History, http://www.history.com/this-day-in-history/railroads-create-the-first-time-zones; PFRA Research, *"Camp and His Followers: American Football 1876–1889,"* Professional Football Researchers Association, http://www.profootballresearchers.org/articles/Camp_And_Followers.pdf; Roger R. Tamte, *Walter Camp and the Creation of American Football* (Urbana: University of Illinois Press, 2018), 312.

24. Leon Fink, ed., *Major Problems in the Gilded Age and the Progressive Era* (Lexington, MA: D. C. Heath, 1993), 448, 466, 480; Reyburn, *Football Nation*, 36.

25. John White, "Andrew Carnegie and Herbert Spencer: A Special Relationship," *Journal of American Studies* 13, no. 1 (April 1979): 57–71; Richard Hofstadter, "William Graham Sumner, Social Darwinist," *New England Quarterly* 14, no. 3 (September 1941): 457–477. Hofstadter parlayed his research on social Darwinism into a published manuscript, *Social Darwinism in American Thought: 1860–1915* (Philadelphia: University of Pennsylvania Press, 1944), which portrays Spencer's theories as the ideological basis of various turn-of-the-century conservative causes like imperialism and laissez-faire capitalism. Robert C. Bannister rejects Hofstadter's thesis and thinks twentieth-century liberals were the ones who made the most effective use of Spencer's theories by falsely connecting them to Sumner and other like-minded conservatives, whose views were in reality far more complex. See Bannister, *Social Darwinism: Science and Myth in Anglo-American Social Thought* (Philadelphia: Temple University Press, 1979). My own view is that Sumner's teachings—eagerly devoured by his brother-in-law Walter Camp—contain enough Spencerian logic in them (whether by choice or by coincidence) to justify describing nineteenth-century football as a "Darwinian" game.

26. William E. Winn, "*Tom Brown's Schooldays* and the Development of 'Muscular Christianity,'" *Church History* 29 (March 1960): 64–73; Clifford Putney, "Muscular Christianity," *Encyclopedia of Informal Education,* http://www.infed.org/christianeducation/muscular_christianity.htm.

27. Walter Licht, *Industrializing America: The Nineteenth Century* (Baltimore: Johns Hopkins University Press, 1995), 102.

28. James E. Herget, *American Football: How the Game Evolved* (CreateSpace, 2013), 51–54; Kaye, *Good Clean Violence,* 25.

29. "Henry W. Grady Heralds the New South," 104–107.

30. "Henry W. Grady Heralds the New South," 105; "Frederick Douglass Describes a Legacy of Race Hatred, 1883," in Fink, *Major Problems,* 110–112.

31. *Hopkins Medley* (1890), 114, and *Hopkinsian* (1891), 23, Special Collections Library, Johns Hopkins University, Baltimore, Maryland; Melvin Patrick Ely, *The Adventures of Amos 'N' Andy: A Social History of an American Phenomenon* (New York: The Free Press, 1991), 28.

32. Reed, *Crusading for Chemistry,* 4–5; *Debutante* (1889), 66–67.

33. Mike Jernigan, "The Life and Times of George Petrie," lecture delivered at Auburn University Library, August 23, 2007, https://vimeo.com/14591733; "Woodrow Wilson Coached Princeton's First Football Team, Says Historian," *Harvard Crimson,* November 8, 1924, http://www.thecrimson.com/article/1924/11/8/woodrow-wilson-coached-princetons-first-football; August Heckscher, *Woodrow Wilson: A Biography* (Newtown, CT: American Political Biography Press, 1991), 95.

34. Brenda Harper Mattson, "George Petrie, the Early Years, 1866–1892" (master's thesis, Auburn University, December 9, 1983), 107–108.

35. Heckscher, *Woodrow Wilson,* 107.

36. James C. Whorton, *Crusaders for Fitness: The History of American Health Reformers* (Princeton, NJ: Princeton University Press, 1982), 270–273.

37. John Higham, "The Reorientation of American Culture in the 1890s," in *The Origins of*

Modern Consciousness, ed. John Weiss (Detroit: Wayne State University Press, 1965), 25–48; Whorton, *Crusaders for Fitness,* 282–283.

38. Whorton, *Crusaders for Fitness,* 283–284.

CHAPTER THREE

1. *Raleigh News and Observer,* October 19 and October 20, 1888.

2. *Raleigh News and Observer,* October 19, 1888; Jim L. Sumner, "The North Carolina Inter-Collegiate Foot-Ball Association: The Beginnings of College Football in North Carolina," *North Carolina Historical Review* 65, no. 3 (July 1988): 263–286; *Raleigh News and Observer,* November 18, 1888, reprinted in Bill Cromartie, *Battle of the Blues: Duke vs. Carolina* (Atlanta: Gridiron, 1992), 3.

3. Reyburn, *Football Nation,* 40.

4. Ayers, *Promise of the New South,* 310–312; David A. Martin, "Henry W. Grady, the Atlanta Constitution, and the Inaugural Season of the Southern League" (master's thesis, University of Tennessee, 2006), http://trace.tennessee.edu/cgi/viewcontent.cgi?article=3082&context=utk_gradthes; *Randolph Macon Monthly* 15, no. 3 (December 1893): 143, and no. 6 (April 1894): 291, Randolph-Macon College Library, Ashland, Virginia; "UNC Baseball History," http://grfx.cstv.com/photos/schools/unc/sports/m-basebl/auto_pdf/Pages42-51.pdf; *Southern Collegian* 4, no. 15 (May 4, 1872), and no. 18 (June 15, 1872).

5. Schlereth, *Victorian America,* 223.

6. Sumner, "North Carolina Inter-Collegiate Foot-Ball Association," 266–267; John Franklin Crowell, *Personal Recollections of Trinity College North Carolina, 1887–1894* (Durham, NC: Duke University Press, 1939), 225–227.

7. Cromartie, *Battle of the Blues,* 7–9; Sumner, "North Carolina Inter-Collegiate Foot-Ball Association," 269; Crowell, *Personal Recollections,* 46.

8. William E. King, "A Great History," 4i–5i, Duke University Archives, Athletics Reference Collection, Subject Files, Club Sports—Victory Bell, Box 2, Duke University, Durham, North Carolina; Sumner, "North Carolina Inter-Collegiate Foot-Ball Association," 270–271; Crowell, *Personal Recollections,* 45–46.

9. Ratcliffe, *University of Virginia Football Vault,* 7–9; Ben Cohen and Andrew Beaton, "A Final Four Mystery Unraveled: Why UVA and Auburn Have the Same Team Colors," *Wall Street Journal,* April 5, 2019.

10. *Hullabaloo* (1899), Special Collections Library, Johns Hopkins University, Baltimore, Maryland, 170–171; Sumner, "North Carolina Inter-Collegiate Foot-Ball Association," 268.

11. G. Rouquie, "Furman vs. Wofford," *Wofford College Journal* 2, no. 1 (January 1890): 20–21. https://archive.org/details/woffordcollegej02189woff/page/n25?q=G.+Rouquie%2C+%E2%80%9CFurman+vs.+Wofford%2C%E2%80%9D+1890.

12. Reed, *Crusading for Chemistry,* 5–7.

13. Other sources claim the final score was Princeton 116, Virginia 0. See Andrew Doyle,

"Turning the Tide: College Football and Southern Progressivism," in *The Sporting World of the Modern South,* ed. Patrick B. Miller (Urbana: University of Illinois Press, 2002), 102.

14. Ratcliffe, *University of Virginia Football Vault,* 10.

15. "The McKinley Tariff of 1890: October 1, 1890," History, Art & Archives, United States House of Representatives, http://history.house.gov/Historical-Highlights/1851-1900/The-McKinley-Tariff-of-1890/.

16. Paul K. Conkin, *Gone with the Ivy: A Biography of Vanderbilt University* (Knoxville: University of Tennessee Press, 1985), 137; "SEC Charter Member! Vanderbilt Commodores," *Sarasota Herald-Tribune,* September 25, 1957, 13, https://news.google.com/newspapers?nid=1755&dat=19570925&id=Aq8qAAAAIBAJ&sjid=_GQEAAAAIBAJ&pg=7489,4125676&hl=en; Bill Traughber, "William Dudley: A Father of Vanderbilt Athletics," VUCommodores.com, August 25, 2005, http://www.vucommodores.com/sports/m-footbl/spec-rel/082505aaa.html; Traughber, *Vanderbilt Football: Tales of Commodore Gridiron History* (Charleston, SC: History Press, 2011), 18–19.

17. Conkin, *Gone with the Ivy,* 138–140; Jim L. Sumner, "John Franklin Crowell, Methodism, and the Football Controversy at Trinity College, 1887–1894," *Journal of Sport History* 17, no. 1 (Spring 1990): 5–20.

18. Branch, "Shame of College Sports," 80–110; Warren Goldstein, "Walter Camp's Off-Side: A Tarnished Football Legacy," *Hartford Courant,* March 14, 2014, https://www.courant.com/opinion/op-ed/hc-op-commentary-goldstein-yales-walter-camp-bent--20140314-story.html.

19. Albert J. Figone, *Cheating the Spread: Gamblers, Point Shavers, and Game Fixers in College Football and Basketball* (Urbana: University of Illinois Press, 2012), 61–62.

20. "A Great Day for Harvard," *New York Times,* November 23, 1890, 1; Julie Des Jardins, *Walter Camp: Football and the Modern Man* (New York: Oxford University Press, 2015), 92–94.

21. Gregory H. Nobles, *American Frontiers: Cultural Encounters and Continental Conquest* (New York: Hill and Wang, 1997), 240–242.

22. Camp, *American Football.*

23. John F. Stegeman, *The Ghosts of Herty Field: Early Days on a Southern Gridiron* (Athens: University of Georgia Press, 1966), 2–5.

24. Russ Bebb, *The Big Orange: A Story of Tennessee Football* (Huntsville, AL: Strode Publishers, 1973), 24–26; *Cap and Gown* (1892), University of the South Library, 71, https://dspace.sewanee.edu/handle/11005/17. Bebb quotes a *Knoxville Journal* article that reported a score of 24–0 in favor of Sewanee. However, the *Cap and Gown* claims the score was 26–0, which is the number I choose to reprint, based on a guess that the winner would have had less incentive to distort the score.

25. Stegeman, *Ghosts of Herty Field,* 5–7.

26. Mattson, "George Petrie," 133–138.

27. Mattson, "George Petrie," 146–151.

28. Stegeman, *Ghosts of Herty Field,* 9–10; Mattson, "George Petrie," 146, 152; Doyle, "Causes Won, Not Lost," 150.

29. Stegeman, *Ghosts of Herty Field,* 12–13; Doyle, "Causes Won, Not Lost," 13–14.

30. "Traditions," Auburn University, http://www.auburn.edu/main/welcome/traditions/index.php.

CHAPTER FOUR

1. "Historical State Timelines: Athletics," North Carolina State University Libraries, https://historicalstate.lib.ncsu.edu/timelines/athletics; "The Foot Ball Game," *Raleigh News and Observer,* March 13, 1892.

2. This Leonidas Polk should not be confused with a well-known Confederate general of the same name who was killed in 1864, during the Atlanta campaign.

3. "The Omaha Platform: Launching the Populist Party," History Matters, http://history-matters.gmu.edu/d/5361.

4. Bruce Palmer, "The Southern Populist Creed," in Fink, *Major Problems,* 197–207.

5. "1892," American Presidency Project, UC Santa Barbara, https://www.presidency.ucsb.edu/statistics/elections/1892.

6. "The First 120 Seasons of Football at Virginia Tech," Virginia Tech Athletics, https://hokiesports.com/sports/2018/4/30/the-first-120-seasons-of-football-at-virginia-tech.aspx; Chris Colston, *Virginia Tech Football Vault* (Atlanta: Whitman, 2009), 7–8.

7. Jack Wilkinson, *Georgia Tech Football Vault: The History of the Yellow Jackets* (Atlanta: Whitman, 2008), 7–11; Miller, "The Manly, the Moral, and the Proficient," 37; Des Jardins, *Walter Camp,* 82.

8. Clyde Bolton, *The Crimson Tide: A Story of Alabama Football* (Huntsville, AL: Strode, 1972), 21–23; Jay Barker, *The University of Alabama Football Vault: The Story of the Crimson Tide, 1892–2007* (Atlanta: Whitman, 2007), 9. According to Bolton, Ross kicked a sixty-five-yard field goal. Barker claims it was sixty-three yards. I decided to err on the side of caution and present the more conservative of the two estimates. I hope that, by doing so, I have not in any way diminished the significance of Mr. Ross's amazing feat.

9. Some football historians claim that W. G. Little attended Phillips Exeter Academy, and place it in Andover, Massachusetts. However, Phillips Exeter, as the name indicates, is located in Exeter, New Hampshire. It is far likelier that Little attended Phillips Academy in Andover, which has traditionally served as a feeder school for Yale.

10. Bolton, *Crimson Tide,* 17–19.

11. Nelson, *Anatomy of a Game,* 67.

12. Billy Watkins, *University of Mississippi Football Vault: The History of the Rebels* (Atlanta: Whitman, 2009), 7.

13. Reyburn, *Football Nation,* 46–47.

14. Reyburn, *Football Nation,* 46; J. Steven Picou and Duane Gill, "Football," in *Encyclopedia of Southern Culture,* vol. 3, *Literature—Recreation,* ed. Charles Reagan Wilson and William Ferris (New York: Anchor, 1991), 653; Danzig, *History of American Football,* 24–25.

15. Elizabeth Cassidy West, *University of South Carolina Football Vault: The History of the Gamecocks* (Atlanta: Whitman, 2008), 7–8.

16. The Southern Intercollegiate Athletic Association officers for 1893 were J. Breckinridge Robertson from the University of Virginia (president), W. S. Symington from Johns Hopkins University (vice president), and William H. Graham from the University of the South (treasurer and secretary). See *Constitution of the Southern Intercollegiate Athletic Association 1893* (Richmond, VA: J. L. Hill, 1893), University of Virginia Special Collections, Charlottesville, Virginia.

17. "An Athletic Association," *Raleigh News and Observer,* December 29, 1892.

18. Zipp Newman, *The Impact of Southern Football* (Montgomery, AL: Morros-Bell, 1969), 3–4.

19. Michael Hurd, *Black College Football, 1892–1992: One Hundred Years of History, Education, and Pride* (Virginia Beach, VA: Donning, 1993), 28–29; Jared Thompson, "J. C. Smith, Livingstone Mark 125 Years of HBCU Football," *NCAA Champion Magazine,* November 3, 2017, https://www.ncaa.com/news/football/article/2017-11-02/johnson-c-smith-livingstone-showdown-marks-125th-anniversary-first.

20. Patrick B. Miller, ed., "To 'Bring the Race Along Rapidly': Sport, Student Culture, and Educational Mission at Historically Black Colleges During the Interwar Years," in *The Sporting World of the Modern South* (Urbana: University of Illinois Press, 2002), 129–152.

21. Leslie H. Fishel Jr., "The African-American Experience," in *The Gilded Age: Essays on the Origins of Modern America,* ed. Charles W. Calhoun (Wilmington, DE: SR Books, 1996), 137–161; Ayers, *Promise of the New South,* 156–159.

22. Fishel, "African-American Experience, 146.

23. Painter, *Standing at Armageddon,* 116–117; Ronald W. Walker, "Crisis in Zion: Heber J. Grant and the Panic of 1893," *Arizona and the West* 21, no. 3 (Autumn 1979): 257–278.

24. Erik Larson, *The Devil in the White City* (New York: Vintage, 2003), 247.

25. Peter Finney, *The Fighting Tigers: Seventy-Five Years of LSU Football* (Baton Rouge: Louisiana State University Press, 1968), 3–5; Charles E. Coates, "How LSU Became the Tigers of Purple and Gold, Not White and Blue," *LSU Alumni News,* October 1937, http://www.lsusports.net/ViewArticle.dbml?ATCLID=208876760.

26. "Tulane Football History," Tulane Athletics, https://tulanegreenwave.com/sports/2016/6/13/sports-m-footbl-archive-history-html.aspx; Finney, *Fighting Tigers,* 5.

27. Coates, "How LSU Became the Tigers"; Herb Vincent, *LSU Football Vault: The History of the Fighting Tigers* (Atlanta: Whitman, 2008), 7–9; Miller, "The Manly, the Moral, and the Proficient," 32; Terry L. Jones, *Lee's Tigers Revisited: The Louisiana Infantry in the Army of Northern Virginia* (Baton Rouge: LSU Press, 2017), 391.

28. "Tulane Tackles the University Team," *New Orleans Daily Picayune,* November 26, 1893, 9.

29. Watkins, *University of Mississippi Football Vault,* 7–11; "History," Harvard University, https://www.harvard.edu/about-harvard/harvard-glance/history.

30. Watkins, *University of Mississippi Football Vault,* 7–11

31. Steve Richardson, *The University of Texas Football Vault: The Story of the Texas Long-horns* (Atlanta: Whitman, 2007), 7.

32. *Randolph Macon Monthly* 13, no. 1 (November 1891), 13–24, Randolph-Macon College Library, Ashland, Virginia; Chris Preston, "Oldest Small-School Football Rivalry in the South Now 'Goes Across All Sports,' " ESPN, July 8, 2008, http://espn.go.com/college-sports/news/story?id=3476639.

33. Reed, *Crusading for Chemistry,* ix, 12–47; Luana Henderson, ed., "Biographical/His-torical Note," in Charles E. and Ollie Maurin Coates Family Papers, mss. 3579, Louisiana and Lower Mississippi Valley Collections, Special Collections, Hill Memorial Library, Louisiana State University Libraries, Baton Rouge, 4. http://www.lib.lsu.edu/sites/default/files/sc/fin-daid/3579.pdf; Doyle, "Causes Won, Not Lost," 85, 134.

34. Doyle, "Causes Won, Not Lost," 77; Miller, "The Manly, the Moral, and the Proficient," 41.

35. C. G. Montgomery, ed., *Journal of the Western North Carolina Annual Conference of the Methodist Episcopal Church, South, Third Session, held at Winston, N.C., Nov. 30th to Dec. 5th, 1892* (Greenboro, NC: C. F. Thomas, 1892), 44.

36. Crowell, *Personal Recollections,* 223–227.

37. Washington and Lee Trustees Papers, June 19–December 1894, Leyburn Special Collections, folder 272, Washington and Lee University, Lexington, Virginia; George Washington Paschal, *History of Wake Forest College,* vol. 2, *1865–1905* (Wake Forest, NC: Wake Forest University, 1943), 316–317; Watkins, *University of Mississippi Football Vault,* 13; Barker, *University of Alabama Football Vault,* 10.

38. University of North Carolina Archives Trustee Affairs (UNC) subgroup 1: Minutes, volumes 5–8, June 1883–February 1891, University of North Carolina, Chapel Hill; Ken Rappoport, *Tar Heel: North Carolina Football* (Huntsville, AL: Strode, 1976), 99.

39. Kent Stephens, *The College Football Hall of Fame: A Chronicle of the Game's History and America's Premiere Sports Museum* (Virginia Beach, VA: Donning, 2000), 56; Paschal, *History of Wake Forest College,* 2:316.

40. Michael Oriard, *Bowled Over: Big-Time College Football from the Sixties to the BCS Era* (Chapel Hill: University of North Carolina Press, 2009), 191, 237; Reyburn, *Football Nation,* 41.

41. Herget, *American Football,* 69–70.

CHAPTER FIVE

1. Richard L. McCormick, *Public Life in Industrial America, 1877–1917* (Washington, DC: American Historical Association, 1997), 12.

2. Herget, *American Football,* 70–71; Nelson, *Anatomy of a Game,* 71; *Hullabaloo* (1895), 141–145; *Debutante* (1889), 63–64.

3. Nelson, *Anatomy of a Game,* 74; Jacqueline Sahlberg, "Memorable Games in Harvard–Yale History," *Yale Daily News,* November 18, 2011, http://yaledailynews.com/blog/2011/11/18/memorable-games-in-harvard-yale-history.

4. Herget, *American Football,* 71–72; Watterson, *College Football,* 33–36.

5. Sumner, "North Carolina Inter-Collegiate Foot-Ball Association," 263–286; Board of Trustees minutes, June 20 and August 1, 1894 meetings, Washington and Lee Trustees Papers, June 19–December 1894, Leyburn Special Collections, folder 272, Washington and Lee University, Lexington, Virginia; Conkin, *Gone with the Ivy*, 139.

6. "SIAA 1894 Constitution," William Lofland Dudley Papers, MSS 123, box 3, Special Collections and University Archive Library, Vanderbilt University, Nashville, Tennessee; Ray Glier, *How the SEC Became Goliath: The Making of College Football's Most Dominant Conference* (New York: Howard, 2012), 23.

7. See Andrew Doyle, "Foolish and Useless Sport: The Southern Evangelical Crusade Against Intercollegiate Football," *Journal of Sport History* 24, no. 3 (1997): 317–340.

8. Rusty Burson, *Texas A&M University Football Vault* (Atlanta: Whitman, 2009), 7–9; Rick Schaeffer, *University of Arkansas Football Vault* (Atlanta: Whitman, 2008), 7–8; Doyle, "Causes Won, Not Lost," 55–56.

9. Mike Nemeth, *Mississippi State University Football Vault: The History of the Bulldogs* (Atlanta: Whitman, 2009), 7–9.

10. Heisman and Schlabach, *Heisman*, 81–82.

11. Heisman and Schlabach, *Heisman*, 83–84.

12. Sam Blackman, "The Clemson–Auburn Connection," Clemson Tigers, August 30, 2016, https://clemsontigers.com/the-clemson-auburn-connection; West, *University of South Carolina Football Vault*, 9–12.

13. Chris Chase, "The 10 Best Pranks in College Sports History," *USA Today*, March 7, 2013, https://www.usatoday.com/story/gameon/2013/03/07/best-college-rivalry-pranks/1968429.

14. "1896 Presidential General Election Results," Dave Leip's Atlas of US Presidential Elections, http://uselectionatlas.org/RESULTS.

15. James Oliver Horton and Michele Gates Moresi, "Roberts, Plessy, and Brown: The Long, Hard Struggle Against Segregation," *OAH Magazine of History* 15 (Winter 2001): 14–16.

16. Christopher C. Meyers, " 'Unrelenting War on Football': The Death of Richard Von Gammon and the Attempt to Ban Football in Georgia," *Georgia Historical Quarterly* 93, no. 4 (Winter 2009): 388–407.

17. Meyers, "Unrelenting War," 388–407.

18. Ratcliffe, *University of Virginia Football Vault*; Meyers, "Unrelenting War," 388–407.

19. Meyers, "Unrelenting War," 388–407.

20. Ratcliffe, *University of Virginia Football Vault*, 14; Tracy Coley Ingram, "Classic Places: A Symbol of Georgia's Athletic Traditions," *Athens Banner-Herald*, October 4, 2000.

21. Humphreys, *Yellow Fever and the South*, 137, 145; Finney, *Fighting Tigers*, 14; Watkins, *University of Mississippi Football Vault*, 15; Trustees' papers, Department of Physical Education, Annual Report for the Session 1897–1898, June 11, 1898, folder 292, January–June 12, 1898, Washington and Lee University Special Collections and Archives Department, Washington and Lee University, Lexington, Virginia; Paschal, *History of Wake Forest College*, 2:320; Barker, *University of Alabama Football Vault*, 10; Nemeth, *Mississippi State University Football Vault*, 9; Bebb, *Big Orange*, 35.

22. Reyburn, *Football Nation*, 55–56.

23. Wilkinson, *Georgia Tech Football Vault*, 9; Theodore Roosevelt, *The Rough Riders* (Dallas: Taylor, 1997), 14, 41–42.

24. Kevin Hillstrom and Laurie Collier Hillstrom, *Defining Moments: The Spanish–American War* (Detroit: Omnigraphics, 2012), 57.

25. Harry D. Temple, *V.P.I. in the Spanish American War,* Virginia Tech Special Collections, https://spec.lib.vt.edu/archives/spanamer/spamwar1.htm; "Spanish–American War Memorial," August 27, 2013, *My Aggie Nation,* http://www.myaggienation.com/campus_evolution/landmark_statues/spanish-american-war-memorial/article_24c3ce-ba-0f40-11e3-a871-001a4bcf887a.html; Bebb, *Big Orange,* 46; Barnhart, *Southern Fried Football,* 3; Colin F. Baxter, "Spanish–American War," *Tennessee Encyclopedia of History and Culture,* December 25, 2009, http://tennesseeencyclopedia.net/entry.php?rec=1239; Virginia Military Institute, Historical Rosters Database, accessed December 31, 2016, http://archivesweb.vmi.edu/rosters/index.php?ID=&basic=spanish+american+war ; Citadel Alumni Association History Committee, "Brief History of the Citadel," Spring 2007, http://www.citadel.edu/citadel-history/brief-history.html.

26. "William Jennings Bryan Opposes US Occupation of the Philippines, 1900" and "Theodore Roosevelt Links War in the Philippines to the Ideal of the Strenuous Life, 1899," in Fink, *Major Problems,* 489–494.

27. See Judy Hilkey, *Character Is Capital: Success Manuals and Manhood in Gilded Age America* (Chapel Hill: University of North Carolina Press, 1997).

CHAPTER SIX

1. Terri Jo Ryan, "Brazos Past: Toby's Practical Business College Flourished in Waco for Nearly 50 Years," *Waco Tribune-Herald,* July 7, 2012, http://www.wacotrib.com/news/waco_history/brazos-past-toby-s-practical-business-college-flourished-in-waco/article_b49f28a1-7b6a-5872-9ee1-3912f4f58184.html; Dan Jenkins, *Texas Christian University Football Vault: The History of the Horned Frogs* (Atlanta: Whitman, 2008), 13; Baylor University Official Athletic Site—Football, section 9, "History," http://www.baylorbears.com/sports/2018/5/16/sports-m-footbl-spec-rel-06-fb-media-guide-html.aspx; Miller, "The Manly, the Moral, and the Proficient," 24.

2. T. S. Parrott, "Rah! Rah! Ree! Victory!," *Sewanee Purple* 14, no. 7 (October 24, 1899); Doyle, "Turning the Tide," 111.

3. Intercollegiate Football Association rule changes enacted in 1898 made a touchdown worth five points and a point after touchdown worth one.

4. Parrott, "Rah! Rah! Ree! Victory!"; Doyle, "Turning the Tide," 111; Fuzzy Woodruff, *A History of Southern Football, 1890–1928,* vol. 1 (Atlanta: Georgia Southern, 1928), 88–91.

5. Parrott, "Rah! Rah! Ree! Victory!".

6. Parrott, "Rah! Rah! Ree! Victory!"; John McCardell, *The Idea of a Southern Nation: Southern Nationalists and Southern Nationalism, 1830–1860* (New York: W. W. Norton, 1979),

220–225; Wendell Givens, *Ninety-Nine Iron: The Season Sewanee Won 5 Games in 6 Days* (Birmingham: Seacoast, 1992), 27–34.

7. "Tennessee Downed, Sewanee Wins Easily," *Sewanee Purple* 14, no. 8 (October 31, 1899); *Volunteer* (1900), 117, University of Tennessee Library Digital Collections, https://digital.lib.utk.edu/collections/yrbcollection?_ga=2.155827899.1435763528.1530714328-506273920.1530714328; *Cap and Gown* (1900), University of the South Library, 153, https://dspace.sewanee.edu/handle/11005/21.

8. *The Sou'wester* (1900), Rhodes College Digital Archives, http://hdl.handle.net/10267/11247.

9. Arthur Chitty to Gioia Grieme, November 5, 1954, and J. G. de Roulhac Hamilton to Arthur Chitty, October 11, 1954, Sewanee Football 1899: Vertical file, Jessie Ball duPont Library, Archives and Manuscript Collections, Sewanee: University of the South.

10. Givens, *Ninety-Nine Iron,* 26, 44; Parrott, "Rah! Rah! Ree! Victory!."

11. John Durant, "The Miracle of Sewanee," *Sports Illustrated* (October 16, 1961): S5–S8.

12. Durant, "Miracle of Sewanee"; W. B. Wilson to Arthur Ben Chitty, October 18, 1954, Sewanee Football 1899: Vertical file, Jessie Ball duPont Library, Archives and Manuscript Collections, Sewanee: University of the South.

13. Givens, *Ninety-Nine Iron,* 51–55.

14. Rachel Zoll, "1899 Sewanee 'Iron Men' Remembered," *Spartanburg Herald-Journal,* November 28, 1999; Givens, *Ninety-Nine Iron,* 60–62; "U. of S.! Rah! Rah!," *Sewanee Purple* 14, no. 10 (November 14, 1899).

15. Ralph S. Black to Arthur Ditty, August 25, 1949, Sewanee Football 1899: Vertical file, Jessie Ball duPont Library, Archives and Manuscript Collections, Sewanee: University of the South; Burson, *Texas A&M University Football Vault,* 10.

16. Richard Scott, *SEC Football: 75 Years of Pride and Passion* (Minneapolis: Voyageur, 2008), 22; Arthur Chitty to Gioia Grieme, October 21, 1954, Sewanee Football 1899: Vertical file, Jessie Ball duPont Library, Archives and Manuscript Collections, Sewanee: University of the South.

17. Givens, *Ninety-Nine Iron,* 31, 73–74; "U. of S.! Rah! Rah!."

18. Givens, *Ninety-Nine Iron,* 34; "U. of S.! Rah! Rah!."

19. Letter to John Musemeche, October 16, 1962, Sewanee Football 1899: Vertical file, Jessie Ball duPont Library, Archives and Manuscript Collections, Sewanee: University of the South; "Plantation Life," Ardoyne Plantation, http://www.ardoyneplantation.com/about.html.

20. Letter to John Musemeche, October 16, 1962; Durant, "Miracle of Sewanee."

21. "Sewanee Keeps It Up," *Nashville Tennessean,* November 14, 1899.

22. Durant, "Miracle of Sewanee"; "The Celebration," *Sewanee Purple* 14, no. 11 (November 21, 1899).

23. Woodruff, *History of Southern Football,* 97; Givens, *Ninety-Nine Iron,* 99.

24. Woodruff, *History of Southern Football,* 98.

25. Givens, *Ninety-Nine Iron,* 100.

26. "Auburn–Sewanee Thanksgiving 1899: David Shepherd—as Told by Luke Lea, Mgr.,"

and W. B. Wilson to Arthur Chitty, October 18, 1954, Sewanee Football 1899: Vertical file, Jessie Ball duPont Library, Archives and Manuscript Collections, Sewanee: University of the South; "Champions of the South: The Thanksgiving Game," *Sewanee Purple* 14, no. 13 (December 14, 1899).

27. Givens, *Ninety-Nine Iron,* 100; Woodruff, *History of Southern Football,* 101. Givens's account of the game differs from Woodruff's. Woodruff, who was present at the game, claimed that Ed Huguley scored Auburn's final touchdown. Givens claimed it was Franklin Bivings. Givens's source is W. W. Screws, a reporter for the *Montgomery Advertiser.* It is impossible to know who is right. Unfortunately, play-by-play accounts of the period were often inaccurate, making it difficult for historians to puzzle out precisely what happened during games. I have included what I believe are the most plausible scenarios, based on the available source material.

28. Woodruff, *History of Southern Football,* 101; "Auburn vs. Sewanee: The Alabama Boys Lose a Hotly Contested Game," *Columbus Enquirer-Sun,* December 1, 1899, 6. Again, Givens's account of the game differs from Woodruff's. Givens credits Warbler Wilson with scoring the final Sewanee touchdown and Bart Sims with kicking the point after touchdown.

29. James Young to Ralph Black, October 2, 1954, and letter to Marjorie Miller, November 27, 1954, Sewanee Football 1899: Vertical file, Jessie Ball duPont Library, Archives and Manuscript Collections, Sewanee: University of the South.

30. Ralph Black to Henry Seibels, August 25, 1949, Sewanee Football 1899: Vertical file, Jessie Ball duPont Library, Archives and Manuscript Collections, Sewanee: University of the South; Durant, "Miracle of Sewanee."

31. Ralph Black remembered North Carolina making it inside the ten-yard line instead of the five-yard line and getting stuffed nine times instead of eight.

32. W. B. Wilson to Arthur Chitty, October 18, 1954, and Ralph Black to Henry Seibels, August 25, 1949, Sewanee Football 1899: Vertical file, Jessie Ball duPont Library, Archives and Manuscript Collections, Sewanee: University of the South; "Champions of the South."

33. "All-America Team for 1899," *Collier's Weekly* 24, no. 14 (January 6, 1900): 20; Ayers, *Promise of the New South,* 409–410.

34. "Seibels, Henry Goldthwaite ('Ditty')"; "Kilpatrick, Ringland Fisher ('Rex,' 'Kil')"; "Wilson Jr., William Blackburn ('Warbler')"; "Pearce, Hugh Miller Thompson ('Bunny')"; "Claiborne, William Sterling ('Rev,' 'Bishop,' 'Wild Bill')"; and "Simkins, Ormond," Sewanee Football 1899: Vertical file, Jessie Ball duPont Library, Archives and Manuscript Collections, Sewanee: University of the South.

35. Durant, "Miracle of Sewanee"; "Sports Release: The University of the South," September 20, 1973, Sewanee Football 1899: Vertical file, Jessie Ball duPont Library, Archives and Manuscript Collections, Sewanee: University of the South; Cam Martin, "Sewanee Puffs Out Chest with Historic Title," ESPN, May 9, 2012, http://www.espn.com/blog/playbook/fandom/post/_/id/2254/sewanee-puffs-out-chest-with-historic-title.

CHAPTER SEVEN

1. H. W. Brands, *T. R.: The Last Romantic* (New York: Basic Books, 1997), 418.

2. "Booker T. Washington Advocates Self-Help, 1895," and "W. E. B. Du Bois Rejects Washington's Strategy of Accommodation, 1903," in Fink, *Major Problems*, 223–227.

3. Brands, *T. R.*, 421–423.

4. Nemeth, *Mississippi State University Football Vault*, 9.

5. Finney, *Fighting Tigers*, 331; "History," University of Louisiana Lafayette, https://louisiana.edu/about-us/history.

6. Ratcliffe, *University of Virginia Football Vault*, 17.

7. "Dixie Championship Goes to Vanderbilt," *Atlanta Constitution*, November 29, 1901, 2, Newspapers.com, https://www.newspapers.com/clip/2916508/the_atlanta_constitution.

8. The section reads, "A student who has been connected with an institution where he has participated in an inter-collegiate contest shall not participate in an inter-collegiate contest at any other institution in this association until he has been a student there for one collegiate year."

9. *Constitution of the Southern Inter-Collegiate Athletic Association* (Oxford, MS: Eagle Job Printing Office, 1903), 5–14, William Lofland Dudley Papers, MSS 123, box 3, Special Collections and University Archive Library, Vanderbilt University, Nashville, Tennessee; "Athletic Blacklist Has Widespread Effect," *Charlotte News*, December 14, 1901, 11, Newspapers.com, https://www.newspapers.com/clip/3116130/the_charlotte_news; "Fight Is Against Professionalism," *Atlanta Constitution*, December 22, 1901, 11, Newspapers.com, https://www.newspapers.com/clip/3116190/the_atlanta_constitution; Finney, *Fighting Tigers*, 17–18.

10. Bert McGrane, "Dan McGugin," *Des Moines Register*, http://data.desmoinesregister.com/hall-of-fame/single.php?id=540.

11. David Ignatius, "The Right Roosevelt?" *Washington Post*, March 5, 2009, http://www.washingtonpost.com/wp-dyn/content/article/2009/03/04/AR2009030403067.html.

12. Bradford E. Burns, "Panama: A Search for Independence," *Current History*, February 1977, 65–82; "Panama Secedes From Columbia: Independence of Isthmus Proclaimed," *New York Times*, November 4, 1903, 1.

13. Wilkinson, *Georgia Tech Football Vault*, 14–15, 17, 19–20.

14. Traughber, *Vanderbilt Football*, 30–31; "Coach McGugin to Wed," *Atlanta Constitution*, December 3, 1905.

15. "Michael 'Iron Mike' Donahue," National Football Foundation, http://www.football-foundation.org/Programs/CollegeFootballHallofFame/SearchDetail.aspx?id=10001.

16. "Bobcat History," 110, 127, http://graphics.fansonly.com/photos/schools/txst/sports/m-footbl/auto_pdf/109-FBMGHistory.pdf.

17. "Bobcat History," 110, 127; Wilkinson, *Georgia Tech Football Vault*, 16; Traughber, *Vanderbilt Football*, 31.

18. Fabian Lange, Alan L. Olmstead, and Paul W. Rhode, "The Impact of the Boll Weevil, 1892–1932," *Journal of Economic History* 69, no. 3 (September 2009): 685–715; Theodore Roosevelt, "Fourth Annual Message," December 6, 1904, American Presidency Project, UC Santa Barbara, https://www.presidency.ucsb.edu/node/206208.

19. "1904 Presidential General Election Results," Dave Leip's Atlas of US Presidential Elections, http://uselectionatlas.org/RESULTS.

20. Katie Zezima, "How Teddy Roosevelt Helped Save Football," *Washington Post,* May 29, 2014, https://www.washingtonpost.com/news/the-fix/wp/2014/05/29/teddy-roosevelt-helped-save-football-with-a-white-house-meeting-in-1905/?utm_term=.279be194412b; "Hears Football Men: Coaches in Conference with President Roosevelt," *Washington Post,* October 10, 1905.

21. Watterson, *College Football,* 67.

22. Watterson, *College Football, 67*; Reyburn, *Football Nation,* 70.

23. Christopher Klein, "How Teddy Roosevelt Saved Football," History, September 6, 2012, http://www.history.com/news/how-teddy-roosevelt-saved-football; Michael Beschloss, "T. R.'s Son Inspired Him to Help Rescue Football," *New York Times,* August 1, 2014, https://www.nytimes.com/2014/08/02/upshot/trs-son-inspired-him-to-help-rescue-football.html.

24. Reyburn, *Football Nation,* 74; Zezima, "How Teddy Roosevelt Helped Save Football."

25. Rappoport, *Tar Heel,* 105.

26. Stephens, *College Football Hall of Fame,* 14–16; Reyburn, *Football Nation,* 77; Roger R. Tamte, *Walter Camp,* 313–314.

27. "Theodore Roosevelt and Conservation," National Park Service, https://www.nps.gov/thro/learn/historyculture/theodore-roosevelt-and-conservation.htm.

28. Ayers, *Promise of the New South,* 435–437.

29. David McCullough, *The Path Between the Seas: The Creation of the Panama Canal, 1870–1914* (New York: Simon and Schuster, 1977), 492–496.

30. J. W. Heisman, "Dixie's Football Hall of Fame," *Tennessean,* January 21, 1915, Newspapers.com, https://www.newspapers.com/clip/6578898/the_tennessean. For more information on the Carlisle Indians, see Sally Jenkins, *The Real All Americans: The Team That Changed a Game, A People, A Nation* (New York: Broadway, 2008).

31. Norm Carlson, *University of Florida Football Vault: The History of the Florida Gators* (Atlanta: Whitman, 2007), 7–13. Carlson, the official historian of Florida athletics, says it is unclear whether 1903 or 1906 should be considered the first year of Gator football: "Technically, either answer is correct." Carlson seems inclined toward the latter date, however, since the University of the State of Florida, created under the Buckman Act, opened its doors to students in September 1906.

32. Carl Van Ness, pers. comm., April 29, 2019; Van Ness, "UF's First Gators: In Search of the Gator Nickname," *University of Florida Today* (September 2000): 35–38; Carl Van Ness and Kevin McCarthy, *Honoring the Past, Shaping the Future: The University of Florida, 1853–2003* (Gainesville: University of Florida 150th Anniversary Committee, 2003), 30–31.

33. Edmund Morris, *Theodore Rex* (New York: Random House, 2001), 473.

34. Barnhart, *Southern Fried Football,* 4.

35. Michael T. Wood, "American Football in Cuba: LSU vs. University of Havana, 1907," *Sport in American History,* December 31, 2015, https://ussporthistory.com/2015/12/31/american-football-in-cuba-1-s-u-vs-university-of-havana-1907; Finney, *Fighting Tigers,* 26.

36. "Albert Beveridge Defends US Imperialism, 1900," in Fink, *Major Problems,* 494–497.

37. Rich Remsberg, "Found in the Archives: America's Unsettling Early Eugenics Movement," NPR, June 1, 2011, http://www.npr.org/sections/pictureshow/2011/06/01/136849387/found-in-the-archives-americas-unsettling-early-eugenics-movement; Andrea DenHoed, "The Forgotten Lessons of the American Eugenics Movement," *New Yorker,* April 27, 2016, http://www.newyorker.com/books/page-turnerthe-forgotten-lessons-of-the-american-eugenics-movement.

38. "Annual Meeting of the SIAA," *Bulletin of Vanderbilt University* 1, no. 26 (January 1909): 30–31; Finney, *Fighting Tigers,* 33–37; "From 'The LSU Football Vault': The 1908 Season," November 12, 2008, LSU Sports, http://www.lsusports.net/ViewArticle.dbml?ATCLID=1621833; Jenkins, *Real All Americans,* 288.

39. See Jeremy Henderson, "Auburn's 1908 Team Went Undefeated Despite Losing to Professional LSU Team," *War Eagle Reader,* September 25, 2013, https://www.thewareaglereader.com/2013/09/auburns-1908-team-goes-undefeated-despite-losing-to-professional-lsu-team.

40. "1908 Presidential General Election Results," Dave Leip's Atlas of US Presidential Elections, http://uselectionatlas.org/RESULTS; James West Davidson, *Nation of Nations: A Concise Narrative of the American Republic* (Boston: McGraw-Hill College, 1999), 618.

41. Mike McKinley, "Cruise of the Great White Fleet," *Naval History and Heritage Command,* April 1, 2015, https://www.history.navy.mil/research/library/online-reading-room/title-list-alphabetically/c/cruise-great-white-fleet-mckinley.html.

42. John C. Mitcham, "Troy University Football," *Encyclopedia of Alabama,* August 22, 2009, http://www.encyclopediaofalabama.org/article/h-2406; "Vergil Parks McKinley," Troy University Athletics, Hall of Fame, http://www.troytrojans.com/hof.aspx?hof=6.

43. "Taft's Sail Ended: President Speaks on Waterways at New Orleans," *Washington Post,* October 31, 1909, 1.

44. Ratcliffe, *University of Virginia Football Vault,* 23–24; "Dies of Injuries in Football Game: Young Christian of University of Virginia Had Cerebral Hemorrhages, Due to Concussion," *New York Times,* November 15, 1909, 4.

45. Dan Heuchert, "Plaque to Honor Lambeth's Pivotal Role in UVA Athletics, Football's Development," UVA Today, June 6, 2013, https://news.virginia.edu/content/plaque-honor-lambeth-s-pivotal-role-uva-athletics-football-s-development.

46. John Mosby to Thomas Pinckney Bryan, December 7, 1909, Papers of John Singleton Mosby, Albert Small Special Collections Library, University of Virginia, Charlottesville, Virginia.

47. Jeffry D. Wert, *Mosby's Rangers: The True Adventures of the Most Famous Command of the Civil War* (New York: Touchstone, 1990), 26–27.

48. Mosby to Bryan, December 7, 1909; Robert Waterman Hunter to John Singleton Mosby, December 3, 1909, Special Collections, University of Virginia Library, MSS 5603-a, Charlottesville, Virginia.

49. Herget, *American Football*, 103–105; Watterson, *College Football*, 120.

CHAPTER EIGHT

1. Traughber, *Vanderbilt Football*, 46.

2. Traughber, *Vanderbilt Football, 46*; "Yale and Vanderbilt Tie," *Chicago Sunday Tribune,* October 23, 1910, Newspapers.com, https://www.newspapers.com/clip/2306640/chicago_tribune; "Vanderbilt Holds Yale to No Score," *New York Times,* October 23, 1910, C7.

3. Traughber, *Vanderbilt Football*, 43–45.

4. Robert L. Scribner, "Now About this Football Situation . . . ," *Virginia Cavalcade* (Autumn 1956): 30–37; "Randolph-Macon Football History," Randolph-Macon Athletics, http://rmcathletics.com/sports/fball/fball-history.

5. Scribner, "Now About this Football Situation . . ."

6. Quoted in "Randolph-Macon Football History."

7. Ida M. Tarbell, "The Oil War of 1872," in *Muckraking: Three Landmark Articles,* ed. Ellen F. Fitzpatrick (Boston: Bedford/St. Martin's, 1994), 23, 60–80.

8. Doyle, "Causes Won, Not Lost," 162; Heisman and Schlabach, *Heisman,* 171.

9. Wilkinson, *Georgia Tech Football Vault,* 23; Scott, *SEC Football,* 24. Bill Traughber's version of the story has McGugin telling his team, "You are going against Yankees, some of whose grandfathers killed your grandfathers in the Civil War." See Traughber, *Vanderbilt Football,* 33.

10. Mark Owens, *2017 Media Information Guide* (Murfreesboro: Middle Tennessee Athletic Communications), 107, http://goblueraiders.com/documents/2017/8/7//2017_Football_Fact_Book.pdf?id=14304; *2014 Reference Guide: Arkansas State* (Jonesboro: Arkansas State University), 112, http://www.astateredwolves.com//pdf9/2761286.pdf?DB_OEM_ID=7200.

11. Howard Zinn, *A People's History of the United States* (New York: Harper Perennial Modern Classics, 2005), 326–327.

12. Zinn, *A People's History,* 330–331.

13. "The Socialist Party's Platform, 1912," in Fink, *Major Problems,* 312–315; "1912 Presidential General Election Results," Dave Leip's Atlas of US Presidential Elections, http://uselectionatlas.org/RESULTS.

14. "1912 Presidential General Election Results"; Ayers, *Promise of the New South,* 110–125.

15. "1912 Presidential General Elections Results."

16. Herget, *American Football,* 106.

17. *2014 Southern Miss Football Media Guide* (Hattiesburg: University of Southern Mississippi Department of Intercollegiate Athletics), 140, 162, http://publications.provationsgroup.org/publications/14-Somiss-football/#?page=0; *Rice Owls 2017 Football Factbook* (Houston, TX: Rice University) 187, http://grfx.cstv.com/photos/schools/rice/sports/m-footbl/

auto_pdf/2017-18/misc_non_event/2017FactBook.pdf; *Memphis Tigers Football Media Guide* (Memphis, TN: University of Memphis Athletics Communications, 2017), 14, 260, http://goti-gersgo.com/documents/2017/9/11/2017MemphisMediaGuide.pdf.

18. "The History of the CIAA," Central Intercollegiate Athletic Association, https://the-ciaa.com/sports/2018/9/25/information-about-ciaa-index-7-2018.aspx

19. "Oldest and Boldest," NAACP, http://www.naacp.org/oldest-and-boldest; David Housel, *Auburn University Football Vault: The Story of the Auburn Tigers, 1892–2007* (Atlanta: Whitman, 2007), 27–28.

20. *"The Yucca,* Yearbook of North Texas State University, 1965," 20–21, University of North Texas Digital Library, https://digital.library.unt.edu/ark:/67531/metapth61034/m1/24; *2017 UTEP Football Media Guide,* UTEP Athletics Media Relations Office, https://utepathlet-ics.com/documents/2017/7/11/UTEP_FB_Media_Guide_2017_WEB.pdf; Traughber, *Vanderbilt Football,* 47.

21. Jeremy Henderson, "Football Rankings Guru Richard Billingsley Says Auburn Should Claim Century-Old Crown: 'My National Championship for Auburn in 1913 Is a Very Valid National Championship,' " War Eagle Reader, August 21, 2013, http://www.thewareaglereader.com/2013/08/football-rankings-guru-richard-billingsley-says-auburn-should-crown-centu-ry-old-champions-my-national-championship-for-auburn-in-1913-is-a-very-valid-nation-al-championship/#.VF81IcnYqqk.

22. Housel, *Auburn University Football Vault,* 24. Michael Skotnicki, a Birmingham lawyer and Auburn alumnus, believes that the 1910, 1913, 1914, 1958, 1983, 1993, and 2004 Auburn teams all deserve to be recognized as national champions. See Skotnicki, *Auburn's Unclaimed National Championships* (Michael C. Skotnicki, 2012).

23. Bebb, *Big Orange,* 97.

24. Bebb, *Big Orange,* 98–99; Lester Barnes, "Clemson Defeated by Tennessee Team," *Atlanta Constitution,* October 11, 1914, 6B, Newspapers.com, https://www.newspapers.com/clip/8726520/the_atlanta_constitution.

25. Tom Siler, *The Volunteers* (Knoxville, TN: Archer and Smith, 1950), 25; Bebb, *Big Orange,* 102.

26. Andrew Glass, "US Proclaims Neutrality in World War I, August 4, 1914," Politico, August 4, 2009, http://www.politico.com/story/2009/08/us-proclaims-neutrality-in-world-war-i-august-4-1914-025751.

27. Traughber, *Vanderbilt Football,* 58–65.

28. Ratcliffe, *University of Virginia Football Vault,* 27–28; "Eugene 'Buck' Mayer, Virginia Sports Hall of Fame, https://vasportshof.com/inductee/eugene-buck-mayer.

29. Ratcliffe, *University of Virginia Football Vault,* 32–33.

30. Ratcliffe, *University of Virginia Football Vault,* 33–34; "Eddie Mahan, 83, Harvard Back and 3 Times All-America, Dies," *New York Times,* July 24, 1975, http://www.nytimes.com/1975/07/24/archives/eddie-mahan-83-harvard-back-and-3-times-allamerica-dies.html.

31. "South Atlantic Colleges to Organize," *Daily Tar Heel,* February 20, 1912, Newspapers.com, https://www.newspapers.com/clip/7779842/the_daily_tar_heel.

32. Chase, "10 Best Pranks"; Margaret Catherine Berry, "Student Life and Customs, 1883–1933, at the University of Texas" (PhD diss., Columbia University, 1965), 130–136.

33. Wilkinson, *Georgia Tech Football Vault*, 26–28; Heisman and Schlabach, *Heisman*, 143.

34. *The Volunteer* (1917), 114, Volunteer Yearbooks, University of Tennessee Knoxville Library, https://digital.lib.utk.edu/collections; Bebb, *Big Orange*, 109.

35. *Pandora* 31 (1918), University of Georgia, Athens, 23, http://hdl.handle.net/10724/18829; *Cactus Yearbook* (1918), University of Texas Libraries, University of Texas at Austin, 336, http://hdl.handle.net/2152/61696.

36. Wilkinson, *Georgia Tech Football Vault*, 30; Heisman and Schlabach, *Heisman*, 150.

37. Ken Sugiura, "Georgia Tech: A Century Ago, 'the Most Powerful Team in the Country,'" *Atlanta Journal-Constitution*, October 5, 2017, http://www.myajc.com/sports/college/century-ago-the-most-powerful-team-the-country/MsYY0D7Ima0t7pqMUWFsEN; Heisman and Schlabach, *Heisman*, 155.

38. Heisman and Schlabach, *Heisman*, 155.

39. Eric Foner, *Reconstruction*, xix–xx; Charles Reagan Wilson, *Baptized in Blood: The Religion of the Lost Cause 1865–1920* (Athens: University of Georgia Press, 1980), 1.

40. *Quips and Cranks* (1918), Davidson College, 94, DigitalNC, http://library.digitalnc.org/cdm/singleitem/collection/yearbooks/id/2184/rec/1.

41. *Calyx* (1918), Special Collections and Archives, Washington and Lee University Library, Lexington, Virginia, 120, https://archive.org/details/calyx18wash.

42. *Vanderbilt Commodore* (1918), Vanderbilt University, 136, http://www.library.vanderbilt.edu/specialcollections.

43. *Jambalaya* (1918), Tulane University Archives, https://tuarchives.tulane.edu/collections/digital-collections/yearbooks-jambalaya.

44. "Tech Smothers Indians," *The Technique* 7, no. 8 (November 20, 1917), 4, https://smartech.gatech.edu/handle/1853/7740/browse; *Glomerata* (1918), Auburn University Digital Library, http://diglib.auburn.edu/collections/gloms.

45. Heisman and Schlabach, *Heisman*, 162; *Blue Print* (1918), Georgia Tech Library, https://smartech.gatech.edu/handle/1853/14412. For more on the significance of Alabama's win over Washington during the 1926 Rose Bowl, see Andrew Beaton, "How the South Conquered Football," *Wall Street Journal*, December 21, 2016, A14.

46. *Blue Print* (1918); Heisman and Schlabach, *Heisman*, 164.

47. *Calyx* (1919), Special Collections and Archives, Washington and Lee University Library, Lexington, Virginia, 100, https://repository.wlu.edu/handle/11021/26929/browse?-type=alldates&value=1919; *Ole Miss* (1919), University of Mississippi Libraries, 19, https://archive.org/details/olemiss23univ; *Cactus Yearbook* (1919), University of Texas Libraries, University of Texas at Austin, 110, http://hdl.handle.net/2152/61680; "Minutes of Meeting of the Board of Trust of Vanderbilt University, June 9, 1919," 141, Special Collections and University Archive Library, Vanderbilt University, Nashville, Tennessee.

48. John M. Barry, *The Great Influenza: The Story of the Deadliest Pandemic in History* (New York: Penguin, 2004), 5, 397.

49. "Football Player Dead," *Washington Post,* October 23, 1918, 8, Newspapers.com, https://www.newspapers.com/clip/10112994/football_player_dead; *Yackety Yack* (1919), University of North Carolina, 179, Digital NC, http://ia600208.us.archive.org/32/items/yacketyyackseria1919univ/yacketyyackseria1919univ.pdf; Paul Evans, "Once and Future Plague," *Virginia* (Spring 2006), http://uvamagazine.org/articles/once_and_future_plague; "Minutes of Meeting of the Board of Trust of Vanderbilt University, June 9, 1919," 141; *Glomerata* (1919), Auburn University Digital Library, 67, http://diglib.auburn.edu/collections/gloms.

50. Wilkinson, *Georgia Tech Football Vault,* 33–34.

51. Reyburn, *Football Nation,* 96–97. For more information on the link between mass-circulation magazines and college enrollment numbers during the Progressive Era, see Daniel A. Clark, *Creating the College Man: American Mass Magazines and Middle-Class Manhood, 1890–1915* (Madison: University of Wisconsin Press, 2010).

EPILOGUE

1. *Kaleidoscope* (1927), Hampden-Sydney College, 88–93, https://archive.org/details/kaleidoscope1927hamp.

2. Beaton, "How the South Conquered Football."

3. Beaton, "How the South Conquered Football."

4. Beaton, "How the South Conquered Football"; Warren St. John, *Rammer Jammer Yellow Hammer: A Road Trip into the Heart of Fan Mania* (New York: Three Rivers, 2004), 35.

5. Marc Tracy, "Alabama Win in 1926 Rose Bowl Put Southern Stamp on College Football," *New York Times,* December 27, 2016, https://www.nytimes.com/2016/12/27/sports/ncaafootball/alabama-crimson-tide-washington-huskies.html.

6. Reyburn, *Football Nation,* 117, 150.

7. Reyburn, *Football Nation,* xx; John F. Kennedy, "September 30, 1962: Address on the Situation at the University of Mississippi," Miller Center, University of Virginia, https://millercenter.org/the-presidency/presidential-speeches/september-30-1962-address-situation-university-mississippi.

8. Reyburn, *Football Nation,* xx; Zach Helfand, "Separated From the Myths, Sam Cunningham's Story Remains an Inspiration," *Los Angeles Times,* August 31, 2016, http://www.latimes.com/sports/usc/la-sp-usc-cunningham-alabama-20160831-snap-story.html.

9. James A. Michener, *Sports in America* (New York: Ballantine, 1976), 316.

INDEX

Index

Doyle, Leo Andrew, 9, 96, 157n22

Du Bois, W. E. B., 109, 133

Dudley, Alfred, 149

Dudley, William, 52, 63–64

Duke University, 48, 49–50, 53, 63, 69, 70, 85, 115

Dunning, William, 143

Dwyer, Frank, 100

Dwyer, Tom, 134

Edison, Thomas, 32

Eldridge, Edwin, 122

Eliot, Charles, 72, 85, 115–16

Espionage Act (1917), 141

ESPN: amount paid by for television rights to the College Football Playoff over twelve years, 1

Eton, "Wall Game" and "Field Game" played at, 13

eugenics, 120

Feagin, Arthur, 104

Fellers, Jim, 145

Fenton, George E., 119, 120

Fifteenth Amendment, 23, 24

Filipino-American War, 95

Fincher, Bill, 141

Fisher, Marion, 127

flying wedge, origin of, 62–63

football: Arthurian metaphors used to describe football in the South, 3; attempts to abolish after the death of Richard Gammon, 90–92; attempts to organize based on the Rugby Football Union code, 4, 13, 28; attempts to organize the English version of football, 4; concerns over the dangers of, 2, 70–71, 84–85, 115–16, 124–25; corruption in northern college football, 53–54; development of football helmets, 71; early attempts to adopt a uniform set of rules for, 5; emergence of from provincialism, 15; as "gridiron"

football, 31; head injuries caused by, 8; long history of in the South, 3–4; inaugural game played in the Midwest, 31; as a means of finding common ground with fellow Americans, 3; mob football games in England, 3–4; origin and legalization of the forward pass, 116; player eligibility concerns, 71–72; playing of during the American Revolution and the American Civil War, 4; record number of deaths caused by (1905), 115. *See also* Ivy League football; "scientific football"; southern college football

Football Association (FA), 4

Football Facts and Figures (Camp), 85

Football Nation: Four Hundred Years of America's Game (Reyburn), 10

Forsythe, James, 118

Fourteenth Amendment, 24; failure of former Confederate states to ratify, 18

Franklin, John Hope, 20, 21

Frazier, Bob, 57–58

Frick, Henry Clay, 59

Furman University, 51, 63

Futrall, John, 87

Gammon, Richard Vonalbade, 90–91, 95; national response to the death of, 91–92

Gammon, Rosalind Burns, 91–92

Gandy, Marshall, 120

Garfield, James A., 35

Georgia, attempt by the Georgia General Assembly to abolish football, 91–92

Georgia Tech (Georgia Institute of Technology), 64, 91, 97, 112, 130, 150; debut football game of, 61; decision to continue football during World War I, 146–47; defeat of Penn garnering national respect for southern football, 142–43; perfect season of (1917), 142–43, 143–45

Givens, Wendell, 170nn27–28

Glenn, John, 34

Index

Index

National Grange of the Order of Patrons of Husbandry, 159n13

National Origins Act (1924), 35

Native Americans: decimation of, 54; and football, 8, 54–55, 88

Needham, Henry Beach, 115

Newell, Kirk, 133

Newman, Zipp, 10

North Carolina: establishment of an intercollegiate football association in, 49–50; first intercollegiate football game in, 46–47, 49

North Carolina State Fair, 46

North Carolina State University, debut of football at, 59

Northwestern University, banning of football at, 115

Norton, Charles, 127–28

Oklahoma Colored Agricultural and Normal University, 65

Oneida Football Club, 5

Oriard, Michael, 10

Panama Canal Zone, establishment of, 111–12

Pancho Villa, 140

Panic of 1873, 16–17, 24

Panic of 1893, 65–66, 83

Parker, Alton, 114

Pay for Play (Smith), 9

payment, for student athletes, 2

Pearce, Hugh, 100, 101, 106

Pender, J. W., 134

Perkins, F. D., 86

Pershing, John J., 140, 147

Petrie, George, 41–42, 56–57

Philippines, the, 94, 119–20; rebellion in, 95

Phillips, G. M., 141, 145

Pickens, William, 64

Pike, James, 24–25

Pinchot, Gifford, 128

Plessy v. Ferguson (1896), 89–90

Polk, Leonidas L., 59, 97, 164n2

Populist party, 59–60

Potts, Allen, 50

presidential elections: of 1876, 26–27; of 1892, 60; of 1896, 89; of 1904, 114; of 1908, 121; of 1912, 131–32

Prettyman, E. Barrett, 127–28

Princeton University, 45, 84, 106; "ball-down" version of football played at, 5; and the concept of offensive blocking, 30–31; versus Rutgers University (first intercollegiate football game), 6, 14–15

Princip, Gavrilo, 136

progressives/progressivism, 86, 114, 117, 125, 132

Prostrate State, The (Pike), 25

Pulitzer, Joseph, 93

Pullman, George, 83

Racine College, 31

racism, 19–20, 24–25, 119–20. *See also* eugenics

Rammer Jammer Yellow Hammer (St. John), 8

Remsen, Ira, 34, 41

Randolph-Macon College, 35, 51, 68–69, 127, 160n17; defeat of arch rival Hampden-Sydney College, 127; popularity of baseball at, 48

Ratcliffe, Jerry, 20

Reading Football (Oriard), 10

Real All Americans, The (Jenkins), 8

Reconstruction, 17–18, 23–24, 143; and the elections of 1865, 156n14

Reeves, Joe, 71

Reid, William T., Jr., 116

Renouf, Edward, 34, 41

Republicans, 16–17, 19, 23–24; black Republicans, 24; "Radical" Republicans, 18

Reyburn, Susan, 10

Rhea, J. W. S., 68

Rice, Grantland, 100, 120–21

Rice University, 132

Index

Index